James Augustus Weston

Historic Doubts as to the Execution of Marshal Ney

Vol. 1

James Augustus Weston

Historic Doubts as to the Execution of Marshal Ney
Vol. 1

ISBN/EAN: 9783337379148

Printed in Europe, USA, Canada, Australia, Japan

Cover: Foto ©ninafisch / pixelio.de

More available books at **www.hansebooks.com**

HISTORIC DOUBTS

AS TO THE EXECUTION OF MARSHAL NEY, WITH NUMEROUS ILLUSTRATIONS * * *

BY

JAMES A. WESTON

Rector of the Church the Ascension, Hickory, N. C.; Major 33rd N. C. Regiment, Confederate States Army; Chaplain Catawba County (N. C.) Veteran's Association; Honorary Member of the North Carolina Historical Society, etc.

NEW YORK
THOMAS WHITTAKER
2 and 3 Bible House
1895

To the Memory of my Mother,
who taught me to be true to God and man—

To the Memory of Zebulon Baird Vance,
War Governor, United States Senator, the bravest of the brave in all that was best in Statesmanship, and North Carolina's greatest son,

this volume is affectionately inscribed.

PREFACE.

THE book is written. The difficulties have been very great —almost insuperable. The fires have been exceedingly hot. But the mountain-top is reached. Let the dead past bury its dead. I began this investigation more than twelve years ago. When I first heard the report that Peter S. Ney was probably Marshal Ney I said to myself, "It may be true. *I* would not have shot Stonewall Jackson." I began to make inquiries of those who had been intimately acquainted with Peter S. Ney and whose integrity no one could question. I found that P. S. Ney possessed a strong, clear, vigorous, well-balanced mind, and that he was a man of the highest character. From that moment I believed he was Marshal Ney, and now I know it. I am deeply grateful to the many friends who have so nobly aided me in this work of love. I wish I could take each one of them by the hand and express my gratitude in person. I can never forget their kindness. May Heaven's best blessings be theirs. I am under very especial obligations to the following gentlemen: The Rev. Dr. Morgan Dix, rector of Trinity Parish, New York; the Rev. Dr. Joseph N. Blanchard, rector of St. James's Parish, Philadelphia; the Rev. Dr. Arthur C. Kimber, minister in charge of St. Augustine's Chapel, Trinity Parish, New York; the Hon. Seth Low, LL.D., President of Columbia College, New York; Joseph P. Caldwell, editor of the *Observer*, Charlotte, N. C.; Captain Samuel A. Ashe, Raleigh, N. C.; the Rev. Dr. William A. Wood, pastor of the Presbyterian Church, Statesville, N. C.; T. B. Kingsbury, editor of the *Messenger*, Wilmington, N. C.; Hon. James F. Izlar, Orangeburg, S. C.; Robert Macfarlan, Florence, S. C.; and Reuben G. Thwaites, Secretary of the Wisconsin Historical Society, Madison, Wis.

Without the generous aid of these gentlemen, extended in so many ways, this work could not have reached its present state of completeness. A few words as to the dedication. In December, 1889, Senator Vance wrote to me: "You honor me too highly. I hope you will tone down the dedication so far as I am personally concerned." I have studied Senator Vance's record with the utmost care. The dedication must stand.

JAMES A. WESTON.

HICKORY, N. C., March 18, 1895.

TABLE OF CONTENTS.

	PAGE
I. MARSHAL NEY: CHAPTER I.	1
CHAPTER II.	25
CHAPTER III.	53
II. WAS MARSHAL NEY EXECUTED? CHAPTER I.	97
CHAPTER II.: TESTIMONY.	135
III. DOCUMENTARY EVIDENCE AS TO NEY'S IDENTITY.	227
IV. SPECIMENS OF POETRY BY P. S. NEY.	257
V. SUMMARY.	279
APPENDIX A.	299
APPENDIX B.	303
APPENDIX C.	305
INDEX.	307

LIST OF ILLUSTRATIONS.

No.   PAGE
1. MARSHAL NEY..*Frontispiece*
   (From an oil painting at Versailles.)
2. NAPOLEON..*facing* 25
3. MARSHAL NEY...*facing* 38
   (From an engraving by H. R. Cook, 1817.)
4. MADAME LA MARÉCHALE NEY............................*facing* 50
5. MARSHAL NEY...*facing* 62
   (From Meyer's Collection of Portraits of the Grand Officers of the Legion of Honor.)
6. NEY STATUE AT METZ.................................*facing* 74
7. MARSHAL NEY...*facing* 86
   (From an old pen-and-ink sketch.)
8. THE EXECUTION OF MARSHAL NEY.......................*facing* 97
   (From an old woodcut.)
9. SKETCH OF THE DEATH OF MARSHAL NEY................*facing* 115
   (By Gérôme.)
10. THE EARL OF ELGIN..................................*facing* 135
    (Whose portrait bears a striking resemblance to P. S. Ney.)
11. No. 1.—FACSIMILE SIGNATURE OF P. S. NEY................. 156
12. No. 2.—FACSIMILE SIGNATURE OF MARSHAL NEY............... 157
13. No. 3.—EXAMPLES OF P. S. NEY'S HANDWRITING.............. 176
14. No. 4.—EXAMPLES OF MARSHAL NEY'S HANDWRITING........... 177
15. No. 5.—EXAMPLES OF P. S. NEY'S HANDWRITING.............. 196
16. No. 6.—EXAMPLES OF MARSHAL NEY'S HANDWRITING........... 197
17. No. 7.—EXAMPLES OF P. S. NEY'S HANDWRITING.............. 206
18. No. 8.—EXAMPLES OF MARSHAL NEY'S HANDWRITING........... 207
19. CAST OF SKULL AND LOWER MAXILLARY OF P. S. NEY...*facing* 227
20. FACSIMILE OF P. S. NEY'S NOTES......................*facing* 235
21. FACSIMILE OF P. S. NEY'S NOTES......................*facing* 240
22. FACSIMILE OF P. S. NEY'S NOTES......................*facing* 246
23. FACSIMILE OF P. S. NEY'S NOTES......................*facing* 252
24. FACSIMILE OF P. S. NEY'S NOTES......................*facing* 257
25. SPECIMENS OF P. S. NEY'S SIGNATURES.................*facing* 279

PART I.

LIFE OF MARSHAL NEY.

CHAPTER I.

It is not my purpose to write a complete biography of Marshal Ney. I have abundant material for such a work, much of which is new, and it may be used at some future time ; but for the present I design simply to give, as an introduction to my book, a brief sketch or outline of the life and character of this illustrious soldier, the greatest, in some important respects, that the world has ever produced.

There were but two of Napoleon's marshals that would bear any sort of comparison with him—Masséna and Soult. Masséna has generally been regarded by military critics as the ablest of Napoleon's lieutenants. Bonaparte had a very high opinion of him, and Wellington "thought him the best French officer that he had met." But Masséna committed blunders in the Peninsular campaign that Ney never would have committed ; and in the famous retreat from Portugal, Ney, by his consummate skill and valor, saved Masséna's army from total annihilation. Napoleon said that "Soult was the only real *homme de guerre* among his marshals ;" and Napier, in his "History of the Peninsular War," thinks Soult was little inferior to the god of war himself—Napoleon being his god.

Soult was unquestionably an officer of very great merit. He had a sound, well-balanced mind, was a brilliant tactician, strong and vigorous in assault and calm and self-reliant in the hour of danger ; but he was exceedingly cautious and timid. His intellect was slow in all its operations. "Like the lion, he measured his leap before he took it, and if he fell short he measured it over again," and took a long time to measure it.

He had no improvisations of genius, and on more than one occasion he deliberately allowed fine opportunities for attacking or crippling Wellington to pass away unimproved.

Wellington soon found him out, and played with him as he would have played with a child. On one occasion Wellington, with a small body of troops, found himself in presence of Soult with a much larger force. He rode slowly along the lines, and his troops cheered him in the most enthusiastic manner. Wellington stopped and said to one of his aids : "Yonder," pointing toward Soult, "is a great commander, but he is a cautious one, and will delay his attack until he can investigate the cause of these cheers ; that will give time for the Sixth Division to arrive, and I shall beat him." And so he did. Soult's defeat at Oporto is an everlasting stain upon his military fame.*

Ney had faults as a soldier—I am by no means blind to them—but they were neither so many nor so grave as the faults of Masséna and of Soult. In other respects these two men will hardly bear to be named in connection with Marshal Ney.

The six great captains of history—I name them in order—Wellington,† Cæsar, Hannibal, Napoleon, Alexander the Great, Frederick the Great—these world-renowned warriors, it must be granted, possessed greater genius than Marshal Ney for the "higher parts of war," as the phrase goes—organization, supreme command, the direction and control of a large system of operations, etc.—but not one of them could conduct a vanguard or a rear-guard with such ability and such success as Marshal Ney ; not one had so quick, so true, so accurate a *coup d'œil* on the field of battle ; not one could handle troops so readily, so skilfully, so effectively in actual combat ; not one could *create* resources as *Ney created* them in the Russian retreat ; not one had that moral power over men which moulds them anew, as it were, and influences them and *rules* them when all discipline is gone, when all hope is gone. Not one.

---

* Browne's "Wellington ;" "Conversations with the Duke," Earl Stanhope ; Las Cases's "Memoirs," etc.

† "The great world-victor's victor."—Tennyson.

In these important *vital* qualifications of a great soldier Ney's position is simply unique. He stands alone.

Michel Ney was born at Saar-Louis, on the river Saar, province of Lorraine, about twenty-six miles from Metz and thirty miles from Treves, on the 10th day of January, 1769.* His father, Peter Ney, was a cooper by trade, and had been a soldier in the Seven Years' War. He had greatly distinguished himself at the battle of Rosbach, and this circumstance, the crowning glory of his life, he always contrived with pardonable pride to weave into his "tales of fields lost and won." His son Michel, the second of six children, was sprightly and energetic, and at a very early age evinced a decided taste and talent for a military life. He was carefully educated at Saar-Louis at a school kept by the monks of St. Augustine, and at the age of thirteen he began the study of law in the office of the village notary.†

He remained here about twelve months, when, growing tired of the law, he applied for and obtained an appointment as clerk to the Procureur de Roi. "But this was still worse, for if he must be pinned to the desk he by far preferred copying deeds and contracts to conducting criminal proceedings." He therefore abandoned his new duties in disgust, and soon succeeded in obtaining the position of overseer of the Apenwerler mines. He was afterward superintendent of the Saleck Iron Works. He was distinguished for his quickness of perception, strong common sense, general intelligence, and faithfulness to his official duties.

But such occupations were ill adapted to his genius. He was yearning for the excitement and glory of a military life. His parents, however, were bitterly opposed to his entering the army; and young Ney, a most loving and dutiful son,

---

* Napoleon was born in 1769. It is a remarkable circumstance that the *twelve* men who, in one way or another, so greatly influenced the fortunes of Bonaparte, were all born in the same year, 1769—viz., Wellington, Ney, Lannes, Soult, Lavalette, Castlereagh, Arndt, Méhée, Bourrienne, Tallien, Belliard, and Sir Hudson Lowe.

† "The minutes in Ney's handwriting are still preserved in this office as valuable relics."—" Memoirs of Marshal Ney," London, 1833.

hesitated a long time before he ventured to oppose their wishes. But the master passion of his soul finally overpowered every other feeling.

He left his home amid the tears, remonstrances, and threats of his parents, and "without clothes or money," his feet bleeding at every step, set out for Metz, where the Fourth Regiment of Hussars, called at that time the Régiment de Colonel Général, was then quartered. On his arrival at Metz, February 1st, 1787, Ney enlisted in this regiment, being then in his nineteenth year. "His good conduct, his application, and the rapidity with which he made himself master of his duty attracted the attention of his officers, while his patient submission to discipline and his orderly conduct elicited their good will; and, as he wrote a *beautiful hand*, he was soon employed in the quartermaster's office." Whatever leisure time he could command he devoted to hard study, laboring day and night to qualify himself for his new duties. "He distinguished himself among his comrades by his fine, soldier-like appearance, his great dexterity in the use of his weapons, and by the ease and boldness with which he rode the most dangerous horses and broke in those hitherto considered unmanageable.

"On this account every regimental affair of honor was confided to him. The fencing-master of the Chasseurs de Vintimille, a regiment also quartered at Metz, was, like most regimental fencing-masters of those days, a dangerous duellist, and as such dreaded not only by young recruits but by old and experienced swordsmen. This man had wounded the fencing-master of the Colonel Général and insulted the whole regiment. The non-commissioned officers having held a meeting to take measures for the punishment of this bully, Ney, just promoted, was selected, as the bravest and cleverest swordsman, to inflict the chastisement deemed necessary. He accepted the mission with joy; and though prevented at the time by the colonel of his regiment from carrying out his purpose, he afterward met his antagonist in a secret place, and, after a sharp encounter, defeated him, wounding him seriously in the wrist. The fencing-master, thus disabled and disgraced, was speedily dismissed from his regiment. He was afterward reduced to great poverty, and Ney, hearing of his condition, with characteristic warm-heartedness sought him out and settled a pension on him." ("Memoirs.")

Ney's promotion was rapid. So zealous and efficient an officer could not long remain in a subordinate position. He was promoted five times in the year 1792, to wit : Maréchal des logis, February 1st ; maréchal des logis chef, April 1st ; adjutant, June 14th ; sub-lieutenant, October 29th, and lieutenant, November 5th. On March 29th, 1793, he was appointed aide-de-camp to General Lamarche, one of the best soldiers of the revolutionary period. "Thus Ney, almost at the outset of his career, found himself in a situation to study the art of war without being subjected to the painful drudgery of the lower grades. Being placed upon an eminence whence his eye could embrace the whole field of military tactics, he was thus initiated into the secret of grand movements, which he was in a situation not only to study and comprehend, but at times to dissect in person ; and he soon proved that the lessons he received were not thrown away."

Unfortunately, General Lamarche was killed at the storming of the camp at Famars. Ney then served for a short time on the staff of General Coland. He was made a captain in his old regiment April 26th, 1794. After the battle of Fleurus, in which Ney particularly distinguished himself, Kléber appointed him adjutant-general of his division, and shortly afterward placed him at the head of a select body of five hundred men, called Partisans, whose duty it was to act as the vanguard of the army, to execute missions of extraordinary peril, to traverse the enemy's lines, to reconnoitre his positions and strength, to cut off his convoys, and to destroy or make prisoners such separate detachments as they might encounter—to be ready for any enterprise, however daring or desperate.

This was a position of immense responsibility, requiring great courage, energy, judgment, and skill. But Ney not only met Kléber's expectations, but went far beyond them.*

* "Young Ney brought to this perilous service all his mental and physical powers. His iron will seemed to compensate for the loss of sleep and

Kléber could not find words with which to express his admiration of this new Agamemnon. "I can't do without him," he said. "In every operation entrusted to him he displays the most consummate skill and bravery." In fact, Jourdan and Kléber had a hot quarrel about Ney. "I must have him," said Jourdan. "I must have him," said Kléber; and the dispute could be settled only by an appeal to higher authority. It is impossible in this brief sketch to follow Ney through all the battles, skirmishes, reconnoissances, forays, etc., in which his command was engaged. He was almost always successful, even when the odds were fearfully against him. His men had boundless confidence in him. They were willing to go anywhere and attempt anything at his bidding. And they loved him, even at this early stage of his career, with a passion which amounted almost to idolatry.

At the siege of Maestricht, Ney rendered the most valuable services. Indeed, the success of the undertaking was mainly due to his able dispositions and brilliant manœuvres. Bernadotte wrote to Kléber: "Great praise is due to the brave Ney. He seconded me with the ability which you know he possesses; and I am bound to add, in strict justice, that he greatly contributed to the success we have obtained." During the siege of Mayence, in January, 1795, Ney, while cutting his way, single-handed, through the midst of the enemy, was severely wounded in the arm.* "A species of lockjaw ensued, and he became restless and desponding. Being informed that he had been appointed general of brigade, this promotion was only a source of uneasiness to him. He did not think he had done enough to merit that rank, and wished to leave it to those who, as he said, had better claims than his. In vain were his scruples laughed at; in vain was he urged to accept the promotion; it was impossible to shake his resistance or overcome his modesty.

"As his wound continued painful, the representative, Mer-

---

food and rest. Daunted by no danger, exhausted by no toil, caught by no stratagem, he acquired at the head of this bold band of warriors the title of the *Indefatigable*"—HEADLEY.

* Gunshot wound.

lin, recommended him to try his native air. 'My brave friend,' he wrote, 'go and complete your cure at Sarrelibre,* your birthplace. I have dispatched an order to the surgeon of first-class, Bonaventure, to send one of his pupils with you. Return soon and lend us your powerful aid against the enemies of your country.' The spring was advancing, active operations were about to be resumed, and Ney's wound was not yet healed. With anxiety, though resigned, he watched the slow progress of his convalescence. His hopes were still buoyant, and he trusted that his youth and the approaching season would speedily restore him to health" ("Memoirs"). The campaign soon opened, and Ney set out forthwith for headquarters without regard to the condition of his wound and against the express commands of his surgeon. He still persisted in declining the office of brigadier-general. Kléber and his other friends earnestly remonstrated with him, but it did no good. He felt that he was unworthy of so great an honor.

His return to the army was hailed with the liveliest satisfaction. Though his wounds were not altogether healed, he at once entered upon his duties with all the ardor and energy of his nature. At Wurtzburg and Forchheim he was eminently successful. "With one hundred cavalry he took two thousand prisoners and obtained possession of Wurtzburg. He led two columns straight into the river, and, forcing the opposite banks, though lined with cannon, made himself master of Forchheim." Before the river was fairly crossed the imperial army fled in dismay, and Ney quietly "rode up to the gates and summoned the garrison to surrender. The commander hesitated, but Ney swore that he would bombard the place unless his demands were instantly complied with. The commandant wished to parley in order to gain time; but Ney, bursting into a violent rage at such useless obstinacy, swore that he would put the whole garrison to the sword if the surrender were delayed another instant. This threat produced the desired effect, and Forchheim, with its arms, ammunition,

* "The name of Sarrelouis had been Jacobinized into Sarrelibre." ("Memoirs.") This may be a mistake.

and stores of provisions, was immediately surrendered to the French." ("Memoirs.")

Kléber was delighted at Ney's brilliant success. He complimented him in the highest terms, and in the presence of his men said the most flattering things respecting his talents, zeal, and courage. "But," continued he, turning to Ney, "I shall not compliment you upon your modesty, because, when carried too far, it ceases to be a good quality. In sum, you may receive my declaration as you please ; but my mind is made up, and I insist upon your being general of brigade."

The chasseurs clapped their hands in applause, and the officers warmly expressed their satisfaction at the general's determination. Ney alone remained thoughtful. He seemed still in doubt whether he should accept a promotion which he had already declined, and he uttered not a word. "Well," said Kléber in the kindest manner, "you appear very much grieved and confused, but the Austrians are there waiting for you ; go and vent your ill humor upon them. As for me, I shall acquaint the Directory with your promotion."

He kept his word in the following terms : " Adjutant-General Ney in this and the preceding campaigns has given numerous proofs of talent, zeal, and intrepidity ; but he surpassed even himself in the battle which took place yesterday, and he had two horses killed under him. I have thought myself justified in promoting him upon the field of battle to the rank of general of brigade. A commission of this grade was forwarded to him eighteen months ago, but his modesty would not allow him then to accept it. By confirming this promotion, Citizens Directors, you will perform a striking act of your justice."

Ney was accordingly promoted to the rank of brigadier-general, but before his commission arrived he had still further distinguished himself by the capture of Nuremberg, a "great and beautiful city, containing a noble-minded population smarting under recently inflicted injuries."

On August 15th, 1796, Ney received his commission of general of brigade with the following complimentary letter from Jourdan, the general-in-chief : " I inclose you, general.

your commission of general of brigade, which I have just received from the War Minister. Government has thus discharged the debt which it owed to one of its worthiest and most zealous servants ; and it has only done justice to the talents and courage of which you daily give fresh proofs. Accept my sincere congratulation." Ney determined to prove himself worthy of so high an honor, and in the very next engagement (near Sulzbach) he conducted his operations with so much ability and vigor that the Austrians were beaten at every point (though they occupied almost impregnable positions) and forced into a disorderly retreat.

Jourdan resigned the command of the army in September, 1796, and Bournonville was appointed to take his place. This was a most unfortunate selection, for Bournonville, though a man of talent, soon became disgusted with the service, and wished to divide the responsibility of commander-in-chief with his subordinate officers. He wrote as follows concerning Ney :

"*To the Minister of War:*

"I recommend your proposing to the Directory that Brigadier-General Ney be appointed general of division, to command the vanguard in the place of General Lefebvre. This officer, intrepid in action, has, during the campaign, covered himself with glory. He has always commanded corps in the vanguard, and is the only one I know who could efficiently command that of the army of Sambre-et-Meuse."

This was indeed a very high compliment ; but Ney richly deserved it. Bournonville was soon recalled, and that great soldier, Hoche, who had just failed in his expedition to Ireland owing to adverse winds and other unavoidable causes, assumed the command of the army. Hoche and Ney soon became the warmest of friends. "Allow me, general," said Hoche, in a letter to Ney, "to express my satisfaction at serving with you, whose military merit is so generally known and appreciated."

Ney fully reciprocated these kind expressions. "I sincerely participate," he wrote to Hoche, " in the delight of all my comrades at your arrival among us. The confidence with which your presence inspires the whole army is a sure presage of your success. I shall be too happy if I can at all contribute in bringing your undertakings to a successful issue, and thus deserve your esteem."

In his report of the action near Dierdorf, Hoche thus refers to Ney: "Ney proceeded with rapidity to Dierdorf, where he found the reserve of the Austrians, *six thousand* strong, and still untouched. With less than *five hundred* hussars he engaged this body during four consecutive hours, and by his skill and energy succeeded in gaining time until the arrival of our infantry and reserve of cavalry." Shortly afterward Ney, with a small force, attacked the enemy near Giessen. He charged with his wonted intrepidity ; but the Austrians greatly outnumbered him, and his troops were put to flight. Ney's horse fell and rolled with him into a ravine. He was immediately surrounded. Six dragoons made at him with their swords. Still he would not surrender. He was covered with bruises and blood, but he kept his astonished antagonists at bay until his sword snapped in twain. Even then he refused to yield, for, perceiving that the Fourth Regiment was about to make a fresh charge, he wished to give them time to come to his aid. He used the stump of his sword, and struck and parried with so much vigor and skill that for a while his enemies, as numerous as they were (they had increased to a whole company of cavalry), were unable to capture him. Finally his foot slipped and he fell to the ground. They then seized him and bore him in triumph (such as it was) to the Austrian headquarters. Ney's fame had preceded him. As he passed through the streets of Giessen almost the entire population, the women especially, pressed eagerly forward to see one whose deeds seemed to surpass those of the purest days of chivalry.

The Austrian officer who was escorting Ney to headquarters was greatly annoyed. "Really," said he, "one would suppose that he was some extraordinary animal." "Extraordinary indeed," said one of the ladies, "since it required a whole squadron of dragoons to take him."

One day Ney saw an Austrian riding his (Ney's) horse. The animal exhibited the most vicious, lazy, and obstinate spirit. The officers began to laugh at Ney about the worthlessness of his horse. "Let me show you how to manage him," said Ney. Permission was granted. Ney leaped into the saddle, and the noble animal, conscious of bearing his master, stepped proudly away. He made directly for the French lines, and Ney came very near effecting his escape. The Austrians were greatly alarmed. The trumpets were sounded, the heavy and light cavalry rode off in every direction, and soon every avenue was closed. Ney wheeled, and with equal speed rode back to the Austrian camp. There was no more jesting about his horse.

Ney's absence was deeply felt by Hoche and by the entire army. Hoche wrote to Ney as follows: "You know me sufficiently, my dear general, to give me credit for the affliction I feel at your misfortune. . . . I am awaiting in the most anxious impatience the moment when I shall embrace you. Write to me and inform me what pecuniary assistance you require. Adieu, my dear Ney; rely upon my sincere and constant friendship." Hoche rewarded Ney's men for their gallantry and good conduct. He gave a horse to one, a sword to another, a sash to a third. He also sent to Ney a magnificent belt, with a letter couched in the most flattering terms. "In sending you," he wrote from Friedberg, "the belt which the bearer will deliver to you, I do not pretend, my dear general, to reward either your success or your merit. Pray, therefore, accept it only as a feeble pledge of my personal esteem and unalterable friendship. Give me news of your health." The Directory also sent him a very kind and complimentary letter.

Ney was at length exchanged, and was soon put at the head of part of the forces destined for the invasion of England. But this project was chimerical, and came to nothing. In 1798 Ney's command formed part of the corps under Bernadotte, called the Army of Observation, on the Rhine. Bernadotte was exceedingly anxious to capture the city of Manheim. It was a most important place. It was separated from the French army by the river Rhine, and was defended by a powerful garrison. Its position was so strong and so advantageous every way that it was called the key of Germany on that part of the frontier. It also abounded with provisions and stores of almost every description; but it seemed to be almost impossible to take it by force. Ney therefore proposed to take it by stratagem.

After a careful reconnoissance, Ney was convinced that a few brave, determined men might cross the river a short distance from the city, march round the enemy's cantonments, and fall upon him in the rear before a force sufficient to repel them could be collected at that particular point of attack. Before engaging in this bold enterprise, Ney resolved to cross the river in disguise and reconnoitre the enemy's position in person.

"Accordingly one evening he assumed the garb of a Prussian peasant, passed the Rhine, entered Manheim with a basket upon his arm, proceeded through the streets, made his observations, and obtained precise information as to the force which defended it, and the provisions it contained.

"No one suspected him of being a spy, as the German was his native language, and his manners not above those of his assumed character. Besides, Ney had a great deal of tact and address, which upon occasion he well knew how to use. He was about to leave the fortress full of hope when he perceived a soldier of the garrison supporting a woman in the last stage of pregnancy. Having accosted the woman, he expressed an interest in her situation, and his fear that her illness might begin before the night was over. 'No matter if it does,' the soldier replied; 'should this be the case, the commandant will allow the drawbridge to be let down at any hour of the night, so that the instant she is taken ill she can have assistance.'

"This was all Ney wanted to know, and he soon recrossed the Rhine to make his preparations. He selected a hundred and fifty of his bravest soldiers, crossed the river with them in skiffs, went rapidly forward, and concealed them under the walls of Manheim in the hope that the woman's labor pains would soon come on. She did not disappoint him; her sufferings began, the bridge was lowered, and an instant after

Ney and his men took possession of it. The latter, with their general at their head, then pushed forward, and the weakness of their force was masked by the darkness of the night. They assailed the garrison with such fury and determination that they were utterly demoralized, and after a short struggle he obtained complete possession of the place. This achievement put the seal to his celebrity." ("Memoirs.")

Being master of Manheim, they advanced toward Philipsburg. Upon arriving there he demanded an interview with the governor of the town. The governor dispatched the chief of the advanced posts to represent him with authority to accept any reasonable proposals which Ney might make. Ney, who had but a small force, feigned to be desirous of sparing the garrison, and offered a suspension of arms. The chief of the advanced posts at first eluded the proposal, but being a man of weak judgment and devoid of energy, he soon suffered himself to be led by Ney, and the suspension was accepted. Thus was Philipsburg blockaded upon parole, and Ney became free in his movements.

On March 28th, 1799, Ney was appointed general of division. His modesty at once took the alarm, and he received his commission only to send it back. He felt that he might be competent to command a brigade, but not a division. He therefore wrote to the war minister as follows :

"I have received your letter of the 8th of Germinal (March 28th), in which was inclosed the decree appointing me general of division. The Directory, in conferring this promotion upon me, probably yielded to advantageous reports of my conduct ; but it is my duty to be more severe on my own merits. If my talents were truly such as the Directory have conceived, I should not hesitate to accept the promotion ; unfortunately such is not the case, and I am forced to decline the honor the Government would confer upon me. I trust that this refusal will be considered nothing more than a proof of the sincere patriotism by which I am actuated, and of the disinterestedness with which I perform my professional duties. May I beg you will assure the Directory that I shall never have any other aim than that of deserving its esteem."

But the Directory paid no attention to Ney's refusal. The minister who forwarded Ney's letter was directed to make known to him that the Government persisted in its decree. He wrote to Ney:

"The Executive Directory, before whom I laid your letter requesting me to tender your refusal of the rank of general of division to which you had been appointed, has directed me to inform you that it persists in the decree which promotes you to that grade. It sees in your modesty only a stronger claim to reward for the services you have already rendered, and a valuable earnest for those you will hereafter render to the republic. In consequence of which, I herewith again forward the decree of your appointment."

Still Ney hesitated. He had already performed the duties of the new office to which he was appointed, but he was afraid to accept the title.

Bernadotte wrote to him not to displease the Directory by refusing the promotion which it persisted in conferring upon him. "Look around you, my dear Ney," he wrote, "and say candidly whether your conscience does not call upon you to lay aside a modesty which becomes out of place and even dangerous when carried to excess. We must have ardent souls and hearts as inaccessible to fear as to seduction to be able to lead the armies of France. Who more than yourself is gifted with these qualities? It would be an act of weakness, then, to shrink from the career that is open to you. Adieu, my dear Ney. . . . You will, I know, listen to everything from one who is attached to you by the ties of the warmest friendship and the most perfect esteem."

Ney yielded to Bernadotte's advice, and assumed the rank to which the Directory had raised him. In May, 1799, he was transferred to the Army of Switzerland, commanded by Masséna. At Andelfingen and Altikon, on the banks of the Thur, and at Winterthur, he more than sustained his high reputation. At the very commencement of the action at Winterthur, Ney "was struck with a musket-ball, which, after passing through his thigh, spent itself in the shoulder of his horse. He remained on the field, however, after allowing some of the men to bind up his wound and stanch the blood with their pocket-handkerchiefs. Afterward, at the head of a small body of cavalry, they charged a whole squadron of Hungarians, and being attacked by a foot soldier just as he had struck down a hussar, he had not time to turn aside the bayonet, which pierced through the sole of his foot. He succeeded in cutting down his rash assailant, who, however, in falling, fired his piece and shattered Ney's wrist." * ("Memoirs.")

The severity of Ney's wounds forced him to retire for awhile from the command of his troops, but at the end of two months his wounds were healed, and he again joined Masséna. But he was soon ordered by the Directory to join the Army of the Rhine. Masséna was deeply grieved at this order. His circumstances were too critical to permit the departure of so able an officer as Ney, and he therefore begged Ney to remain with him until the danger was past. "I was aware, my dear general," he wrote to Ney, "of the order given you to join the army on the Rhine, but I must request you will defer your departure for some days. Indeed, I most earnestly entreat you to do so. You are necessary, nay, indispensable, to your division ; and I should feel the most lively regret if you were to leave until the arrival of the general appointed to succeed you. At all events, be assured that it is with great regret I see you taken from an army to whose success you have so powerfully contributed." Ney therefore remained a short time longer.

At Heilbronn, Ney gained a magnificent victory over a greatly superior force almost solely by the use of his artillery. Never were three guns served with more skill and effect. The Austrian cavalry, a large and fine body of men, made repeated and desperate charges, but Ney's artillery mowed them down by hundreds, until at last, tired out and demoralized, they fled tumultuously from the field. A few days afterward the Austrians appeared in overwhelming numbers, and the French army was compelled to retreat, owing to the

* Wounded in thigh (*knee*, according to Ney's official report to Masséna), foot, wrist (or *hand*, according to Ney's official report).

bad dispositions and faulty arrangements in general of the commanding officer. Ney warmly protested against them, but it did no good. Nothing was left but "patient resignation to events." The end soon came. The Austrians attacked the French in their ill-chosen position, and, after a spirited resistance, completely routed them. The French were compelled to evacuate Manheim, and the Austrians, flushed with victory, boldly attacked their communications.

"General Vandermassen and Adjutant-General Lefol, having collected a few men, threw themselves in front of the enemy, but being almost immediately surrounded, some of their soldiers were put to the sword and the remainder unconditionally surrendered. The French army was now in open flight, and the greater part of it would have been destroyed had not Ney come to its assistance. In the action which followed Ney was twice wounded. He received a musket shot in the chest, and his thigh was dreadfully contused by a Biscayan." ("Memoirs.")

General Muller, the commander-in-chief, was a patriotic but a very slow and incompetent officer. He had succeeded, with the best intentions, in getting the French army into a most miserable and critical condition. Ney was disgusted with his operations, but he continued faithfully to perform his duties. General Muller was soon recalled by the Directory, and Ney was appointed (September, 1799) to take his place as commander-in-chief. He at first refused to accept the appointment. "The difficult situation in which the army was placed and his own ill health—two wounds being yet unhealed—induced him to do all in his power to get rid of the perilous honor conferred upon him. But the Directory had forwarded his commission, and the generals and other officers unanimously entreated him to put himself at their head. He therefore acceded to their wishes, but rather as a self-immolated victim than as an officer whose ambition is crowned by fortune.

"His first act was to claim the indulgence of his colleagues, and to invoke the aid of their talents and exertions. 'The Executive Directory,' said he in his circular, 'has called upon me to assume the provisional command of the army in the room of General Muller. You are aware of the inefficiency of my military talents for this important station, particularly in our present critical situation. I shall perhaps become the victim of my obedience, but under the circumstances in which we are placed I am bound to accept the appointment. I therefore claim your kind solicitude for the safety of the troops under your command, as also your individual kindness toward myself. I must, moreover, inform you that I have signified to the Directory my intention of not retaining the command beyond ten days.'

" Nothing could be more modest than this address, nor show a stronger proof of the most devoted zeal. But every officer in the army had the strongest confidence in Ney's talents. The different commanders of corps, whose assistance he solicited, had fought with him, some in Helvetia, others in the Army of Sambre-et-Meuse ; all knew his ability and daring courage, and all were delighted at seeing him assume the command."

General Gillot congratulated the army upon having Ney at its head. He wrote to Ney as follows : " I have learned with real pleasure your appointment to the provisional command of the Army of the Rhine. . . . You may depend, Citizen General, upon my vigilance for the safety of the troops under my command, and believe me when I say that I will always exert myself to deserve your esteem and friendship."

General Leval was still warmer in his congratulations. He wrote : " If, in the whole course of my life, my dear comrade, I ever experienced satisfaction, it was on receiving the news of your appointment to the chief command of this army. It is of a certainty weak, but it is composed of soldiers who greatly esteem you. You are calculated to inspire confidence ; and it is with redoubled zeal that I shall study to execute scrupulously the orders you may give me. . . . You may rely, my dear general, upon my neglecting nothing to contribute to the success of your undertakings. That is the first proof I will give you of the satisfaction I experience at being under your command. Rely, also, upon my sincere devotion and friendship."

General Legrand was equally delighted. In his letter he says : " The last courier, my dear general, brought me the news of General Muller's departure from Paris, and your appointment to the chief command of the army. This gives me the most lively pleasure. . . . The promptitude with which I will proceed to whatever post you may assign me will prove to you how much pleasure I feel in serving under your orders, and the sincere attachment of your comrade and friend."

Ney at once acted with decision and vigor. The army was in a measure reorganized. Incompetent and sore-headed officers were weeded out and new men put in their places. His soldiers were comparatively well fed, well clothed, and well armed. The strictest discipline was enforced in every department ; the frontiers were carefully fortified and guarded ; the enemy, closely watched, was foiled in every movement, and confidence, even enthusiasm, was infused into every branch of the service. The wily Archduke Charles endeavored to surprise Ney, but was soundly punished for his presumption. At Frankfort the Austrian militia were quickly overthrown and almost entirely destroyed.

The French army was daily gaining important advantages, though Ney had almost insuperable obstacles to overcome, and its *morale* was of the highest order. Grosgeran and Trebbin were easily taken, and at Heidelberg (October 15th) Ney gained a decisive victory over Prince Lichtenstein, who commanded during the action. The Austrians made a most heroic resistance, but they were at length cut to pieces and driven in confusion from the field. On October 29th Ney encountered and routed the enemy at Haslach. The next day there was an engagement near Slocksberg, and the Imperialists, under Prince Hohenlohe, were again defeated. On both occasions Ney was greatly outnumbered, but he made up for this disproportion of force by the skill, prudence, and valor with which he combated the enemy.

General Lecourbe now assumed command of the army, and victory at once deserted its standards. Lecourbe had some military talent, but he was petulant, jealous, and wanting in energy. The French army met with several reverses, and was forced into a retrograde movement. Lecourbe was greatly disheartened, and made a strong appeal to Ney to help him out of his difficulties. He asked him to "employ his influence in rekindling the courage of the men, in rousing the energy they were capable of displaying, and again exciting that confidence in themselves which had so often led them to victory."

Ney readily promised to aid him in every way that he could, and in the very next engagement, near Wislok, Ney taught the enemy a severe lesson. Prince Hohenlohe, in strong force, attacked Ney, with a mere handful of men. The action was long and obstinately contested. Hohenlohe made repeated charges with the most determined bravery, but every attack was successfully resisted, until at length Ney, seizing the opportune moment, executed a brilliant manœuvre and decided the fortunes of the day. Hohenlohe retreated, and the French were left masters of the field.

This victory, entirely due to Ney, restored the confidence of the army, and the soldiers were eager to be led against the enemy. In the campaign of 1800–1801 Ney served under Moreau in the Army of the Rhine.* Here he won fresh laurels. He foiled and defeated the enemy at every point. At Stettin he made a night attack upon the Austrians, who occupied a strong position in the gorges of the mountains, and before day they were entirely routed. At Ingolstadt, Ney gained an important victory over the Austrian General Neu, who had great reputation in his army as a bold, dashing, and successful officer. He endeavored to surprise Ney, but was himself surprised and ignobly defeated. The French were so confident of victory that they formed and marched against the

---

* Ney seems to have suffered a good deal from his wounds. Before he joined Moreau he had for some time been "living in retirement at Malgrange, where his still unhealed wounds confined him to his bed." The two wounds which he received in September, 1799 (chest and thigh) were not serious, as he did not leave the army, but continued in active service. It is probable that he received *other wounds* of which no account is given.

enemy amid shouts of laughter and derision. "Here we are," said an old hussar, "*nez à nez** (Ney à Neu). Let us see how matters will come to pass." Ney broke through the Austrian ranks, put them to complete flight, and took six pieces of cannon and six hundred prisoners.

At the great battle of Hohenlinden (so graphically described by the poet Campbell, who viewed the conflict at a safe and convenient distance), Ney was foremost in those terrible onsets which decided the fortunes of the day. His talents, his energy, his *staying* qualities had never been more conspicuously displayed. Ney's last feat in this war added to his renown as the ablest strategist in the French army. I quote from the "Memoirs."

"Ney, in pursuit of the enemy, had arrived upon the Ems and nearly overtaken the Austrian rear-guard. He was directed to continue the pursuit; but he could not reach the enemy without crossing the plain, and he was not sufficiently strong to encounter the cavalry by which it was covered. Unable, therefore, to employ force, he had recourse to stratagem. He demanded an interview with Schwartzenburg, represented to that general the hopelessness of the struggle, and the danger of resistance; in short, he performed his part so well that he obtained, without firing a shot, that which he did not feel himself strong enough to carry by arms. The prince gave up the whole country to him, and peaceably withdrew behind the Ips."

A treaty of peace between Austria and France was signed at Luneville on February 9th, 1801, and Moreau and his army returned to France. Ney was warmly received by the First Consul. He had taken no part in the revolution of the 18th Brumaire, but subsequent events had seemed to him fully to justify the change which had taken place, and he heartily supported the new government.

Bonaparte was lavish in his praises. He was anxious to

---

* "*Nez à nez* (nose to nose), pronounced Ney-à-Ney. The pronunciation of the German *Neu* is between the name Ney and the English monosyllable nigh. Thus the English reader may easily understand the *double entente*."—"Memoirs."

attach Ney to his person and his fortunes, and he therefore plied him with all the arts of which he was capable. Josephine ably seconded him. She invoked the aid of love—a power which moves the world. " She brought about an attachment between Ney and a young favorite of hers (Mlle. Aglae Louise Auguié), and wound up the romance with the marriage of the lovers."

The following letter to Ney explains itself:

"I inclose you, general, the letter which you requested for Citizen Auguié. May I beg that you will read it? I have not mentioned in it all the good which I know and think of you; for I would leave this amiable family the satisfaction of discovering your good qualities themselves. But I here repeat the assurance of the interest which both Bonaparte and I take in this marriage, and of the satisfaction which Bonaparte will feel in promoting the happiness of two persons toward whom he entertains very particular feelings of regard and esteem. I share with him in this double feeling.

"LAPAGERIE BONAPARTE.

"MALMAISON, May 30, 1802."

Ney went, saw, conquered. Mlle. Auguié was a beautiful woman, of gentle heart and rare accomplishments. She was a niece of Madame Campan, and had been educated at the famous school of St. Germain. One of her intimate friends was Hortense Beauharnais, afterward Madame Louis Bonaparte, Queen of Holland. The marriage was celebrated at the château of Grignon, the residence of M. Auguié, on the 26th day of July, 1802.*

Ney was quite poor. He had had abundant opportunities for amassing wealth of almost every description, but he was no plunderer like Masséna or Augereau. "Everything for France and her soldiers," said he; "nothing for myself." There never was a more generous, a more unselfish patriot. He required the inhabitants of the countries through which

---

* Goodrich says Ney was married on August 4th, 1802. But, according to the official record, he was married " le 6 Thermidor an dix de la République Française à 10 heures du matin"—July 26th, 1802.

he passed to feed and clothe his starving and naked soldiers, but he permitted no stealing or marauding of any character. He punished with severity those who were guilty of such acts. His wife's fortune was also small. But both of them were young, happy, and hopeful.*

"In the village where Ney was married dwelt an old couple who had been married half a century. Ney clothed them and made them receive their second † nuptial benediction on the same day and at the same altar with himself and his young bride, thus marking his own marriage by an act of benevolence. 'These old people,' he observed, 'will recall to my mind the lowliness of my own origin ; and this renewal of their long union will prove of happy augury for my own.' The thought was the emanation of a noble mind ; but the presage which it expressed was, unhappily, not to be accomplished." ("Memoirs.")

Prior to his marriage Ney had been appointed inspector-general of cavalry in the Third, Fifth, and Twenty-sixth Divisions, and the zeal and ability with which he performed his duties gave much satisfaction to the First Consul. Ney corrected abuses, disciplined wrong-doers, introduced many needed reforms, and gave new life and energy to this important arm of the service.

But a still higher honor awaited him. In the fall of 1802 Bonaparte appointed Ney Minister Plenipotentiary to the Republic of Switzerland. This country was torn in pieces by intestine feuds of the most formidable character. Ney's mission under ordinary circumstances would have been delicate and difficult, but it was rendered doubly so by the fact that he went as a kind of armed mediator, with peace in one hand and a sword in the other.‡

---

* "Le brave homme !" écrit Mme. Campan ; "je m'abonnerais volontiers à la moitié de ses qualités pour chacune de mes nièces !"—"Le Maréchal Ney, le Général," etc.

† "In France, when a couple has spent half a century in the joys of wedded life, the nuptial benediction is renewed."—"Memoirs."

‡ Ney had about thirty thousand soldiers in Switzerland. We must also remember that England and other foreign powers were violently opposed to French mediation in Switzerland, and were quick to throw every possi-

We may make people obey us, but we cannot make them love us. Still, Ney, in spite of seemingly insurmountable difficulties, conducted his negotiations with so much patience, prudence, and tact (qualities which it is generally supposed he did not possess) that in a little more than twelve months he had accomplished the object of his mission to the entire satisfaction of the First Consul (always hard to please), and, what is still more wonderful, to the entire satisfaction of the Swiss people themselves. He had established "peace and concord" in Switzerland, and had won the love and confidence of his bitterest foes—indeed, of a whole nation, suspicious, embittered, rebellious, and at times exasperated almost beyond endurance.* The glory of this achievement is second only to that which encircled the hero's brow in the Russian retreat.† Nor were the honest Swiss either slow or ungenerous in testifying their sense of the value of Ney's services. There were public rejoicings everywhere, and all felt that the French general had rendered an invaluable service to the entire nation.‡

ble obstacle in the way of such mediation. Rapp, too, as the forerunner of Ney, was a total failure, adding (though with the best intentions) fuel to the flame wherever he went.

* The spirit of revolt had been aroused by French aggression in 1798, only four years before Ney's mission to Switzerland.

† Ney's fame as a soldier is so great that historians have been accustomed lightly to pass over this important period of the Marshal's life, and to seek for laurels only in his military career. But Ney was almost as great in the Cabinet as he was in the field. A short time before he left Switzerland, Talleyrand, prince of diplomatists, wrote to him as follows : "The Government relies upon your talents and zeal. You are equally distinguished, General, both as a soldier and a politician." Every one must admit that Ney's diplomatic career in Switzerland reflected infinite credit alike upon his head and his heart.

"Sent as a plenipotentiary to Switzerland, Ney displayed much adroitness and vigor, and was exceedingly successful in difficult circumstances."
—" Imperial Dictionary of Universal Biography."

‡ Prior to Ney's departure the Landamman was authorized to express the regret of the confederated cantons at losing him, and in their name to forward to him a snuff-box with the monogram of Switzerland set in diamonds on the lid, and accompanied with the following letter :

GENERAL : At the moment of your departure from us, . . . allow me to fulfil a most agreeable duty, that of speaking of the good you have done us and of our gratitude toward you. It is not solely the expression of my

A great soldier, a great statesman, a great man, Ney was the brightest star in the consular or the imperial galaxy.

own private sentiments that I now offer you. Having for the last ten months enjoyed the most delightful intercourse with you, it is quite natural that I should entertain toward you much esteem and personal attachment; but as chief magistrate of all Switzerland it is in her name that I now address you. All the cantons, on being made acquainted with your intended departure, have expressed the most lively regret. They all set a proper value upon the share you have taken in the beneficial changes which the present year has brought us. Switzerland is restored to peace ; order is everywhere established ; the diversity of opinions among us merges each day into a spirit of moderation and harmony. . . . An act of kindness attaches him who performs it as well as him upon whom it is conferred ; we therefore do not fear that you will forget us ; we would even, on every occasion, continue to rely upon your support, for you have conferred upon us at once the right and the habit of so doing. The cantons have expressed a wish that you would accept a feeble pledge of their attachment and gratitude ; and seeing the preparations for your departure, I have requested M. Maillardoz to present it to you at Paris. It is a token of remembrance and nothing more ; but we should esteem ourselves happy if, by calling to your recollection a nation whom you have so essentially obliged, it should prove the means of your not forgetting the sentiments which every member of that nation will forever feel toward you.

LOUIS D'AFFRY,
Landamman of Switzerland.
MAUSSON,
Chancellor of the Confederation.

FRIBOURG, December 28, 1803.

" The citizens of Berne determined to perpetuate the remembrance of Ney's mission by the erection of a public monument ; they likewise had a medal struck upon which were represented the disorders to which he had put an end and the peace he had established."—" Memoirs."

Murat wrote to Ney : " This campaign of an instant has covered you with glory. It is a noble thing to have obtained, by mild proceedings, combined with a formidable appearance, that which another would have effected by force of arms."

Had Ney's mission failed, the flame of civil war would have burst forth in every part of the Swiss Republic.

NAPOLEON.

CHAPTER II.

UPON his return from Switzerland, Ney was appointed commander-in-chief of the camp at Montreuil, where Bonaparte was making active preparations for the invasion of England. Many historians have supposed that this was a mere feint, that he had no serious intention of invading England. But Bonaparte himself repeatedly declared at St. Helena that such was his intention, and there seems to be no good reason to doubt it. It was about the silliest project that ever entered his head, for had he succeeded in crossing the Channel, he would, in all probability, have found his grave on English soil. Ney, however, was a firm believer in the feasibility of the plan.*

* His observations are interesting. I quote from the "Memoirs": "Moreau dwelt at great length upon the dangers of the invasion of England. He deemed it nothing short of madness to confront line-of-battle ships with gunboats, and to hope that the passage across the Channel could be won with such a craft. Ney was not of the same opinion. Barring the accidents of the sea, he thought that by taking advantage of light winds, of calms, and of long nights, it was not impossible to elude the vigilance of the Channel fleet and escape from the overwhelming superiority of the British naval force. He had procured a journal of the winds prevalent in the Channel, and was well acquainted with their course, their variation, the periods when they blow with violence, and those when their action is suspended. He had, therefore, no doubt that by seizing a favorable opportunity, the French army might escape the fleet which alarmed Moreau so much, and effect a landing upon the shores of England. 'The British nation,' he said, 'were convinced of this, for the British admirals, who in 1756 were consulted on the possibility of such an event, had unanimously declared that they could not answer for preventing a landing, even had they ten times the force they commanded; and in 1770 the same answer had been given. The Duke of Argyle and some of the most distinguished British officers of the period had often declared their conviction in Parliament that situations and conjunctions might often arise at sea which would give a hostile army every possible opportunity of landing in England without the British fleets, even were they collected together, being able to secure the safety of the coast. The reason of this,' he said, ' was very clear. The westerly winds and those from the south and south-

His activity at Montreuil was unceasing. Like Wellington, he would trust to nobody, but insisted on seeing everything for himself, and knowing beyond a doubt that everything was properly done. No man can be great in war or great in any-

> west blow from France to England, and during their prevalence vessels sailing from the ports of France make good way, while those of England cannot leave their ports; thus the most formidable fleets are of no use during the continuance of those winds, and an attempt might be successfully made. A sudden cessation of wind,' continued Ney, ' might produce the same effect as a violent and continued gale; for if the British fleet were overtaken in a dead calm, either in the middle or at the end of a voyage from one part of the coast to another, it would baffle the talents of its officers and render the valor of its seamen of no avail. What could be done with ships of the line under such circumstances? Have recourse to oars? That would be impracticable. Use their boats? What chance would these have against our host of gunboats, *péniches*, and light vessels, armed and equipped as they are? Besides, the tides and fogs will again increase our chances of success. How many of our squadrons are there which have escaped from the British cruisers in a fog or during a dark night? Remember how the Prince of Orange crossed the Channel, and that during six hours his fleet passed close to that of James II. without being perceived. The Earl of Dartmouth, having ascertained at length that it had sailed, bore up in pursuit of it; but as he began to brace up his yards the wind became more ahead, having veered to the south, and he was unable to interrupt the prince's landing. The same thing afterward occurred to the French fleet cruising off Brest. It suffered the ships under the command of Admiral Anson to pass without perceiving them; and this distinguished officer did not know the danger he had run until his return to England. But these are not our only chances. The English are terror-stricken at our preparations, and the malcontents among them are excited with hope. Such vessels as ours have always terrified those islanders. In the reign of Elizabeth one of her ministers frankly declared that England had never been more exposed to the dangers of an invasion than since the King of Spain had built small boats similar to those used by the Flemish and the French. The same description of vessels has even more recently excited the alarms of Boscawen. This admiral knew the amount of our force in the Mediterranean; he knew that, having been defeated in a great naval action on the 20th of November, 1759, we were not in a state to attempt any enterprise. Still, such was the impression made upon him by our gunboat on the coast, that on seeing a few sails appear on the horizon he had no doubt of their forming a part of an invading expedition, and he immediately stated his apprehensions to the king and the government. In an incredibly short space of time all England was in rumor, while the dreaded expedition turned out to be nothing but a convoy of colliers.' " See also " Lord Dudley's Letters," p. 37.

thing unless he adopts a rule of this kind. And yet Napier, Jomini, Goodrich, and others say that Ney was " notoriously indolent." His " Memoirs" show, his whole career from beginning to end shows, that no assertion could be more false. Indeed, Ney worked so hard and required others to work so hard that Napoleon was compelled gently to remonstrate with him. He told Ney that all men were not so richly endowed as he was, and therefore could not stand so much physical and mental toil. Ney neglected nothing. He established schools of instruction both for officers and men ; he drilled his soldiers several hours daily ; his inspections were frequent and thorough ; his discipline was rigorous, yet tempered with mercy ; the health and comfort, even the recreations * of his soldiers received his most careful attention ; every branch of the service was put on the soundest, the most efficient footing ; and it was universally conceded that Ney's soldiers at Montreuil were the very best in the French army.

Amid his arduous labors Ney found time to write a valuable treatise on the art of war, which he modestly styled " Military Studies," a work, indeed, which is everywhere regarded as a masterpiece of its kind.†

* " The barraques, or wooden huts, being all built upon the same model, and perfectly uniform, had the most agreeable appearance. They were whitewashed and divided into groups ; these again were intersected by streets, or, rather, alleys, each bearing the name of some distinguished soldier or of some great battle won. In front were avenues ; the parade was surrounded by plantations ; and in the rear were kitchens, dancing rooms, and gardens. . . . Farther on were the eating huts, with their fireplaces and benches, and racks for the firelocks and pegs for the knapsacks."—" Memoirs."

† This work has been translated into English by G. H. Caunter, with an Introduction by Major A. James, of the British army, author of " Battalion Movements," " Brigade Formations," etc. It is dedicated to the " officers of the British army." Major James says : " In the ' Military Studies of Marshal Ney ' we see the hand of a master ; like the cartoons of Raphael, they constitute a monument which bids fair to be *ære perennius*. . . . Many of his formations constitute the most valuable portion of the French regulations, . . . and his officers at Montreuil were confessedly the best instructed, the most ready, and the most intelligent in the army. *Fas est etiam ab hoste doceri*. If a military genius like Dundas or the Duke of Elchingen appears once in a century, their labors become the

On the 18th day of May, 1804, the army made Bonaparte Emperor of France. The *Senatus Consultum* did not amount to a row of pins. Ney had been quite active in getting up and forwarding addresses to the First Consul, urging him to assume the imperial purple, in order that he might "consolidate the glorious work which he had so auspiciously begun."

On the 19th day of May, 1804, eighteen general officers were made marshals of the empire. Ney was included in this "new aristocracy," as it was popularly called, and it is but just to say that no man ever wielded more worthily or more brilliantly the "staff of supreme command."

Bonaparte's plans for the invasion of England failed through the notorious incompetency of the French naval officers, and because of the very great competency of the British naval officers. His land preparations were most excellent. It would have been difficult to better them. Two of his best officers, Ney and Soult, were in command of the troops destined for the English expedition, and they neglected nothing which was calculated to insure the success of the undertaking. Soult, commanding at Boulogne, was almost as active as Ney. From daybreak to nightfall he was on horseback, inspecting his troops, superintending their various evolutions, or directing their labors in the intrenchments. Ney's preparations for the embarkation of his troops were almost perfect. I quote from the "Memoirs":

"The troops on the coast received orders to hold themselves in readiness to embark at a moment's notice. Ney had only to see to the exact execution of the orders transmitted by

property of the world, and, like the sacred fire of the temple, should be religiously preserved."—Caunter's "Military Studies of Marshal Ney."

"That Ney united profound science to the experience of a life of active warfare is placed beyond a doubt by the manuscripts left in his own handwriting, containing his own observations upon the various campaigns in which he served, and also his military studies for the use of his own officers when he commanded the camp at Montreuil. To this we may add that he first improved upon the old system of military tactics and founded the system now followed by the French armies."—"Memoirs."

And yet Napier and Jomini say that Ney "was *unlearned in the abstract science of war!*"

the minister. He distributed his ammunition and the tools he was to take with him among the several transports. He then arranged the distribution of the flotilla ; he directed that each battalion and each company should make themselves acquainted with the vessels assigned to them, and that every man should be ready to rush on board at the very first signal. But as dispatch necessitates great precision of movement, he resolved to drill his troops into such precision by making them execute sham embarkations. The divisions composing his corps were successively assembled on the shore, and by turns escaladed the gunboats in which they were to embark. This they executed in the most beautiful style, and Ney was satisfied with it ; but the divisions had only performed it separately ; when together they might display less coolness and promptitude, and he resolved to put them to the test. The infantry, cavalry, and artillery assumed their arms ; each column placed itself opposite to its own vessels. All were formed into platoons for embarking, at a little distance from each other, and divided by sections. The whole, from left to right, were in a parallel line to the anchorage. A first gun was fired ; the general officers and staff officers alighted from their horses and placed themselves at the head of the troops which they were respectively to lead. The drums had ceased rolling and the men had unfixed their bayonets. Everything was ready and each man prepared. A second gun was heard nearer to them, and the generals of divisions gave the word of command : ' Prepare to embark ! ' The brigadier-generals received it, transmitted it to the colonels, and the latter to the officers under them. A dead silence now succeeded ; each man was attentive and motionless, and each controlled the intense excitement under which he labored. A third gun gave forth its thunder, and the word ' Forward, columns ! ' immediately followed. Each soldier now yielded to an almost uncontrollable emotion. When a last report was heard, the word ' March ! ' was pronounced ; it was almost drowned by acclamations ; the columns immediately put themselves in motion and got into the boats. *In ten minutes and a half twenty-five thousand men were already on board.* The troops felt assured that they were immediately to set sail ; they took their places, and were engaged in making their quarters comfortable when a shot was unexpectedly fired. The drums rolled and called the men to arms ; they formed upon the decks of their respective boats. A fresh discharge soon followed the first ; they fancied it was the signal for weighing anchor, and they received it with cries of ' Long live the Emperor ! ' but it was only an order to land. They were unable to control the expression of their disappointment, which broke forth in murmurs. They resigned themselves, however ; and scarcely had *thirteen minutes elapsed before they were again upon the beach, formed in line of battle.* The marshal now saw that he could depend upon his preparations, and calculate to a minute the time his troops would occupy in embarking."

But these splendid troops (about equal, under Ney, to Wellington's army which broke up at Bordeaux in 1814) * were destined never to cross the English Channel. Pitt soon stirred up a powerful coalition against France, and Bonaparte quickly changed his plans. Indeed, a general European war was inevitable. Bonaparte's restless and sinister ambition ; his forcible annexation of territory to which he had not the shadow of a claim ; his avowed purpose to continue such aggressions ; his dark, his ceaseless intrigues ; his underhand system of espionage with respect to other nations ; his swaggering, *novus homo* insolence—these things were simply unbearable, and they would at no distant period have produced a general war in Europe even if Pitt had not succeeded in organizing a coalition against Napoleon.

In August, 1805, the French army suddenly quitted the coast and marched rapidly to the Austrian frontier. Austria was concentrating her troops on the banks of the Danube and the Rhine, and the Russian forces were *en route* for the seat

---

* " Speaking of Waterloo, Wellington one day said to two of his general officers, sweeping the table with his closed hand : ' Had I had the army that broke up at Bordeaux I should have swept Bonaparte off the face of the earth in two hours."—" Words on Wellington," Fraser. " Voice from Waterloo," Sergeant-Major Cotton.

of war. Napoleon knew that his safety consisted in rapid movements and in bold surprises. He was terrible in attack and in victory, but nothing, or next to nothing, in defence and in defeat. This one fact must forever place him at the tail end of great generals. He had the best of lieutenants—Ney, Soult, Lannes, Murat, Bernadotte, Davout. He could hardly fail to accomplish his purposes, especially when contending with an inferior foe.

Ney was in command of the Sixth Corps. He left Montreuil on the 28th day of August, and arrived at Lauterburg on September 24th. "In this short interval Ney's division had executed a march of more than three hundred leagues, which was upward of ten leagues a day. History has no example of such rapidity." *

During this long and toilsome march Ney's arrangements and dispositions of every kind were so complete that the war minister wrote to him that he had "no orders to give him; that he had left nothing for him" (the war minister) "to do." In the operations leading up to the capitulation of Ulm Ney's troops bore no unimportant part. At Guntzburg (October 9th) and Haslach (11th) they fought with a courage and determination which nothing could withstand; which, indeed, so appalled and demoralized the enemy that he knew not which way to turn. At Elchingen (14th) Ney gained a glorious victory. He and "His Serene Highness," Prince Murat, had had a stiff quarrel a few days before.†

Murat, as the Emperor's brother-in-law and chief lieutenant, had given orders to Ney which Ney considered absurd and very dangerous to the safety of the troops and the general success of the Emperor's plans. Indeed, it is now known that Murat would have almost ruined the grand army by his ill-considered and violent measures but for the energetic and continued remonstrances of Marshal Ney. Ney again and again

---

* "Memoirs."

† "They came very near fighting. . . . Already had Ney written to appoint a place of meeting, when, recollecting that he was in the presence of the enemy, he altered his mind and resolved to bear that which he could not prevent."—"Memoirs."

pointed out to the war minister and the major-general the inevitable consequences of Murat's false dispositions, "and the Emperor, at last seeing that his communications had been given up to the Austrians by Murat's rashness, revoked some of his arrangements, and Ney had the satisfaction of receiving orders from the Grand Duke himself" (Murat) "to re-occupy the positions whose importance he had so vainly endeavored to point out." ("Memoirs.)"

"Napoleon," says Thiers ("Consulate and Empire") "coincided entirely with Marshals Ney and Lannes against Murat, and gave instructions for repairing immediately the egregious blunders * committed during the preceding days. . . . For Ney was reserved the honor of executing in the morning of the 14th, at Elchingen, the vigorous operation which was again to put us in possession of both banks of the river. This intrepid marshal was deeply mortified by some indiscreet expressions used by Murat in the recent altercation

* Napoleon, in my opinion, was responsible in a great measure for these *egregious blunders.* He didn't believe that *Mack* had the slightest idea of crossing the Danube and cutting his way into Bohemia; he was slow to act when his attention was called to Murat's "blunders," and he was too far from the scene of operations fully to understand and appreciate the critical situation in which that portion of his army occupying the left bank of the Danube was placed. If Mack had possessed even middling military talent he would have crossed the Danube, overthrown Dupont's division (the only one left to oppose him), destroyed Napoleon's communications, and marched in triumph to the Bohemian mountains. It could have been done with the utmost ease, and it would have been done, in part at least, but for Ney's vigilance and unceasing protests. As it was, a portion of the Austrian army "crossed the Danube on October 10th and spread like a torrent over the French-communications." ("Memoirs".) Dupont's division (of Ney's corps) alone saved Napoleon and the army from disgrace. Dupont fought a battle at Haslach which would have done honor to the greatest generals. Neither Ney nor Wellington could have shown more skill, firmness, or courage. It was a miracle that he was not overpowered. After the battle of Haslach Napoleon woke up and "repaired immediately Murat's egregious blunders." But suppose Wellington or even Lord Hill had been in command at Ulm! What would have become of Napoleon? His famous "Campaign of Ulm" reflects no credit upon him whatever. It is easy to gain victories over steel-plated fools, or traitors, or both, like the Austrian General Mack. See **Lanfrey's** "History of Napoleon."

which he had with him. Murat, as if impatient of too long arguments, had told him that he understood nothing of all the plans that were explained to him, and that it was his own custom not to make his till he was facing the enemy. This was the proud answer which a man of action might have addressed to an empty babbler.

"Marshal Ney, on horseback, early in the morning of the 14th, in full uniform and wearing his decorations, laid hold of Murat's arm, and shaking him violently before the whole staff and before the Emperor himself, said haughtily, 'Come, prince, come along with me and make your plans in face of the enemy.' Then, galloping to the Danube, he went, amid a shower of balls and grape, having the water up to his horse's belly, to direct the perilous operation assigned to him. This operation consisted in repairing the bridge, of which nothing was left but the piles, without flooring ; passing it ; crossing a small meadow that lay between the Danube and the foot of the eminence, then making himself master of the village, with the convent of Elchingen, which rose amphitheatrically, and was guarded by twenty thousand men and a formidable artillery. It was, indeed, an extraordinary, difficult, and perilous task ; but Marshal Ney was fully equal to the emergency.

"Undaunted by all the obstacles which presented themselves, he ordered an aide-de-camp of General Loison and a sapper to lay hold of the first plank and to carry it to the piles of the bridge for the purpose of re-establishing the passage under the fire of the Austrians. The brave sapper had a leg carried away by a grape-shot, but his place was immediately supplied. One plank was first thrown in the form of flooring, then a second, and a third. Having finished one length, they proceeded to the next, till they had covered the last piles under a murderous fire of small arms, poured upon the laborers by skilful marksmen on the opposite bank."

Ney crossed the bridge only to encounter fresh difficulties ; but these, instead of dampening, served but to increase the ardor and determination of himself and his men. He marched on from victory to victory until he "gloriously reconquered the left bank," shut up Mack and his army in Ulm, and virtually forced them to one of the most ignominious surrenders to be found in the history of war.* The Emperor freely acknowledged the value of Ney's services by according to his corps the place of honor in the final surrender of the Austrian army and in the bulletin announcing the victory.†

After the capitulation Ney was sent to the Tyrol, to "drive from the mountain fastnesses the Austrian forces there assembled under the Archduke John and the Prince of Rohan. By a series of masterly movements, the enemy, occupying positions hitherto considered impregnable, were defeated at every point, and barely escaped total destruction. The Archduke John retreated in great confusion to Vienna, his army disheartened and demoralized by a succession of disasters, and in the beginning of December, Ney, having accomplished with the most brilliant completeness the purpose of his detachment, marched to Salzbourg to communicate with the main body of the army." (Goodrich, Thiers, Alison.)

Ney was not at Austerlitz. He was doing better work in the Tyrol. At Jena, Ney was simply superb. Some historians say he was rash ; but war was Ney's trade, and he was master of his trade. What would have been rash in others was not rash in him. A giant can easily do many things which a pigmy may not attempt. Not unfrequently Ney, by his very audacity, united as it was with perfect poise and calmness amid the greatest dangers, and a consummate knowledge of his art, was enabled to gain victories which he clearly could not have gained by a more timid and circumspect course.

* Lanfrey gives Ney the highest praise for the skill and judgment which he uniformly displayed throughout the campaign.

† "It is from this glorious action that Marshal Ney's title of Duke of Elchingen is taken. He exposed his person without hesitation throughout the day, and seemed even to court death ; but fate reserved him for greater and more melancholy destinies."—JOMINI.

"Dressed in full uniform, Ney was everywhere to be seen at the head of the columns leading the soldiers to the conflict, or rallying such as were staggering under the close and murderous fire of the Austrians."--Alison's "History of Europe."

Ney was created Duke of Elchingen March 19th, 1808. The honor, it strikes me, was rather long deferred, as the battle was fought October 14th, 1805.

Ney's attacks at the battle of Jena were, it is true, exceedingly bold, but they were also exceedingly effective. No one can doubt that Ney, by his fearless, rapid, and vigorous movements, coupled with his matchless skill on the field of battle, greatly contributed to the success of the day. There was not a general in the French army, Bonaparte included (or in the English army), who could have done what Ney did on that memorable day. With a mere handful of soldiers he successfully defended himself against an army which no other man would have thought of resisting. He was attacked by the whole Prussian cavalry, justly celebrated as the finest in Europe ; but after repeated and desperate charges, Ney's two weak squares, though suffering severely, remained unbroken. As soon as reinforcements arrived Ney coolly formed his men again into column, marched straight upon Vierzehn-Heiligen, the centre of the enemy's position, and after an obstinate conflict captured it. Napoleon, who at first was displeased at Ney's seeming impetuosity, was highly delighted when he saw his invincible marshal in the very heart of the enemy's lines. The Austrians were dismayed and confounded. They knew that such soldiers under such a leader could not be whipped.*

On the 8th day of November the great fortress of Magdeburg, by far the most important of the Prussian fortresses,

---

* General Jomini says that at Ulm, Jena, and some other places he was Marshal Ney's "*providence.*" This is a piece of insufferable vanity on the part of this *dilettante* warrior. He was a splendid fighter on paper, but not once did he distinguish himself on the field of battle. Jomini was chief of Ney's staff, but Ney seldom consulted him as to his military operations. Now and then he would ask Jomini's opinion about some particular plan or movement, but he invariably fell back upon his own sound judgment. Bonaparte often held war consultations with Berthier, his chief of staff ; but no one will for a moment suppose that Berthier was Napoleon's " providence."

At Ulm, it is well known, Ney rejected the advice of his entire staff— Jomini included—and gained his great victory by carrying out his own plans. It can be proved by the official records that Jomini was not even acquainted with them.

Jomini Ney's " providence !" " In cornu tauri parvulus quondam culex consedit."

containing a garrison of twenty-two thousand men, eight hundred pieces of cannon, and immense magazines, surrendered to Ney, with a greatly inferior force, and almost without resistance. Ney swore a little, made great threats, threw a few bombs into the town, and the frightened garrison capitulated. Ney's passage of the Vistula and capture of Thorn, despite almost insuperable obstacles, was fully equal in daring and skill to Wellington's passage of the Douro and capture of Oporto—a feat which, when reported to Napoleon, caused him to exclaim, "Wellington is a good general!"

At Soldau, Ney won imperishable laurels. "The village of Soldau is situated amid a marsh impassable except by a single causeway, from seven to eight hundred fathoms in length, resting sometimes upon the ground, sometimes upon bridges, which the enemy had taken care to break down. Six thousand Prussians, with cannon, guarded this causeway. A first battery enfiladed it longitudinally; a second, established on a spot judiciously chosen in the marsh, took it obliquely. Ney, with the Sixty-ninth and the Seventy-sixth, advanced impetuously along it. They threw planks over the broken bridges, they carried the batteries at a run, they overturned with the bayonet the infantry drawn up in column on the causeway, and entered the village of Soldau pell-mell with the fugitives. A most obstinate conflict with the Prussians took place then. The French had to storm Soldau house by house. This was not accomplished without unparalleled efforts, and not till nightfall. But at this moment the gallant General Lestocq, rallying his columns in rear of Soldau, made his soldiers swear to recover the lost post. The Prussians, treated by the Russians since Jena as the Austrians had been treated since Ulm, determined to avenge their honor, and to prove that they were not inferior in bravery to any nation. And so they did. Four times, from seven in the evening till midnight, they attacked Soldau with the bayonet and four times they were repulsed. At last they retired, having sustained an immense loss in killed and wounded and prisoners" (Thiers).

Many portions of the army suffered greatly in their winter

cantonments; but Ney's corps was well cared for. Thiers says:

"The indefatigable Ney had, by his industry and boldness, opened a source of abundance for himself. He had approached very near to the German country, which is extremely rich; nay, he had even ventured to the banks of the Pregel. Sallying forth on daring expeditions, he placed his soldiers on sledges when it froze and went foraging to the very gates of Königsberg, which, indeed, he had once well-nigh surprised and carried."

Napoleon, Thiers says, reprimanded Ney for these bold incursions; and when his advanced guard was attacked by the Russians, "Napoleon conceived at first that it was the excursions of Marshal Ney which had brought reprisals upon him. *But he was soon enlightened* concerning the real cause of the appearance of the Russians, and he could not but discover that they meditated a serious enterprise, having a totally different aim from that of contending for the cantonments." The fact is, Marshal Ney's "bold excursions" were of immense benefit to Napoleon's army. They saved it from surprise, and, scattered as it was, from probable defeat.

Ney was so active and enterprising that he detected the first movements of the enemy and promptly communicated them to Bernadotte and Soult, who were near him, and to Napoleon. But for this timely and certain intelligence a considerable portion of Bonaparte's army would, in all probability, have been cut off and captured—certainly it would have been exposed to very great peril. Thiers frankly admits this. Ney made some mistakes; but I do not hesitate to say that he made *fewer* mistakes than any general of his time.

Napoleon knew what Ney was worth, or he would not have placed him, as he always did, in the most important and responsible positions. In the present instance Bernadotte, even with the early intelligence which Ney gave him, was barely able to save himself from destruction. I quote from Thiers:

"The troops of Marshal Bernadotte, scattered as far as Ebling, near the Frische Haff, had great distances to go in order to rally; and if General Benningsen had marched rapidly he might have surprised and destroyed them before their concentration was effected."

Eylau was a drawn battle. Ney saved Bonaparte from an absolute and serious defeat. Lestocq would have ruined him; but Ney struck Lestocq almost as soon as Lestocq struck Napoleon. No thanks to Napoleon for Ney's timely arrival at Eylau. It was due to Ney's irrepressible energy and to a warlike instinct which never deceived him.*

Fezensac, in his "Memoirs," says:

"Selon M. Thiers, Napoleon envoya dans la soirée du 7 plusieurs officiers aux Maréchaux Davout et Ney pour les ramener sur le champ de bataille. C'est une erreur en ce qui concerne le Maréchal Ney; il ne reçut aucun avis, et ne se doutait pas de la bataille quand je le joignis le 8 à deux heures, dans la direction de Kreutzbourg."

Ney's retreat from Deppen was a marvellous feat. It has few equals. Let Plotho, the Russian historian, describe it:

"The French, consummate masters in the art of war, resolved on that day this very difficult problem—to execute a retreat that is become indispensable, in the face of an enemy who is much stronger and urgently pressing, and to render it as little prejudicial as possible. They extricated themselves from the situation with the utmost skill. The calmness and order and, at the same time, the rapidity shown by Ney's corps in assembling at the signal of three cannon shot; the coolness and attentive circumspection with which it executed its retreat, during which it opposed a resistance renewed at every step, and knew how to avail itself in a masterly manner of every position—all this proved the talent of the captain who commanded the French and the habit of war carried by them to perfection as strongly as the finest dispositions and the most scientific execution of an offensive operation could have done. For attacking with success, as well as for opposing a regular resistance in a retreat, there are required rare qualities, virtues difficult to practise; and yet it is necessary that all these

---

* Thiers says that Napoleon, the evening before the battle, dispatched several officers to Marshal Ney to bring him to the field of battle, etc. This is positively untrue. Ney received no order from Napoleon.

MARSHAL NEY.
(From an Engraving by H. R. Cook, 1817.)

should be combined in the same person to form the great captain."

At Friedland, Ney occupied the post of honor, and more than met the expectations of Napoleon. The Emperor appointed him to commence the action. The Russians were huddled together in an elbow of the river Alle. They had nobody to command them, but they were ready to fight and die. Napoleon surveyed them with attention. Surrounded by his lieutenants, he "explained to them the part which each had to act in that battle. Grasping the arm of Marshal Ney, and pointing to Friedland, the bridges, the Russians crowded together in front, ' Yonder is the goal,' said he ; ' march to it without looking about you ; break into that thick mass, whatever it costs you ; enter Friedland ; take the bridges, and give yourself no concern about what may happen on your right, on your left, or on your rear. The army and I shall be there to attend to that.' Ney, boiling with ardor, proud of the formidable task assigned him, set out at a gallop to arrange his troops before the wood of Sortlack. Struck with his martial attitude, Napoleon, addressing Marshal Mortier, said, ' That man is a lion.' " (Thiers.)

In 1808 Ney was sent into Spain, but the Spanish war did not suit him. He opposed it in council from beginning to end ; and had Napoleon listened to him, he would have avoided one of the greatest errors of his life. Ney foresaw nothing but disaster, yet he labored in general as faithfully in this new field as if success were absolutely assured. A French officer has related a singular scene which occurred at Madrid :

" After a grand review at Madrid, the Emperor entered the room where Ney and many other officers were assembled. He was in the best of spirits, from some favorable dispatches which he had just received. ' Everything goes on well,' said he. ' Romana will be reduced in a fortnight ; the English are defeated, and will be unable to advance. In three months this war will be finished.' None of the other generals ventured to reply, but the Duke of Elchingen shook his head, and with a dissatisfied look, said : ' Sire, the war has lasted long already, and I cannot perceive, like you, that our affairs are much improved. These people are obstinate; even their women and children fight; they massacre our men in detail. To-day we cut the enemy in pieces, to-morrow we have to oppose another twice as numerous. It is not an army we have to fight; it is a whole nation. I see no end to the business.' While he was speaking, the Emperor regarded him with a fixed look. When Ney had ceased, he turned to the other officers and said : ' This country is a Vendée—but have I not subdued Vendée? The Calabrians were formerly insurgents; wherever there are mountains there will be insurrections; but now the kingdom of Naples is peaceable enough. Here the people are instigated to resistance by the clergy; but the Romans subdued them; so did the Moors; and they are not to be compared with their ancestors. I will strengthen the government; I will bind the grandees to my interest, and fire on the rabble. If Julius Cæsar had been daunted by difficulties, would he have conquered Gaul ? The population is said to be against us; this Spain is but a solitude—not five inhabitants to a square league ! But let the question be decided by numbers. I will bring all Europe over the Pyrenees." (" Court and Camp of Bonaparte.")*

At Soria, Napoleon blamed Ney for his circumspection—a queer charge to bring against him; but the truth is, Napoleon himself was in error. Ney was right. A careful study of Napoleon's orders to Ney,† and of the whole situation, will

---

* Ney, of course, was right, as the sequel proved. Napoleon was a very poor judge of human nature. He could easily detect talent, cunning, and selfishness, but of the higher, nobler part of man's nature he knew little or nothing. This marked defect in his understanding was one of the prime causes of his ruin.

† "Napoleon's order to Ney was inexact and ill conceived, and the manœuvre which the marshal was instructed to perform was of a most hazardous description. The perplexity which he has been reproached for having felt on this occasion does us much honor to his *coup d'œil* as to his patriotism. . . . The order, dated at four P.M., November 21st, stated that the battle was to take place at Calahorra. Ney could not, at the earliest, have received it until five or six o'clock in the afternoon of the 22d, and it must then have appeared too late to begin a march of twenty leagues in order to take part in a *battle that would be over before he could start.*"—Lanfrey's " History of Napoleon."

show that Ney did precisely what any good, prudent general ought to have done.

"Napoleon," says Marshal Grouchy, "oftentimes gave vague and ambiguous orders, so that if anything went wrong he could easily throw the blame upon some of his lieutenants. If Ney had had command of the troops at Corunna, Sir John Moore's army would not have gotten off so easily."*

Napoleon seems originally to have intended that Ney should

---

* Colonel Napier, in his "History of the Peninsular War," relates an incident which reflects the highest credit both upon Marshal Soult and Marshal Ney. It is a silver lining to the murky clouds of war. Major Napier, Colonel Napier's brother, was wounded and made prisoner at the battle of Corunna. He was reported killed. "The morning after the battle," says Napier, "the Duke of Dalmatia (Soult), being apprised of Major Napier's situation, had him conveyed to good quarters, and with a kindness and consideration very uncommon wrote to Napoleon, desiring that his prisoner might not be sent to France, which (from the system of refusing exchanges) would have been destructive to his professional prospects. The marshal also obtained for the drummer (who had saved him from being murdered by a French soldier) the decoration of the Legion of Honor. The events of the war obliged Soult to depart in a few days from Corunna, but he recommended Major Napier to the attention of Marshal Ney, and that marshal also treated his prisoner with the kindness of a friend rather than the rigor of an enemy, for he quartered him with the French Consul, supplied him with money, gave him a general invitation to his house on all public occasions, and refrained from sending him to France. Nor did Marshal Ney's kindness stop there ; for when the flag of truce arrived, and he became acquainted with the situation of Major Napier's family, he suddenly waived all forms, and instead of answering the inquiry by a cold intimation of the captive's existence, sent him, and with him the few English prisoners taken in the battle, at once to England, merely demanding that none should serve until regularly exchanged. I should not have dwelt thus long upon the private adventures of an officer, but that gratitude demands a public acknowledgment of such generosity, and the demand is rendered imperative by the after misfortunes of Marshal Ney. That brave and noble-minded man's fate is but too well known. He who had fought five hundred battles for France—not one against her—was shot as a traitor! Could the bitterest enemy of the Bourbons have more strongly marked the difference between their interests and those of the nation ?"

A noble tribute from a noble man. No wonder the English people were opposed to Ney's execution. No wonder Wellington thought that his conduct as to Ney would be made the subject of parliamentary investigation.

pursue the English to the coast, but unavoidable circumstances prevented him from carrying out this intention. Soult was nearer the English, and he was put in command of the army. Ney behaved very generously toward him. He offered to join him at once; but Soult was jealous of Ney, and after considerable hesitation and delay, requested him to send him one of his divisions when it was too late for that division to be of any use to him. Ney and Soult together could have destroyed the Marquis de la Romana; but Soult deceived Ney, broke his promises, and refused to act with him. Ney's dispositions were good, but he could do nothing without the co-operation of Soult. Napoleon, away off in Austria or Germany, knew little about the real condition of affairs in Spain, and had most unwisely placed Marshals Ney and Mortier under the command of Soult. He afterward deeply regretted this act. He blamed Soult severely for his conduct toward Ney,* and authorized Ney to return to France to relieve him from the embarrassing position in which he had been placed.

During Ney's occupation of Galicia and the Asturias, he defeated the organized forces, put down most of the insurgent bands, and governed the country with a firm yet not ungentle hand. He had a sea of troubles to contend against. The English constantly menaced the coast (he had more than one hundred leagues to guard), and the guerilla parties, composed of men, women and children, attacked him fiercely from every quarter and in every imaginable way. This was a new species of warfare, to which Ney was unaccustomed, and for awhile it greatly annoyed him. But he finally reduced the country to something like orderly submission, and, what was still better, succeeded by his kindness and humanity in gain-

---

* "Soult behaved toward Ney in a manner that no proud man forgives."—LANFREY.

The truth is, Soult was exceedingly jealous of Ney; but Ney, though very angry with him, and taking little pains to conceal his anger, treated him with great magnanimity. "Soult's army came from Oporto exhausted by fatigue, their clothes torn in shreds, without shoes, baggage, ammunition, or artillery." Ney supplied all their wants, and afterward took care of Soult's sick and wounded.

ing no small share of the love and confidence of the people whom he governed.*

If Ney had literally carried out Napoleon's instructions he could not have succeeded in Galicia. He was cut off from the other troops, and he was compelled to exercise his best judgment as to his military operations or fail utterly in the accomplishment of his purpose. Lanfrey says :

"The Emperor had instructed Ney to fortify himself at Lugo. . . . Lugo, no doubt, was the *geographical* centre of Galicia, but it was far from being its centre from the point of view of population, riches, influence, or political importance. Corunna united all these conditions, . . . and as the danger which chiefly threatened us in Galicia was to be sought, not in the centre, but along the seaboard of that province, where we had perpetually to defend ourselves against the landing of the English, it may be said that, even from a strategic point of view, Ney acted very wisely in preferring to station himself at Corunna rather than at Lugo."

In 1810 Ney acted under Masséna in the invasion of Portugal,† and if Masséna had followed Ney's advice he would not have left Portugal, as he did leave it, a disgraced and broken-hearted man. Ney captured the strong fortresses of Ciudad Rodrigo and Almeida, and at the battle of the Coa, on July 24th, defeated General Crawfurd, of the English army. If General Montbrun had obeyed Ney's order to seize the bridge over the Coa (the only line of retreat open to the English), the greater part of Crawfurd's division would undoubtedly have been captured. At Busaco, on the 27th,

---

* "Galicia and Salamanca, provinces particularly hostile to the French, have nevertheless preserved the recollections of Ney's integrity while governor of them. One only spoil of a conquered country did Ney bequeath to his descendants : this is a relic of St. James of Compostello, with which the monks of St. Jago presented him, in testimony of his humanity toward them."—"Memoirs of Ney."

† "I have been informed that Marshal Ney resumed the command of the Sixth Corps under the impression that he was to conduct the enterprise against Portugal, but that the intrigues of Marshal Berthier, to whom he was obnoxious, frustrated his hopes." (Napier's "Peninsular War." See also Thiers' "History of the Consulate and the Empire.)"

Masséna met with a signal repulse. Ney, who was in advance, was very anxious to attack the English two days before, but Masséna would not permit him to do so.

Clinton ("History of the Peninsular War") says : "Ney, on the 25th, observing that the heights of Busaco were yet only half occupied, and that the allies were moving up in some disorder, sent off to Masséna, who was about ten miles in the rear, to obtain permission for an immediate attack. But Masséna kept Ney's messenger waiting two hours, and then replied that no action could take place before his own arrival at the front. The French thus lost the opportunity of almost certain victory, and when Masséna came up at noon on the following day (the 26th) the allies were securely posted along the sierra."

Napier, speaking of Ney's eagerness to attack on the 25th, says : "Ney, whose military glance was magical, perceived in an instant that the position—a crested, not a table mountain—could not hide any strong reserve ; that it was scarcely half occupied, and that the allied troops were moving from one place to another with that sort of confusion which generally attends the first taking up of unknown ground. He therefore desired to make an early and powerful attack ; but Ney's aide-de-camp was told at headquarters that everything must await Masséna's arrival. . . . Thus a most favorable opportunity was lost ; for the first division of the allies, although close at hand, was not upon the ridge ; Leith's troops were in the act of passing the Mondego, and Hill was still behind the Alva. Scarcely twenty-five thousand men were actually in line, and there were great intervals between the divisions."

When Masséna arrived at Busaco, Wellington's position was so strong that few officers of either army believed that Masséna would be foolish enough to attack it. Ney, in a council of war, held on the evening of the 25th, frankly told Masséna that two days before the heights could have been captured, but that now they were almost impregnable. But Masséna was determined to fight, and nothing could stop him. He failed, as Ney and others predicted that he would. A few loose historians allege that Ney gave Masséna but a half-hearted support. This is false. Ney's attacks were as bold and determined as any that he ever made.* No one could have captured those heights. Wellington retired behind the formidable lines of Torres Vedras, and in the following March Masséna was compelled to make a disastrous retreat. Ney commanded the rear-guard, and by his marvellous energy and ability saved the French army from complete destruction.†

In the very beginning of the retreat Ney adroitly deceived Wellington, and thus gained time for the army to get a running start of the great duke. The marshal's movements were so bold, so mysterious, so happily conceived, that Wellington thought, as Ney wished him to think, he was meditating a return to Torres Vedras. This uncertainty as to Ney's movements caused Wellington to suspend offensive operations for several hours. Meanwhile, the French army was marching rapidly to the rear. At Pombal, Wellington overtook Ney, and a considerable combat occurred. Ney drove back the English to the little river Arunca, where several of them were drowned, set fire to the village of Pombal, and continued his retreat leisurely on the right bank of the Arunca in defiance of the British, who were strongly posted on the opposite bank. This spirited and well-executed movement retarded the march of the English army for several hours. After leaving Pombal, Ney disputed every inch of ground with the pursuing enemy. General Picton, of the English army, says that every movement which Ney made was a "perfect lesson in the art of war. Moving at all times on his flank, I had an opportunity of seeing everything he did, and I must be dull in the extreme

---

* " During the whole day of September 27th the corps of Regnier and of Ney fought desperately on the abrupt slopes of the mountain, but success was impossible."—LANFREY.

† He had previously saved it from starvation. " We shall hereafter show the wonders he (Ney) effected in providing food for his forces during the Portuguese campaign in a country ravaged by war, when by almost superhuman exertions he succeeded in meeting not only the consumption of the Sixth Corps, which he commanded, but that of the whole army, during the six months it remained upon the banks of the Tagus."
—" Memoirs of Ney."

if I had not derived some practically useful knowledge from such an example."*

At Redinha, Ney was grand. "He resolved to remain several hours before Redinha with the Mermet division alone and his three regiments of cavalry and some guns, as if to show what might be done with seven thousand against twenty-five thousand by skilful manœuvring on a ground well adapted for defence. Proudly resting on the heights which he was about to dispute, he had his four infantry regiments deployed in two ranks, his artillery a little in advance, numerous bands of *tirailleurs* scattered right and left in convenient positions, and his three cavalry regiments in the rear, in the centre, ready to charge through the intervals of the infantry at the first favorable moment.

"The English, drawn out in the plain, continued their manœuvre practised during the day, and endeavored to outflank us. Generals Picton and Pack attempted to climb the heights on our left to dispute with Ney the retreat upon Redinha, while Generals Cole and Spencer advanced in deep columns to the centre, and Erskine's light infantry endeavored to cross the river on our right by the fords previously selected by our cavalry. But Ney, employing every arm with equal presence of mind, began by riddling with bullets Picton's troops; and, by destroying whole lines, he obliged them to escape by an oblique movement; but having succeeded in mastering the heights after great loss, they advanced against the flank of Ney almost on a level, and were within gunshot when the latter, bringing to bear upon them six guns, covered them with shot, and then directed against them a battalion of the Twenty-seventh and one of the Fifty-ninth, and all his *tirailleurs*, who had rallied and been formed into a third battalion. These three small columns vigorously charged Picton's English with the bayonet, and threw them to the foot of the heights after killing and wounding a considerable number.

"In a few moments the rout at this spot was complete.

---

* "Life of Sir Thomas Picton," by H. B. Robinson, vol. ii.

Lord Wellington then advanced his centre to rally and rescue his right, and to attack the position of the French in front. . . . After a discharge of artillery and musketry, Ney charged them with the bayonet, driving them to the sloping ground. He then sent against them the Third Hussars, who broke their first line and sabred many of their foot. At this moment the confusion in the whole body of the English was extreme; and if Ney, by having kept near him the Marchand division, had been able more fully to engage that of Mermet, the rout would have been general and irrevocable. However, Ney, unwilling to compromise his troops, recalled them, drew them up in battle array, and remained in position another hour, continually breaking the ranks of the English by ball. It was now four o'clock. Lord Wellington, touched to the quick at seeing himself thus detained and damaged by a handful of men, collected his whole army, formed it in four lines, and advanced with the evident determination to force the position at any cost. Ney effected his retreat with the same decision and vigor as had characterized the day.*

"The English were obliged to halt upon the Soure after a laborious day which had cost them not less than eighteen hundred in killed and wounded, while we had lost scarcely two hundred. The French army, under the command of its ablest manœuvrer, had on this occasion exhibited every form of perfection which it attains when it combines education with natural qualifications. . . . If on this occasion Ney had been as bold in command as he had been skilful in manœuvring, he would certainly have driven the English far back; but under the influence of prudential considerations, not ill founded, he confined himself to a combat of the rear-guard, when he might have ventured on a general battle with success. The British

* The battle of Redinha, when taken in connection with the operations leading up to it, was a peerless feat of arms. Ney's positions were so well chosen, his "handful of men" so skilfully arranged, his manœuvres so brilliant, his blows so daring, so hard, so well delivered, that he kept Wellington's whole army at bay for *six consecutive hours*. Wellington thought that Masséna's whole army was before him. The Iron Duke was deeply chagrined when he discovered that he had been so egregiously deceived.

army would probably have experienced a sanguinary defeat, and would have paid dear for the honor of having forced us to quit the Tagus" (Thiers' " History of the Consulate and the Empire." See also Alison's " Lives of Castlereagh and Stuart," and Wright's " Wellington").

At Condeixa, at Casalnovo, at Miranda do Corvo, at Foz d'Aronce, at the Sierra de Murcelha—at every point of the retreat Ney maintained himself with matchless steadiness, vigor, decision, and judgment. He has been blamed by Koch, Masséna, and others for burning Condeixa and making a hasty retreat; but it was simply unavoidable. Wellington, finding that he could not force Ney's position in front, although he had three times as many men as the French marshal, sent Picton's division by a long and circuitous route unknown to Masséna to cut off Ney from his only line of retreat. When Ney saw that he was about to be separated from the main body of the army, " he would have been frantic," says Napier, " to have delayed his movement."

Koch, in his " Memoirs of Masséna," also says that Ney ought to have remained longer at Ponte de Murcelha; but he is either dishonest or densely ignorant of the facts of the case. Ney did everything in his power to carry out Masséna's orders at the Sierra de Murcelha, but General Regnier prevented him from doing so. Masséna had directed Regnier to connect with Ney's left to protect him from a flank movement by the English; but Regnier, engaged in pillaging, refused to obey Masséna; and Ney, seeing the English advance beyond his left, was compelled to abandon the position of Ponte de Murcelha.*

Ney had saved the army. No one can doubt that. This retreat alone would make Ney immortal. Napier says: " Ney, with a wonderfully happy mixture of courage, readi-

---

* " General Regnier has put me in the greatest embarrassment. I shall be obliged to set out at once, as every moment of delay may induce the ruin of the army, which has hitherto escaped as if by a miracle. This conduct of General Regnier is frightful."—Ney to Masséna.

This extract proves conclusively that Ney was willing and anxious to execute Masséna's instructions.

ness, and skill illustrated every league of ground by some signal combination of war" ("History of the Peninsular War").

"The glory of this memorable retreat was the only considerable advantage derived by Marshal Ney from his services in Spain. That retreat was a most brilliant one, and conferred as much honor on the Duke of Elchingen as the proudest victory he had ever gained. He sustained unmoved the incessant assaults of Lord Wellington's overwhelming forces, though the corps which he commanded consisted of no more than six thousand men, and thus enabled the army to retire in perfect order to Miranda do Corvo" ("Court and Camp of Bonaparte").

At Celorico, Masséna and Ney had an open and a bitter quarrel. Ney flatly refused to obey Masséna. Masséna deprived him of his sword, sent him into the "interior of Spain to await the Emperor's orders," and gave the command of his corps to General Loison. It is not my purpose to enter fully into the details of this unfortunate quarrel between Ney and the commander-in-chief of the Army of Portugal. One thing, however, is perfectly clear: Ney ought to have obeyed Masséna, whether Masséna was right or wrong; whether the orders were good, bad, or indifferent. And no one knew this better than Marshal Ney himself. But the provocation was exceedingly great. Ney was disgusted with Masséna, and he had a right to be. Masséna was constantly complaining of weariness and fatigue, loss of energy, etc., which complaints, under the circumstances, made him the laughing-stock of the whole army.

"He had the weakness," says Thiers, "to seek a solace for his protracted labors in a species of pleasure which should never be presented to the eye of those whom we may be required to command. He was followed by a woman who had never quitted him during the whole campaign, and whose carriage the soldiers were required to escort in the most difficult and dangerous roads. In victory the soldier laughs at the irregularities of his commander; in ill fortune they are regarded as crimes" ("History of the Consulate and the Empire").

Such conduct on the part of the commanding officer was destructive of all discipline in the army, and filled Ney with supreme disgust. Besides, Masséna had treated Ney's suggestions and recommendations—most of which were eminently sound—at all times with disrespect, and sometimes with disdain. Masséna's slowness—he moved like a snail—his unaccountable delays, his obstinacy in trying to carry out impracticable plans,* his want of energy, his peculations, his rapacity, his intense selfishness, his littleness of soul, his avarice, his dissipations, his inability to govern himself or to maintain discipline in the army—these things had borne their legitimate fruit. Officers and soldiers alike had lost all respect for him as a man, and almost all for his genius as a soldier. As to the merits of the controversy between Masséna and Ney, it is clear, to my mind, that Ney was right. Masséna wished to make a second invasion of Portugal, notwithstanding the disastrous issue of the first; but Ney, Regnier, Junot, and almost all the officers and men in the entire army were bitterly opposed to it. It was, indeed, a mad project. Even Thiers, who worships Masséna, condemns it. But Masséna was insanely bent upon a second campaign on the Tagus, and nothing could stop him.

With this end in view, he ordered Ney to march his corps to a "rocky desert, dry and poor, where could be found neither bread, meat, nor vegetables; where the only recreation was to behold a well-fed enemy, to be subject to continual alarms in the rear, and to be deluged with torrents of rain. To announce that after three or four days of inaction and famine in that detestable place it should be considered rested and required to defile before Old Castile, to descend into Estremadura, where it had remained awhile at the time of the battle of Talavera without meeting with abundance, though the country was hitherto untouched, was to drive the corps to despair" (Thiers).

This was the straw which broke the camel's back. Ney refused to obey Masséna unless he produced the Emperor's orders for a new invasion of Portugal. Masséna very prop-

* Napoleon rebuked Masséna sharply for his bad management of the Portuguese campaign.

MADAME LA MARÉCHALE NEY.

erly deprived him of his sword and sent him into the heart of Spain. Ney ought to have obeyed his commanding officer, regardless of the Emperor's orders. And I repeat, no one knew this better than Ney himself.*

Masséna undertook no second invasion of Portugal. Indeed, after Ney left the army he was compelled to adopt the very plans which Ney suggested.

Alison ("History of Europe") says: "These checks" (by Wellington) "convinced Masséna of the justice of Ney's opinion—that the army must seek for rest behind the cannon of Ciudad Rodrigo; and he therefore threw a garrison into Almeida and retreated with the bulk of his forces across the frontier to that fortress, and thence to Salamanca."

On March 29th Wellington attacked Masséna, strongly posted on the summit of the Guarda Mountain. This position, one of the "strongest in Portugal," says Captain Sherer, "was abandoned by the French with the utmost precipitation without one effort for its defence." This result was due, says Napier, to the "absence of Ney."

The English, who had so often felt the strong arm of the French marshal, knowing that he had quitted the army, attacked Masséna with increased confidence and vigor; and the French, feeling that they were deprived of the only man who was able to cope with the English, were panic-stricken, and fled pell-mell down the mountain sides like a flock of senseless

---

* Ney thus wrote to Masséna: "I know that I assume great responsibility in opposing you. But even if I am to be dismissed, or to lose my head, I will not follow the movement on Placencia and Coria unless it is ordered by the Emperor." It turned out, as Ney suspected, that Napoleon had not ordered the movement. Indeed, the Emperor condemned it in no measured terms. After Ney had written his letter to Masséna, the English again set themselves in motion, and a battle seemed imminent. Ney immediately wrote Masséna a kind and conciliatory letter, stating that "at the approach of the enemy he felt in duty bound to abide by the army." But Masséna was inflexible, and "Ney," says Thiers, "quitted the Sixth Corps, filled with regret for his loss, but with no disposition to revolt." They did not revolt, he might have said, simply because Ney positively forbade them to do so. The Sixth Corps idolized Ney. A word from him would have set the corps on fire (see "Memoirs of Ney"). Thiers adds: "Marshal Ney followed up a momentary error by a praiseworthy submission."

sheep. Napier pays Ney the highest compliment in his power when he says : "The absence of Ney was at once felt by *both* armies ; the appearance of the allied columns for the first time threw the French into the greatest confusion, and, without firing a shot, this great and nearly impregnable position was abandoned." * Thus terminated a campaign which brought fame and glory to Ney and dishonor and shame to Masséna. With undoubted genius for war, Masséna yet lacked that moral force without which genius is worth nothing. He never recovered from the shock. The dying embers flashed up a little on the hard-fought field of Fuentes-d'Onore. It was his last battle. Over his tomb in Père la Chaise is a splendid obelisk of white marble, with the simple inscription : MASSÉNA. "Take him for all in all," he deserves such a monument.

* The author of "Cyril Thornton," in his "Annals of the Peninsular War," says with great justice and force : "In this retreat it was impossible to exceed the skill and boldness with which this officer [Ney], taking advantage of every favorable position, foiled and delayed the pursuit of a force *ten* times more numerous than that which he commanded. Resistance was uniformly made till the very last moment when it could be continued with safety. All his movements were marked by a promptitude and precision highly admirable ; by a fearless confidence, ever bold, yet never degenerating into rashness. From the moment when Ney quitted the army a decrease of energy and vigor was discernible. Worn by privation and fatigue, and looking back on a campaign which presented few features calculated to lighten and redeem the gloom by which it was overspread, the French soldiers no longer felt confidence in their leader. All that was gallant and daring in the retreat was attributed to Ney ; while the timid policy of Masséna was made responsible for the misfortunes of the campaign. The departure of Ney was regarded as a misfortune by the whole army, and the lingering hope that the campaign might yet terminate in some honorable and distinguished achievement gave place to forebodings of misfortune. These anticipations were not belied by the event. Masséna was driven disgracefully from his position at Guarda ; and he at length entered Spain with an army whose moral confidence was gone."

CHAPTER III.

IN 1812 Ney accompanied Napoleon in his famous expedition to Russia. He was placed in command of the Third Corps, numbering 37,400 men, to which three divisions of the First Corps were subsequently added. In common with most of Napoleon's best officers, Ney was opposed to this foolish invasion; but Bonaparte was determined to destroy, if possible, the power of Russia, and, through Russia, the power of England, and nothing could turn him from his purpose. "Whom the gods intend to destroy, they first make mad." But though Ney was opposed to the invasion, he was yet the right arm of Napoleon from the beginning to the end of the campaign. Indeed, before the close of the war the Emperor had entirely disappeared, the grand army had disappeared, and Ney alone remained.

The Emperor, the grand army, the French Empire itself lived only in Ney. Before Moscow was reached, Ney was constantly in the vanguard, pursuing the Russians with his wonted vigilance and vigor. His steady valor and sound judgment were of great benefit to Napoleon on many a critical occasion. At Krasnoi, Ney had quite a serious brush with the enemy, but his dispositions were so good that the Russians were quickly defeated and retired in considerable confusion. At Smolensko a ball struck him on the neck and tore away a portion of his coat-collar. He was not so successful here as he had been at Krasnoi, because the orders issued by Napoleon to those who were to assist in the movement were not promptly executed.

Ney now made a last effort to induce Bonaparte to suspend his operations, to winter at Smolensko, to establish a fortified camp, to recruit his army, to collect stores of all kinds, and be ready for a general advance in the spring. He was fully convinced that to penetrate into the heart of Russia at so late a period of the year, especially when Bonaparte's losses of every kind had already been so great, could but result in defeat and ruin to the entire army. His was the counsel of a wise man, but Napoleon was displeased with Ney's frankness of speech. At a council held at Smolensko, Ney spoke his mind so freely that the Emperor replied with considerable asperity : " Duke of Elchingen, I am well aware that in bravery and attachment to my person and interests you have no superior ; but you do not know the Russians ; they are not like the Germans ; they will receive us with open arms—they sigh for our arrival as earnestly as the Jews for the coming of their Messiah. I will give freedom to the people civilized by Peter the Great. I will put the finishing hand to his great work by providing the Russians with the Code Napoleon."

Caulaincourt agreed with the Emperor, using many flattering expressions which were exceedingly distasteful to Ney. " Would to Heaven," said he, with characteristic bluntness, " the honeyed language of this diplomatic general may not prove more injurious to the army than the most bloody battle !"

His words were prophetic. At Valoutina there can be little doubt that Ney would have almost destroyed Barclay de Tolly but for the inactivity and impotence of Junot. That general, surnamed *la tempête*, was anything but a tempest on this occasion. Ney had attacked the Russians in front, and after an obstinate conflict had completely routed them. Junot was on their flank with the Westphalian troops ; but at the critical moment his mind became paralyzed, and he failed utterly to execute the orders which had been given him. A vigorous charge by this unfortunate officer would have completed the victory. Napoleon was very angry with him. " What was Junot about ?" said he. " I shall deprive him of his command. He has irretrievably lost his marshal's staff."

At the battle of Borodino, or of the Moskva, the bloodiest, perhaps, of modern times, Ney surpassed himself, and richly earned the title which Napoleon gave him on the battlefield—

Prince de la Moskowa. For a considerable time after the battle began, Napoleon kept Ney close by his side, and would not allow him to engage in the fight, although he was exceedingly anxious to do so. Napoleon wished to save him for a critical moment, when his blows would tell most powerfully for him and his empire. He well knew that he had no officer who could carry his men so far into the battle and hold them there so long as the "bravest of the brave." It was well for Napoleon that Ney was with him, for Ney alone saved him from a crushing defeat. All historians admit that Ney was the hero of the day.

The struggle was terrific. The Russians "fought like devils." For a long time the scales seemed to be evenly balanced. At last Ney, after incredible exertions, his men falling thick and fast around him at every step, marched straight upon the key of the Russian position, and took it. Koutousoff now fought, not for victory, but for life. Murat's cavalry had been previously driven back upon Ney's troops in utter confusion, and but for Ney's prompt assistance Murat and the greater part of his force would have been captured or destroyed. Ney, with Davout and Murat, sent an urgent request to Napoleon for reinforcements to complete the victory, but Bonaparte refused to send them. He had lost, or appeared to have lost, his accustomed decision and vigor. He was moody, spiritless, and dejected. "He was seized," says Ségur, "with a hesitation which he had never shown before. He gave orders and counter orders. Daru, as well as his other officers, asserted that his genius could no longer accommodate itself to circumstances." They were right. Again and again did Ney, Davout, and others ask for reinforcements. Ney had swept away Bagration's corps, and Davout and Murat, seconded by Ney, had been successful at other points; and it really seemed that they needed but the guard to make the victory decisive. "Let the Emperor send us the Young Guard," said they, "and we will finish the Russians."

But Bonaparte was unyielding. "The hour of this battle," said he, "is not yet come. Nothing is yet sufficiently determined. I must see more clearly upon my chessboard before I bring my reserves into play."

"Meanwhile, Napoleon," says Ségur, "remained at a great distance from the battle, of which he could scarcely see anything after it got beyond the heights,* nerveless, crestfallen, and apparently indifferent to the result."

Ney at last lost all patience with the Emperor. "Are we, then," said he, "come so far to be satisfied only with a field of battle? What business has the Emperor in the rear of the army? There he is only within reach of reverses, and not of victory. Since he will no longer make war himself, since he is no longer the general, and wishes to be the Emperor everywhere, let him return to the Tuileries, and leave us to be generals for him."

But Napoleon would under no circumstances part with his guard. It was his only stay and hope. There were many leagues between him and France, and many things might happen before he could get back. To Belliard and Daru, who urged him at the last moment to send forward the guard, he said: "And if there should be another battle to-morrow, where will be my army to fight it?" The victory at Borodino was dearly bought, and almost barren of practical results. The carnage in both armies was simply frightful. Ney earnestly advised a retreat, but Napoleon had no prudence, and his everlasting *star* led him on to his ruin. He had already committed fearful blunders, and he kept on committing them.

---

* Count Mathieu Dumas seems to contradict Ségur in some particulars. He says: "During the whole of this day I was near the Emperor, leaving him only at intervals to visit the most advanced ambulances, etc. . . . The Emperor remained motionless, generally seated on the edge of a ditch, and sometimes walking a few paces to the right or the left. His apparent indifference has excited astonishment. Napoleon had undergone excessive fatigue during the two preceding nights, and he certainly appeared to be indisposed. He placed himself at a short distance from his right wing. The station which he had chosen was the best point of observation. It commanded a view of the whole field of battle, and if any manœuvre, any partial success of the enemy had required new measures, the vigilance of Napoleon would not have failed to meet the emergency of the case."—"Memoirs."

He thought he knew all about the Russian character, and he knew nothing about it. Moscow was his grave.

When the retreat began, Davout was appointed to command the rear-guard ; but he was unfit for the position, and at Viazma he was superseded by Ney. The history of the Russian retreat, as conducted by Ney, has never been written. It is impossible to write it. No pen is adequate to the task. Each day of the forty days had in it enough immortality for a dozen men. There is nothing like it in all history ; there is nothing even approximating it. At first Davout and Eugene were expected to support Ney, but Ney, in fact, had to support them. Indeed, he saved them from total destruction— Eugene twice. Ney was literally forsaken. Every one fled for his life—Napoleon in the van. But Ney was a hero of heroes. There he was, with a few thousand soldiers, surrounded by deadly foes of every kind. His front, flank and rear were swarming with vengeful Russians. Hunger, cold, disease, fatigue, exhaustion, disorder, lawlessness, despair, madness—foes worse than Russians—attacked him pitilessly at every step. But Ney was equal to the occasion. He rose above the occasion. He became the occasion itself. The retreat was NEY.

Between Viazma and Smolensko he fought ten whole days with a skill and heroism that nothing could surpass. "Ney," says Ségur, "saw that a sacrifice was required, and that he was marked out as the victim ; he nobly resigned himself, therefore, prepared to meet the whole of a danger great as his courage ; and thenceforward he neither attached his honor to baggage nor to cannon, which the winter alone wrested from him. An elbow of the Borysthenes stopped and kept back part of his guns at the foot of its icy slopes ; he sacrificed them without hesitation, passed that obstacle, faced about, and made the hostile river, which crossed his route, serve him as the means of defence.

"The Russians, however, advanced under favor of a wood and of our forsaken carriages, whence they kept up a fire of musketry on Ney's troops. Half of the latter, whose icy arms froze their stiffened fingers, became discouraged ; they gave way, excusing themselves by their want of firmness on the preceding day, and fleeing because they had fled before, which but for this they would have considered as impossible. But Ney, rushing in among them, seized one of their muskets and led them back to action, which he was himself the first to renew, exposing his life like a private soldier with a firelock in his hand, the same as though he had been neither possessed of wealth nor power nor consideration—in short, as if he had still everything to gain, when, in fact, he had everything to lose. But, though he had again turned soldier, he ceased not to be general ; he took advantage of the ground, supported himself against a height, and covered his approach by occupying a palisaded house. His general and colonels, among whom he particularly remarked Fezensac, strenuously seconded him ; and the enemy, who had expected to pursue, was obliged to retreat. By this action Ney afforded the army a respite of twenty-four hours, and it profited by it to proceed toward Smolensko. The next day and every succeeding day he displayed the same heroism."

Just before Ney reached Smolensko, and as he had faced about to give battle to the Russians, he suddenly saw upon his left a large body of disbanded men rushing wildly upon his own troops, as if they intended to attack them. They were Eugene's soldiers, who had become utterly demoralized. They were closely followed by the howling Cossacks. Ney was at first astonished, but quickly taking in the situation, he rapidly made his dispositions to meet this threefold danger— the enemy attacking him in the rear, Eugene's crazy corps, and the Cossacks in hot pursuit of them. By exertions almost superhuman he finally succeeded (ably assisted by Fezensac) in arresting the progress of these formidable armies, and then taking Eugene under his wing, marched triumphantly away.

Ney's difficulties, almost insuperable before, were still greater after he left Smolensko. His resources of every kind were rapidly disappearing, and there was no way to replenish them. His little army was thinning out at every step by cold, disease, famine, and the sword, while his enemies were multiplying like locusts in all directions. Napoleon, with the residue of the army, was, if possible, fleeing faster than before, and the line of retreat was almost blocked up by the deep and deepening snow, by fallen trees and treacherous morasses, excavations, hollows, ravines, etc., into which the soldiers were continually plunging, many of them to rise no more ; by dead and dying men, women, and horses, even children ; abandoned baggage,* cannon, caissons, carts, wagons and carriages laden with the spoils of Moscow : every form of danger, suffering, and death seemed to confront the deserted but undaunted leader.†

* " The Emperor was desirous to march leisurely in order to preserve the baggage. In vain Marshal Ney wrote to him that there was no time to be lost ; that the enemy pressed the rear-guard closer and closer ; that the Russian army was gaining on our flanks by forced marches ; and that there was reason to apprehend it would succeed in reaching Smolensko or Orcha before us."—Fezensac's " Russian Campaign."

† " The Third Corps [Ney's], which arrived last at Smolensko, and who were still engaged in defending the approaches to the town, were altogether forgotten by those whom they had protected. Our army had already taken the route of Orcha, and Marshal Ney, now left to his own resources, made his dispositions for defending Smolensko to the utmost, and thus check the pursuit of the enemy. . . . Our situation now became critical. It was necessary at all hazards to repel an attack which, if successful, would render the enemy master of the *tête du pont ;* but finding myself unsupported in the suburb, I dared not engage my regiment further after I had received the order to retire. Luckily Marshal Ney, whom the sound of firing always drew to the scene of action, appeared on the parapet and ordered me to advance against the enemy, drive him out of the suburb, and thus afford time for clearing the passage. I led my men on at the double march through snow and over the ruins of houses. They felt proud of engaging the enemy under the eyes of the marshal and their comrades of the First Division, who were looking on from the ramparts, and charged with the greatest ardor. The Russians retired with precipitation ; they carried off their artillery, but their skirmishers were dislodged from their houses, and in a few moments we were masters of the whole suburb. Marshal Ney sent me orders *not to advance too far*—a very rare recommendation on his part. . . . The same evening I received from Marshal Ney the most flattering testimonials of his satisfaction at our conduct on the preceding day (15th). I communicated them to my officers, and exhorted them to prove themselves worthy of them. Only five hundred rank and file of the Fourth Regiment still remained ; and what had not this small remnant gone through ? How much interest and confidence were not these brave men calculated to inspire, who, under such severe trials, had continued faithful to their colors, and whose courage had only

As Ney approached the banks of the Losmina, near Krasnoi, on the 18th, he was astonished to find the Russian commander, with eighty thousand men, directly in his front. Koutousoff had captured Napoleon's papers near Krasnoi, and from these he had learned the exact situation of Ney's corps, and the deplorable condition to which it had been reduced. Koutousoff now felt that he had Ney completely in his power. A Russian officer appeared and summoned Ney to surrender. The demand, however, was softened with many flattering words. The pill was sugar-coated. "Koutousoff," said the messenger, "would not have presumed to make so cruel a proposal to so great a general, to a warrior so renowned, if there had remained a single chance of safety for him. But there were eighty thousand Russians before and around him, and if he had any doubt of it, Koutousoff would permit him to send a person to pass through his ranks and count his forces."

The officer had not finished his honeyed speech "when," says Ségur, "suddenly forty discharges of grape-shot, coming from the right of his army, and cutting our files to pieces, struck him with amazement, and effectually put a stop to what he had further intended to say. At the same moment a French officer darted forward, seized, and would have at once killed him as a traitor, but that Ney checked his fury, angrily saying to the Russian, "A Marshal of France never surrenders; there is no parleying under fire, you are my prisoner." The officer was accordingly disarmed and detained as a prisoner; nor was he released until they reached Kowno, after twenty-six days of captivity, sharing all their miseries, at liberty to escape, but restrained by his parole of honor.

The enemy's fire meanwhile grew hotter and hotter, and all the hills, which but a moment before looked cold and silent,

increased with their difficulties. I felt proud of the glory *they* had acquired."—"Memoirs of the Duke of Fezensac."

"The headquarters of the Imperial Guard and the corps of the Prince Viceroy and Marshal Davout proceeded pell-mell, and in the most frightful disorder, to reach Orcha, on the right bank of the Dnieper."—Dumas' "Memoirs of the Revolution, Empire, etc."

became like so many volcanoes in eruption; but the courage of Ney was only inflamed by it; he seemed to be but breathing his own appropriate element. Alone, and looking to no one for support, he supported everybody. He resolved to cut his way through this immense host. He made no harangue, but marched silently at the head of his troops, trusting to example, which in a hero is more eloquent than any oratory, and the most commanding of all orders. They all followed him; attacked, penetrated, and overturned the first Russian line; and, without halting, even precipitating themselves upon the second; but before they could reach it a volley of round and grapeshot poured down upon them.

In an instant Ney saw all his generals wounded, and the greater part of his soldiers killed; their ranks were empty; their shapeless column wheeled suddenly round, staggered, fell back, and drew Ney along with it. He waited until his men had once more placed the ravine between them and the enemy, that ravine which was now his sole resource, and then he halted and rallied them. The Russians dared not pursue him. He drew up his four thousand men against eighty thousand, and returning the fire of the enemy's two hundred cannon with his six pieces, made fortune blush at betraying such courage. Night soon came to Ney's aid. He had been anxiously waiting for it. He quietly ordered his men to march back toward Smolensk. They were struck motionless with astonishment. Even his aide-de-camp could not believe his ears; he remained silent, like one who does not comprehend what he hears, and stared at his general in utter amazement. But the marshal briefly repeating the same order in a still more imperative tone, they were no longer at any loss, but all recognized in it resolution taken, a resource discovered, that self-confidence which inspires others with the same feeling, and a spirit which rises superior to its situation, however perilous it may be. They instantly obeyed and turned their backs on their own army, on the Emperor, and on France. Once more they returned into that fatal Russia.*

* " History of the Russian Campaign."
Some of Ney's men said afterward : " It as a.ways been a matter of

"But Marshal Ney's presence," says Fezensac, "was sufficient to infuse confidence. Without presuming to divine what he would or could do, we *knew* that he would do something. His own confidence in himself was equal to his courage. The greater the danger, the prompter was his determination. When he had once taken his line, he was the last to entertain a doubt of its success. At such a moment his countenance indicated neither indecision nor anxiety. The eyes of all were now turned toward him, but no one had yet ventured to ask a question. At length, seeing near him an officer of his staff, the marshal said in a low voice, 'We are in a bad predicament' (*nous ne sommes pas bien*). 'What do you propose doing?' replied the officer. 'Cross the Dnieper.' 'In what direction is the road?' 'We shall ascertain that presently.' 'And suppose the river should not be frozen?' 'It will be soon.' 'Oh, very good' (*à la bonne heure*). This singular dialogue, which I relate word for word, disclosed to us the project of the marshal to reach Orcha by the right bank of the river, and to move with sufficient rapidity to enable us to overtake in that place the French army, now marching by the left bank. The plan was bold, and ably conceived; we shall see with what vigor it was executed. Marshal Ney, endowed with that military instinct of turning to account the most trifling circumstances, remarked that there was ice in the direction we were following, and ordered it to be broken, in the supposition that it might incase some rivulet leading to the Dnieper.* This really proved to be the case. We followed it and soon arrived at the village of Danikowa,

---

astonishment to us that we should have obeyed the marshal when he ordered us to go back into that earthly hell. The truth is, we couldn't help obeying him. We were completely in his power. He had bewitched us, and we had no wills of our own. We followed him as a dog would follow his master."

* Ney halted on the edge of a ravine. His men looked at him mechanically. "What next?" thought they. "Clear away the snow," said the marshal. "Now break the ice." At the bottom was found a small stream flowing to the west. Ney looked at his map behind a deep snow bank. "This stream," said he, "flows into the Dnieper. Follow me, and we shall soon be safe."

MARSHAL NEY.

(From Meyer's Collection of Portraits of the Grand Officers of the Legion of Honor.)

where the marshal allowed it to be supposed he was about to take up his quarters for the night. The fires were lighted, and advanced posts were placed. The enemy left us quiet, flattering himself with the expectation of an easy victory to-morrow."*

Shortly afterward the noise of the enemy's cannon was heard. Ney at first thought it might be the cannon of Marshal Davout. " Has Davout at last recollected me !" he exclaimed ; but he was soon convinced that it was Russian cannon, that the enemy were triumphing over him in advance, thinking he would be an easy prey the next morning. " I will give the lie to their joy," he said, and under cover of the stratagem which he had employed to deceive the enemy (the lighting of fires, placing of advanced posts, etc.), he quietly resumed his march, leaving the enemy to think that he was still at Danikowa.

A lame peasant, whom the marshal's scouts found not far from the line of march, was made to do duty as a guide. He informed them that the Dnieper was only about three miles distant, that it was too deep for fording, and that he was certain it was not frozen over. Ney cut him short with, " It must be frozen." Some one remarked that it was warmer now than it had been, and that a thaw had just commenced. " It makes no difference," replied Ney, " we *must* pass, there is no other resource left us."

When the river was reached, it was found that it was frozen over only in one place, at a sudden bend of the stream, and that it was just strong enough for the troops to pass over in single file. " But," says Ségur, " in this silent, nocturnal march across the fields of a column composed of exhausted and wounded men, and of women and children, they had been unable to keep sufficiently close to prevent them from losing each other in the dark. Ney perceived that only a part of his people had come up ; still he might at once have secured the safety of those who were there, and waited on the other side for the rest. The idea, however, never entered his mind,

---

* " Memoirs of the Duc de Fezensac."

and when some one at length proposed it to him, he rejected it instantly. He allowed three hours for the rallying ; and, without suffering himself to be agitated by the least impatience, or by the danger of waiting so long, he wrapped himself up in his cloak, and passed these three perilous hours in a profound sleep on the bank of the river. So fully did he possess the temperament and character of great men, a strong mind in a sound and robust body."

Toward midnight the passage began. Most of the troops passed over, though with considerable difficulty, as the ice cracked and bent beneath them at almost every step. A few of the horses only were enabled to cross, and the baggage was entirely abandoned. At last several wagons loaded with the sick and wounded and with women and children attempted to pass. About midway the river the ice broke and gave way. The shrieks and cries for help were perfectly awful, and could be heard for miles around. These were succeeded by heavy, stifled moans—then *silence*. Those who were present say these heart-rending screams sounded in their ears for days and days afterward.

" Ney," says Horne,* " fixed his appalled looks on the dismal gulf, and thought he distinguished through the darkness a living man. It was a wounded officer named Briqueville, who had escaped on a large flat of ice, and was approaching the bank on his hands and knees." Ney reached down from the bank and pulled him ashore.

After crossing the Dnieper the Cossacks appeared in increasing numbers, and these were superior in quality and discipline and general efficiency to those whom Ney had encountered on the left bank of the Dnieper. Platoff himself led them on. They attacked Ney almost without intermission, both by day and night, but he, profiting by the least accidents of ground and by every circumstance that could give him the slightest advantage, kept his enemies at bay by his bold countenance, his unconquerable spirit, and by the energy and hope which he infused into those around him. At one time the

* " Life of Napoleon."

Cossacks placed themselves immediately in his front and attacked him with such numbers and such spirit that escape seemed absolutely impossible, but Ney rushed forward as if *he* had planned the attack, exclaiming, "Comrades, now is your time, forward! We have them."

"At these words" (Ségur) "his soldiers, who but a moment before had been in the utmost consternation, now believed they were about to surprise their foes; from being vanquished they rose up conquerors; they rushed upon the enemy, who fled with the utmost precipitation."

Fezensac's account of these movements is most interesting. But for his presence of mind, good judgment, and tireless efforts, General D'Hénin's Brigade, in which he served, would have been cut off and destroyed. He says:

"We continued to move at the same steady pace, amid a storm of bullets which continually thinned our ranks, and heedless of the cries and threatening movements of the Cossacks. It became necessary to quit the main road, and to thread our way through the woods which followed the course of the Dnieper on our left. The Cossacks had already possessed themselves of these, and the Fourth and Eighteenth regiments were ordered, under General D'Hénin, to drive them out. Here Platoff had calculated on completing our destruction. I entered the woods, and the Cossacks retreated a short distance. The thickness of the woods was such that to guard against surprise we were obliged to show a front in every direction. As the night advanced silence succeeded around us, and we deemed it more than probable that Marshal Ney had continued his march. I recommended General D'Hénin to follow the marshal's movement, but he was unwilling to encounter again the reproaches he had before been subject to for quitting his post without orders. We were on the point of being cut off. I knew this by the loud cries in front of us. I renewed my entreaties to General D'Hénin, assuring him that the marshal, whose habits I was well acquainted with, was not likely to send him any order; for he always expected that an officer in command would act as circumstances might require. Besides, he was now too distant to be able to communicate with us, and the Eighteenth Regiment had by this time proceeded some distance. The general persisted in his refusal, and I could only obtain his consent to lead us to the spot where the Eighteenth was supposed to be, in order that the two regiments might form a junction; but the Eighteenth had marched, and in its place we found a squadron of Cossacks. General D'Hénin was at last convinced of the justice of my observations, and was now anxious to rejoin Marshal Ney's column; but we had traversed the wood in so many directions that we were no longer sure of our road, and the fires which we saw lit on different sides only served to distract us more. I will not undertake to describe all that we suffered on that most trying night. I had not more than one hundred men with me, and we found ourselves upward of a league in rear of the column of which we should have formed a part; we had to rejoin it surrounded on every side by enemies; we had to march with sufficient rapidity to recover our lost time, and with sufficient compactness to resist the attacks of the Cossacks. The darkness of the night, the uncertainty of our direction, the difficulties under such circumstances attending a march through woods, all added to our embarrassments. The Cossacks were continually firing into the midst of us and calling upon us to surrender. I had need of all my authority to maintain order on the march, and to keep every one in his place. One of my officers dared hint at a surrender. I reprimanded him loudly, and the more severely, that having shown himself hitherto a meritorious officer, I was desirous of rendering my reprimand more marked. At last, at the expiration of an hour, we got quit of the woods, and found the Dnieper on our left. The direction we had taken was therefore right, and I profited by the fresh spirit which the discovery infused to recommend the perseverance, courage, and coolness which would alone save us; but we were yet by no means extricated from our perilous position. The plain in which we marched favored an attack by the enemy in mass, and enabled him to avail himself of his artillery. From time to time the Cossacks advanced toward us with loud cries. On these occasions we halted a minute to give our fire, and immediately resumed our march. For two leagues we traversed the most impracticable ground, crossed ravines whose sides we ascended with the utmost difficulty, and waded through streams the half-frozen waters of which reached to the knee; but nothing could daunt the perseverance of our soldiers; the greatest order was maintained, and not a man quitted the ranks. The enemy at length relaxed in his pursuit, and the fires which we descried on the heights in front of us proved to be those of Marshal Ney's rear-guard. They had halted, and were now preparing to resume their march. We joined them, and learned that the marshal had on the preceding evening marched direct on the enemy's artillery, and forced a passage through them.*

"The road we followed led over an extensive plain, and Platoff, profiting by the ground, directed his field-pieces, mounted on sledges, to advance against us; and when this artillery, which we could neither get at nor avoid, had carried disorder into our ranks, he ordered a charge by his whole body. Marshal Ney formed each of his two divisions rapidly into square. We obliged by main force every straggler who still carried a musket to fall into the ranks. At the approach of the enemy, and galled by the fire of his artillery, the soldiers began to hasten their march; but the presence of Marshal Ney, the confidence which he inspired, the calmness of his attitude in the moment of danger, still retained them in their duty. We had reached a height which the marshal ordered General D'Hénin to maintain, and there die, if necessary, for the honor of France. General Ledru marched on the village of Teolino. When he had occupied it, we proceeded to join him, and the two divisions took up a position and afforded each other a mutual flank protection. It was not yet noon, and Marshal Ney declared he would defend the village until nine in the evening. Twenty times did General Platoff endeavor to wrest it from us; twenty times was he repulsed, until, tired out with such opposition, he ended with

* How warmly Marshal Ney must have welcomed such a man as Fezensac. I quote largely from Fezensac's "Memoirs" for reasons which will appear in another part of this work.

establishing himself in our front. The marshal had in the morning sent a Polish officer (Pchébendowski, with fifty horsemen) to give intelligence of our proceedings (and to ask for assistance). At a league from Orcha our advanced guard challenged an outpost, and was answered in French. It was a division of the Fourth Corps, which with the Viceroy (Eugene) was on the march to our assistance. The Viceroy was deeply affected, and loudly proclaimed his admiration of Marshal Ney's conduct.* He congratulated the generals and the two colonels who survived, Colonel Pelleport, of the Eighteenth, and myself. His aides-de-camp overwhelmed us with questions on the details, and the respective parts each had played in such eventful scenes. Thus ended this bold and adventurous march, one of the most extraordinary episodes in the campaign. It covered Marshal Ney with glory."†

When Napoleon heard of Marshal Ney's safety he was sitting at the breakfast-table with some of his officers. He fairly leaped from his chair, and exclaimed in transports of joy, " I have saved my eagles, then. I have three hundred millions in my coffers at the Tuileries. I would willingly have given them all to save Marshal Ney."

" Well he might," says Headley, " and half his empire with it, for without him he had been a throneless Emperor. As his eyes fell on the worn yet still proud, unconquerable

* " Eugene and Ney threw themselves into each other's arms. Eugene wept. He was delighted, melted, and elevated at the sight of the chivalrous hero whom he had just had the happiness to succor. Ney, still heated from the combat, irritated at the dangers which the honor of the army had run in his person, severely blamed Davout, whom he wrongfully" (rightfully) " accused of deserting him. Some hours afterward, when Davout sought to justify himself, he could draw nothing from Ney but a severe look and these words : ' Monsieur le Maréchal, I have no reproaches to make to you ; God is our witness and your judge.' "—Ségur.

" Ney, though performing his duty with a sublime devotion, retained a strong feeling of indignation at the treatment he had received in being deserted, especially by Davout. When that marshal left him on the 16th, and sent to warn him of his danger, Ney replied ; ' All the Cossacks in the universe shall not prevent me from executing my instructions.' "—Griswold's " Napoleon and his Marshals."

† " Souvenirs Militaires," par M. Le Duc de Fezensac.

veteran, he exclaimed, 'What a man! What a soldier!' But words failed to express his admiration, and he clasped the stern warrior to his bosom, and embraced him with all the rapture one hero embraces another."

At Krasnoi, at Liadi, at Dombrowno, at Orcha, and all along the route Napoleon's thoughts had turned to Ney as his only hope. Every few moments he was heard to murmur with unconcealed agitation, "And Ney! And Ney!" Indeed, the whole army felt that Ney alone stood between them and destruction. To Rapp and others Napoleon said, "Ney has a thoroughly tempered soul. How true, how accurate his *coup d'œil!* How admirable his military qualities! What a man he is! I have few men about me who have any real energy, firmness, or moral force. How badly am I served! To whom have I trusted myself? Poor Ney; with whom have I matched thee?" *

Later, near Orcha, when Napoleon clasped Ney in his arms, he said to those around him, "Better an army of deer commanded by a lion, than an army of lions commanded by a deer." And yet Napoleon had the meanness to say at St. Helena: "Marshal Ney was the bravest of men; there terminated all his faculties." No bigger falsehood could have been conceived by the brain of man, and Napoleon knew it. He flatly contradicts himself. Even Headley, who worships Napoleon, if any man ever did worship another, quotes this St. Helena statement only to condemn it as unqualifiedly false. Headley says:

"The whole history of Bonaparte's career, the confidence he everywhere reposed in Ney's skill as well as bravery, pronounce this declaration false; while the manner in which he managed the rear-guard in that unparalleled retreat of the grand army from Russia, shows the injustice of the declaration in every way. Something more than bravery was needed to cover the French there, and Bonaparte knew it. He never placed Ney at the head of the army in invading Russia, and in the rear when retreating from it, simply because he was a

---

* "Memoirs of General Rapp."

brave man. His actions and statements here contradict each other. Bonaparte was the last man to estimate the character of his own officers. He rated all military leaders low but himself. There was not a commander among either the French or the allied forces that ever did or ever could accomplish what Ney performed in that memorable flight. Had he fallen, Bonaparte would probably have fallen also ; and Ney really saved the army, which Bonaparte never could have done."

These observations of Headley are eminently just, and such will be the verdict of posterity. Ney continued to command the rear-guard. Bonaparte dared not release him from this post of danger and honor. There was no one to take his place.

" And he had been too much regretted," says Ségur, " and his preservation had excited emotions far too grateful, to allow of any feelings of envy ; besides, Ney had placed himself completely beyond its reach. As for himself, he had in all this heroism gone so little beyond his natural character that, had it not been for the *éclat* of his glory in the eyes, the gestures, and the acclamations of every one, he would never have imagined that he had performed an extraordinary action."

At the terrible passage of the Beresina, Ney again saved the army from destruction.* And it was almost a miracle that he did save it. The army was fearfully encumbered with superfluous baggage and plunder of every kind. " Burn it all up," bluntly said Ney. " No," replied Berthier, " it can be saved." Napoleon, strange to say, agreed with Berthier. The result was all the baggage, private carriages, trophies of Moscow, etc., were lost, and thirty-six thousand persons found their graves at the bottom of the Beresina. It is impossible to account for the Emperor's illusions. General Eblé, an engineer officer of great skill and judgment, told Napoleon that *six* days would scarcely be sufficient for so many carriages and so much baggage, plunder, etc., to pass over.

---

* " This illustrious soldier, who had saved the Third Corps at Krasnoi, now saved on the banks of the Beresina the whole army, and the Emperor himself."—" Memoirs of the Duc de Fezensac."

"Ney," says Ségur, "immediately called out that they had better be burned immediately; but Berthier, instigated by the demon of courts, opposed this; he assured his sovereign that the army was far from being reduced to that extremity, and the Emperor was led to believe him."

On December 5th, at Smorgoni, Napoleon quitted the army, and set out immediately for Paris. "Why," said he to Daru, "should I remain at the head of a routed army? Murat and Eugene will be sufficient to direct it, and Ney to cover the retreat. I will soon return with fresh forces to the assistance of the grand army. I have no time to lose, and must leave at once." After Napoleon left Ney was practically the commander of the army. He was the only one whose orders were obeyed, and who maintained any discipline among his troops. Murat, whom Napoleon in his blindness appointed commander-in-chief, was utterly inefficient. No one paid any attention to his orders, and he fled disgracefully from his post. The whole army leaned upon Ney as their rock of salvation.

"Murat," says Griswold, "fled in consternation; he was seen forcing his way through the crowd from his palace and from Wilna, without giving any orders, but leaving everything in the hands of Ney." But Ney's spirit was unbroken and unbent, and, like a god, he bore the burden that was put upon him. Rear-guard after rear-guard melted away before him, but as fast as one disappeared he would form another, each one smaller than the preceding, until it was finally reduced to sixty men; but he saved the army and the Empire. Nothing could conquer him. He grew stronger instead of weaker. At Kowno he rose to the highest pitch of soldierly greatness. Fezensac says:

"We were now ordered to defend Kowno. It was the last proof of courage and devotion we were called upon to offer. We expected to be buried beneath its ruins. To the credit of officers and soldiers let it be added, that the *order was obeyed without a murmur*, and that *not a man quitted his post in so critical a juncture*.* As regarded myself, I beheld

* This does not agree with the accounts of Ségur, Scott, and others, but Fezensac *was there*, and his word cannot be doubted.

with admiration the heroic perseverance of Marshal Ney, and congratulated myself on being called on to second his last efforts. We again took possession of our quarters. . . . Marshal Ney still prolonged his defence of Kowno, not only to give time to all those unfortunate people" (stragglers, disbanded men, etc.) "to get clear of the pursuit of the enemy, but to cover the retreat of the King of Naples, who had on the evening before taken the road to Königsberg by Gumbinnen. Two pieces of cannon, supported by some companies of Bavarian infantry, were disposed on the ramparts, and this small number were now prepared to receive the enemy's attack. Marshal Ney, having made his dispositions, retired to his quarters to seek some rest. He had scarcely quitted us when firing commenced. The first discharge of the Russian artillery dismounted one of our guns; the infantry took to flight, and the artillery prepared to follow. There was nothing to prevent the Cossacks from entering the city, when the marshal suddenly appeared on the ramparts. We had been well-nigh ruined by his absence; his presence was sufficient to retrieve all. He took a musket in his hand, and the troops returned to their post, renewed the combat, and sustained it till nightfall, when the retreat was continued. We crossed the Niemen, and imagined that we were safe, but the Cossacks had preceded us and gotten in our front; they had placed their artillery in position on the heights before us, and had thus closed the road. This last and sudden attack, as the most unexpected, was that which exercised the greatest effect on the soldiers' minds. It was useless to attempt a passage by force. Our firelocks had become unserviceable, and those who carried them refused to advance. Despair seized every heart, and our destruction appeared certain. It was now that Marshal Ney again made his appearance among us. Without evincing the slightest uneasiness at our desperate condition, his prompt decision in the field saved us once more—the preserver to the last of all that was left to preserve."

Ségur says: "At Kowno, as it had been after the disasters of Wiasma, of Smolensko, of the Beresina, and of Wilna, it was to Ney that the honor of our arms and all the peril of the last steps of our retreat were again confided. When some of his soldiers left him, he collected their muskets, became a common soldier, and with only four others kept facing thousands of the enemy, constantly fighting, retreating, but never flying, marching after all the others, supporting to the last moment the honor of our arms, and for the hundredth time during the last forty days and forty nights putting his life and liberty in jeopardy to save a few more Frenchmen. Finally, he was the last of the grand army that quitted that fatal Russia, exhibiting to the world the impotence of fortune against unconquerable courage, and proving that with heroes everything turns to glory, even the greatest disasters."

"At length" (General Count Dumas) "we were out of that accursed country, the Russian territory. The Cossacks no longer pursued us with the same ardor. In proportion as we advanced into the Prussian territory we found better quarters and more resources. The first place at which we were able to take breath was Wilkowiszki, and the next Gumbinnen, when I put up at the house of a physician, which I had occupied when I passed through the town before. Some excellent coffee had just been brought us for breakfast, when a man in a great brown coat entered; he had a long beard, his face was blackened, and looked as if it were burnt; his eyes were red and brilliant. 'At length I am here,' said he. 'Why, General Dumas, don't you know me?' 'No; who are you, then?' 'I am the rear-guard of the grand army. I have fired the last musket-shot on the bridge of Kowno. I have thrown into the Niemen the last of our arms, and have come hither through the woods. I am Marshal Ney.' I leave you to imagine with what respectful eagerness we welcomed the hero of the Russian retreat."

And yet Napoleon says Marshal Ney was a brave man, and nothing more. Could any slander be more heartless, more impudent, more shameless? Life is too short to discuss such a question.

Ney continued faithful to Napoleon. At the battle of Lutzen (May 2d, 1813) he was foremost and chiefest in the fight. In fact, his persistent and powerful attacks in the centre at Kaya alone gave Napoleon the victory. He commanded the Fourth and the Seventh corps, composed chiefly of conscripts, but these young soldiers fought like veterans. Indeed, Ney said they were better than the old soldiers.* Ney had moulded them to his hand, for they had been under his charge for the past four months.

Napoleon was surprised at Lutzen, but Ney, by his promptness, quickness, energy, and perseverance saved him from a terrible defeat. Napoleon was trying to outflank his enemies, and his enemies surprised him, and came very near ruining him. They attacked with the utmost violence and determination Napoleon's centre at Kaya, and if Ney had not stemmed the torrent, as no other man perhaps could have stemmed it, the grand army would have been annihilated. At the battle of Bautzen, Napoleon's combinations were all but faultless, and his victory correspondingly great. Here, as at Lutzen, Ney rendered the most important service. On the evening of May 20th, Ney, with sixty thousand men, crossed the river Spree at Klix, and early the next morning fell upon the flank of the allied army as Napoleon attacked it in front. It was a difficult and perilous operation, but Ney exhibited great prudence and skill, and routed the enemy at every point. This was one of Napoleon's greatest victories, the importance of which could hardly be overestimated, and to Ney certainly was due no inconsiderable share of the glory. He had practically an independent command, was entirely separated from Napoleon, and compelled to rely upon his own judgment on a "vast, complicated, and unknown field." Yet all his dispositions were made with exemplary coolness and prudence, and he gained one of the finest victories of his life.

Still Jomini, a pure cobweb general, says Ney's victory

---

* Ney's conscripts were first brought into action at Weissenfels, April 29th. In the marshal's hands they exhibited the valor and steadiness of old soldiers. They repulsed the repeated assaults of the enemy with great spirit and even gayety, Thiers says "with imperturbable good humor." Ney was charmed with his conscripts, and praised them to the Emperor in the most enthusiastic manner.

NEY STATUE AT METZ.

would have been still greater if he had followed *his* advice. Heaven save us!

Napoleon was also surprised at Dresden. While he was hotly pursuing Blücher, who eluded him constantly, purposely drawing Napoleon away from his base, Schwarzenberg, with the main body of the allied army, suddenly advanced upon Dresden. This city, which Napoleon had carefully fortified during the armistice of Pleiswitz, was defended by Marshal St. Cyr with about twenty thousand men. The allies numbered about one hundred and fifty thousand men. They reached Dresden on the morning of August 25th, and if they had attacked St. Cyr at once, or at any time during the day, or before twelve o'clock at night, they would undoubtedly have overwhelmed him and destroyed Napoleon's lines of communication with France; but they foolishly delayed the attack until four o'clock the next morning. In a few hours they had swept everything before them, and St. Cyr was about to surrender, when Napoleon was seen advancing rapidly to his relief.

Napoleon had no idea that Dresden would be attacked, and he was astonished when information was brought him that Schwarzenberg in large force had appeared before the heights of that city. He repaired thither with all haste, and arrived just in time to save St. Cyr from an unconditional surrender. Had the allies attacked the day before, as they ought to have done, Napoleon would have been utterly ruined. No one can deny this. Napoleon in turn assumed the offensive, and gained a decisive victory. Ney and Murat were the chief actors in this struggle. They fought with courage and skill under the most disadvantageous circumstances, and were everywhere victorious. Here Moreau was killed.

At Dennewitz (September 6th) Ney was defeated by the Crown Prince of Sweden. He lost in killed, wounded, prisoners, and deserters more than fifteen thousand men, and about twenty-five pieces of cannon. This defeat is to be attributed to three causes: First, the bad conduct of Ney's chief officers; second, the peculiar composition of his troops; and, third, to Napoleon himself. Napoleon had recently suffered very grave losses. On the 29th and 30th General Vandamme, who, after the battle of Dresden, had been sent in pursuit of the flying enemy, encountered the Russian General Ostermann and others between Kulm and Toplitz, and was utterly defeated. Vandamme's loss was very great—six thousand killed and wounded, eight or ten thousand prisoners, and forty-eight guns. Vandamme himself was taken prisoner, and his fine corps of thirty thousand men was almost entirely dispersed. On the very day that the battle of Dresden was fought (26th) Blücher attacked Marshal Macdonald in the plains of the Katzbach, and defeated him with great loss.* Marshal Oudinot had fared little better. He met Bernadotte at Gross-Beeren on the 23d, and the Crown Prince completely routed him, with the loss of several thousand men in killed, wounded, and prisoners. General Girard was defeated at Leibnitz on the 27th, losing six guns, fifteen hundred men, and all his baggage.

Such disasters, in the light of Napoleon's recent victories at Lutzen, Bautzen, and Dresden, were simply appalling, and the Emperor endeavored to repair his losses by despatching Ney at the head of fifty-two thousand men† to check the progress of Bernadotte, and, if possible "to plant his eagles on the walls of Berlin." Ney's troops consisted of three corps—Fourth (Bertrand), Seventh (Regnier), and Twelfth (Oudinot). These soldiers were for the most part of an inferior quality. They consisted chiefly of foreigners, who cared little for Napoleon and his empire, and of young, raw French conscripts, who had already become tired of the seem-

* Blücher issued the following high-sounding address : " Soldiers, Silesia is delivered. Your bayonets and the nervous strength of your arm drove your enemies down the steeps of the raging Neisse and the Katzbach. One hundred and three pieces of cannon, two hundred and fifty tumbrils, the camp hospital of the enemy, his provisions, a general of division, two generals of brigade, a great number of colonels, staff, and other officers, eighteen thousand prisoners, two eagles, and other trophies have fallen into your hands. Let us sing praises to the Lord of Hosts, by whose help you have overthrown your enemies, and return thanks to Him who has given us the victory."

† Thiers gives this number.

ingly endless struggle in which Napoleon was engaged. Indeed, the *morale* of the entire army was seriously impaired by the recent defeats.

Marshal Oudinot was deeply wounded because he was compelled to serve under Marshal Ney. He felt that Napoleon was trying to disgrace him in presence of the whole army because of his defeat at Gross-Beeren, and he was mad with Napoleon, Ney, and everybody else. Regnier was an officer of ability, but he was full of conceit, and believed himself superior to Oudinot, Ney, and even Napoleon himself. Bertrand was a flat-headed incompetent, who, but for the extreme softness and pliability of his character, would never have been given an important command of any kind. He did not like Ney, though Napoleon was his god.

The movement which Ney was ordered to execute was one of extreme delicacy and difficulty. He himself, generally so daring and hopeful, had little confidence in the final result. He had to perform a protracted flank movement with demoralized men and officers, and in the presence of a largely superior force commanded by an officer of rare ability (Bernadotte). Under such circumstances it was all but impossible for Ney to perform the duty assigned him. Still, he would have done so but for the mistake, inefficiency, or treachery of Bertrand,* and the delay of Oudinot to march to the field of battle, owing mainly to Regnier's gross disobedience of orders, but partly to Oudinot's own indifference and sulkiness. One of these causes alone in so critical and dangerous a manœuvre would have been fatal ; as it was, Ney was simply over-

* " The troops of the Crown Prince lay to the left, and the marshal's object was to avoid any encounter with the enemy, throw himself on the road from Torgau to Berlin, and enter into communication with reinforcements from Dresden ; but it was found necessary to pass by Dennewitz, where Tauenstein was stationed, and who might give the alarm to the other corps of the enemy. On the morning of the 6th, therefore, Bertrand was sent forward to attack Tauenstein and draw off his attention, while Ney with the rest of the army pushed rapidly by without being brought to action ; but Bertrand having made his appearance too early, notice was given to the allied troops in the neighborhood, and before Ney arrived they were ready to dispute the passage with him. The engagement consequently became general."—Hazlitt's " Napoleon."

whelmed. His Saxon troops under Bertrand deserted him, and his army was broken and routed. Ney did all that any man could have done. Napoleon did not blame him.* He no doubt felt that he himself was largely responsible for Ney's defeat.† Ney himself wrote to Napoleon as follows :

"It is impossible to derive any advantage from the Fourth, Seventh, and Twelfth corps d'armée in the present state of their organization ; each of the generals-in-chief does nearly what he judges most for his own safety. Things have come to such a pass that it is difficult for me to keep my ground. The moral condition of the generals and the other officers is singularly shaken, the power of command, therefore, is very imperfect, and I had rather be a grenadier. I pray your Majesty to deliver me from this hell. I think I need not speak of my devotion. I am ready to shed all my blood provided it be with some profitable results. The presence of the Emperor can alone restore order and unity."

And, again, on September 23d, he wrote to Napoleon : "It is impossible to obtain obedience from General Regnier ; he will not execute the orders which he receives. The foreign troops of all nations manifest the worst spirit, and it is doubtful whether the cavalry with me is not more injurious than useful."

Marshal Macdonald also wrote a similar letter to Napoleon. In the important operations preceding the battle of Leipsic,

* See "Memoirs of Marshal St. Cyr."
St. Cyr blames Napoleon for Ney's defeat. The Emperor, he says, was altogether mistaken as to the character, composition, and number of the troops which Ney had to encounter, and the orders which he gave him could not be executed.

"On September 5th Marshal Oudinot had received at Seyda the order to leave in the morning with the Twelfth Corps, to direct himself upon Oehna, but only after the Seventh Corps (Regnier's) should have passed before the Twelfth. *Regnier* (the italics are mine) *having taken another way, Oudinot, who expected this passage, did not leave for Seyda till between nine and ten in the morning.*"—"Memoirs of Duc de Fezensac."
Ney certainly cannot be held responsible for the defeat at Dennewitz.

† See Scott's "Napoleon," J. B. Lippincott Co., 1881, p. 600 ; "Souvenirs Militaires," par M. le Duc de Fezensac, Paris, 1863, p. 442, note at bottom ; Hazlitt's "Napoleon," vol. iii., p. 175.

Ney's energy, vigilance, and prudence were of the greatest benefit to Napoleon. Even Thiers admits this. He outmanœuvred Bernadotte and Blücher, and at Düben, Worlitz and Dessau dealt the enemy some vigorous and effective blows. Napoleon committed some fearful mistakes at Leipsic, and for several days preceding the battle. They came very near ruining him. But for Ney's powerful exertions, it is difficult to see how Napoleon could have effected his retreat from Leipsic. Bernadotte and Blücher would have crushed him, especially on the third day, in this great "battle of kings."

The campaign of 1814, as brief as it was, reflects more credit upon Napoleon than any other part of his military career.* In my opinion it is far superior to his Italian campaign. He was warmly seconded by his officers and men, but to no one was he so much indebted for his magnificent victories as to the "bravest of the brave." Ney must share largely in the glory of this campaign. He was peerless at Brienne, Montmirail, Craonne, Laon, Etouvelles, Arcis, and other places. At Craonne and Laon especially he accomplished with the young, ill-trained conscripts what no other officer could have accomplished. But human endurance has its limit. France was exhausted, and Paris surrendered on March 31st.

Ney and the other marshals, seeing that further resistance was useless, advised Napoleon, who was then at Fontainebleau, to abdicate as the only means of saving France. Some writers affirm that Ney's language to Napoleon was very rough and unbecoming. Thiers says it was not. So do Napoleon and Caulaincourt. Napoleon after much indecision consented to abdicate. Ney, Caulaincourt, and Macdonald were appointed to negotiate with the allied powers. Ney and Macdonald pleaded with soldierly eloquence the cause of Napoleon's son, and a regency under the Empress. Ney's speech made a deep impression upon the Emperor Alexander, and he was about to yield to the wishes of Napoleon's commissioners,

* Though his movement in rear of the allies on March 21st was an inexcusable blunder. It ruined him. While he was gone the allies took possession of Paris.

when General Dessolles and others interfered with rudeness and violence, and finally succeeded in turning the Emperor of Russia from his good intentions.

Ney, Caulaincourt, and Macdonald returned with sad hearts to Fontainebleau, and on April 6th Napoleon signed an unconditional abdication. Ney now made his submission to the provisional government, and afterward took the oath of allegiance to Louis XVIII. The king received him with much kindness, and loaded him with the highest honors; but Ney was not happy. His forced inaction did not suit him.

"He was too old," says an elegant writer, "to acquire new habits. Plain in his manners, and still plainer in his words, he neither knew nor wished to know the art of pleasing courtiers. The habit of braving death and of commanding vast bodies of men had impressed his character with a species of moral grandeur which raised him far above the puerile observances of the fashionable world. Of good nature, indeed, he had a considerable fund, but he showed it not so much by the endless little attentions of a gentleman, as by scattered acts of princely beneficence. The sobriety of his manners was extreme, even to austerity. His wife had been reared in the court of Louis XVI., and had adorned that of the Emperor. Cultivated in her mind, accomplished in her manners, and elegant in all she said or did, her society was courted on all sides. Her habits were expensive; luxury reigned throughout her apartments and presided at her board; and to all this display of elegance and pomp of show, the military simplicity of the marshal furnished a striking contrast. His good nature offered no other obstacle to the gratification of her wishes than the occasional expression of a fear that his circumstances might be deranged by them; but if he would not oppose, neither could he join in her extravagance. While she was presiding at a numerous and brilliant party of guests, he preferred to remain alone in a distant apartment, where the festive sounds could not reach him. On such occasions he almost always dined alone. Ney seldom appeared at court. He could neither bow nor flatter, nor could he stoop to kiss even his sovereign's hand without something like self-humiliation. To his princess, on the other hand, the royal smile was necessary as the light of the sun; and, unfortunately for her, she was sometimes disappointed in her efforts to attract it. Her wounded vanity often beheld an insult in what was probably no more than an inadvertence. She complained to her husband, and he with a calm smile advised her never again to expose herself to such mortifications if she really sustained them; but though he could thus rebuke a woman's vanity, the haughty soldier felt his own wounded through hers. To escape these complaints, and from the monotony of his Parisian existence, he retired to his country-seat in January, 1815, the very season when people of consideration are most engrossed by the busy scenes of the metropolis. There he led an unfettered life; he gave his mornings to field sports, and the guests he entertained in the evening were such as, from their humble condition, rendered formality useless, and placed him completely at his ease." *

Ney was thus living on his beautiful estate near Châteaudun, when, on March 6th, he received an order from the Minister of War (Marshal Soult) to join his division (Sixth) at Besançon, and there await further orders. Ney rode immediately to Paris and sought and obtained an interview with the king. Upon leaving, Ney kissed the king's hand, and, in an "effusion of loyalty," promised to bring Bonaparte to Paris in an iron cage; but instead of capturing or opposing Napoleon, Ney joined him with his entire army, and thus destroyed the last hope of Bourbon resistance.

Up to March 14th Ney protested his loyalty to the king. He said Bonaparte's invasion was an act of madness, and that it was impossible for him to succeed; but at Lons-le-Saulnier his mind underwent a complete change. During the night of the 13th he received letters from General Bertrand, stating that Napoleon's success was assured; that everything had been arranged beforehand; that the Emperor had received the secret submission of every regiment in the service; that he was acting in conceit with Austria and England; that General

* "Court and Camp of Bonaparte."

Köhler had come to Elba on the part of Count Metternich; that Napoleon had dined on an English vessel in company with several French generals; that Marshal Soult, the War Minister, had promised him his support; that the Empress Marie Louise and her son were already on the way to Paris; that the whole country had risen up to welcome him, and that if he persisted in his insane attempt to oppose him, he would be responsible for all the horrors of a civil war.* Ney's own troops had manifested a bad spirit. They had no heart for fighting their old Emperor, and their murmurs and threats even were growing deep and loud. The spirit of disaffection was spreading everywhere, and Ney felt that he could not resist the torrent. "I cannot," said he, "keep back the ocean with my hand."

On the 14th he read a proclamation to his troops (sent to him, he said, by Bertrand) announcing that the "cause of the Bourbons was forever lost," and that the Emperor Napoleon was the legitimate sovereign of France. "Soldiers," said he, "I have often led you to victory; I am now going to conduct you to that immortal phalanx which the Emperor Napoleon is conducting to Paris, where it will be in a few days, and then our hope and happiness will be forever realized."

The idea of a civil war horrified the marshal, and he felt that it would be better to direct the torrent than to be swept away by it. "You are babies," said he to those who blamed him for his course. "I was obliged to choose either one party or the other. Could I hide like a coward, shunning the responsibility of events? It is necessary to take a decided part at once in order to avert civil war, and to get a hold upon the man who is about to become again our ruler, and to prevent him from committing new follies, for I do not pretend to give myself to a *man*, but to *France;* and if he should wish to lead us again to Moscow, I shall not follow him."

Ney met the Emperor at Auxerre. Napoleon received him very graciously, embraced him, petted him, and called him

* See "Le Maréchal Ney, le Soldat," etc.; "Life of Marshal Ney," by Welschinger.

the "bravest of the brave." Ney said to the Emperor that he might always rely upon him when the welfare of his country was at stake ; that his blood had often flowed for France, and for France he was prepared to shed it to the last drop. "But times," continued the marshal, "have changed. The people are tired of war, and wish only for liberty and peace." Napoleon replied that it was patriotism alone which had brought him back to France. "In my island home I learned that my people were unhappy, and I came to deliver them from the Bourbon yoke, and to give them all that they expect from me."

Much other conversation occurred between these illustrious warriors which I cannot relate. Napoleon and Ney each indulged in a good deal of *gush*. Napoleon reached Paris on March 20th, and a few days afterward he sent Ney to Lille to inspect the northern fortresses, to regulate the civil and military authorities, to conciliate the malcontents, and to pave the way generally for the new *régime*.*

On June 12th, a little before daybreak, Napoleon started on his last campaign. As he threw himself into his carriage he remarked, "I go to measure myself with Wellington." On the eve of his departure he sent an order to Ney to "join the army at once if he wished to see the first battle."

Since the marshal's return from the north he had stayed quietly at home, refraining almost entirely from the pleasures of the imperial court. He was, as he afterward said, a miserable man, and he wished to avoid the public eye as much as possible. At the ceremony of the Field of Mars, Ney appeared with the other marshals as one of the Emperor's honorary escort. When Napoleon saw him, he said to him in a tone of ill-humor, "I thought you had emigrated." "I *ought* to have done so," replied Ney, "but it is now too late." Napoleon's conduct in waiting almost until the last moment of his departure before ordering Ney to join the

* "Ney, notwithstanding his characteristic faults, was extremely shrewd with regard to everything connected with his profession, and was most useful on the frontier."—Thiers' "Consulate and Empire," vol. v., p. 485.

army has been universally condemned. His staunchest supporters can find no excuse for it. Hon. John C. Ropes, of Boston, an able historian and a great admirer of Napoleon, says:
"It seems like an unpardonable oversight, to say the least. As such Ney certainly regarded it. Ney was given no time for preparation; it was only by the exercise of great diligence that he reached the front when he did, and that was at five o'clock in the afternoon of the 15th, after the Sambre had been crossed. He was assigned to the command of the First and Second corps, commanded by Counts D'Erlon and Reille respectively; but he was ignorant of their organization, and had even to learn the names of the division commanders. It is difficult if not impossible to understand this strange neglect of Napoleon. No one knew better than he how important it is that the commander of an army or of a wing of an army should have ample time to know his troops and to be known by them, and that this was especially necessary where a reorganization had recently taken place."*

Ney himself says: "On June 11th I received an order from the Minister of War to repair to the imperial presence. I had no command and no information upon the composition and strength of the army. Neither the Emperor nor his min-

* "Campaign of Waterloo." 1892.
"Ney arrived at headquarters without any staff, confidential officers, aides-de-camp, equipage or horses, and had received the unexpected command of numerous corps, whose positions he scarcely knew. In a country which had been effaced from his memory for twenty years. He was equally unacquainted with the general officers who commanded these different corps. Some days were necessary to enable him to study the ground, the troops, and the characters he had to deal with."—Lamartine's "History of the Restoration."

"On leaving Paris, Napoleon had sent him [Ney] word to join him as quickly as possible if he wished to be present at the first battle. Ney received this message so late that he had only time to take with him his aide-de-camp, Heymes, and set out for Maubeuge without any military equipage. . . . The marshal arrived knowing nothing of the state of affairs, ignorant of what position he was to take, and of what troops he was to command. Though not possessing all the calmness of mind necessary in difficult positions, because of the discontent he felt with himself and others, his extraordinary energy was never greater than at that moment."—Thiers' "Consulate and Empire."

ister had given me any previous hint, from which I could anticipate that I should be employed in the present campaign. I was consequently taken by surprise, without horses, without accoutrements, and without money, and I was obliged to borrow the necessary expenses of my journey. Having arrived on the 12th at Laon, on the 13th at Avesnes, and on the 14th at Beaumont, I purchased in this last town two horses from the Duc de Trévise, with which I repaired on the 15th to Charleroy, accompanied by my first aide-de-camp, the only officer who attended me. I arrived at the moment when the enemy, attacked by our troops, was retreating upon Fleurus and Gosselies. The Emperor ordered me immediately to put myself at the head of the First and Second corps of infantry, commanded by Lieutenant-Generals D'Erlon and Reille, of the division of light cavalry, of Lieutenant-General Piré, of the division of light cavalry of the guard under the command of Lieutenant-General Lefebvre-Desnouettes and Colbert, and of two divisions of cavalry of Count de Valmy, forming in all eight divisions of infantry and four of cavalry. With these troops, a part of which only I had as yet under my immediate command, I pursued the enemy, and forced him to evacuate Gosselies, Frasnes, Millet, Hépignies. There they took up a position for the night, with the exception of the First Corps, which was still at Marchiennes, and which did not join me till the following day." *

Napoleon's neglect to summon Ney to join the army till the eve of hostilities is simply inexplicable. There is no telling what effect this egregious blunder had upon the entire campaign. It certainly does throw a good deal of light upon some subsequent events. At St. Helena Napoleon said that on the evening of the 15th he ordered Ney to occupy Quatre Bras, and to fortify it against the English. Ney, he said, failed to execute his order, and thus seriously deranged his plans. Quatre Bras was, of course, a very important point. Four roads (as its name imports) meet here, and through it ran the main line of communication between Wellington and

* Letter to Fouché, Duke of Otranto, June 26th, 1815.

Blücher. Colonel Heymes, who was with Ney when he received his instructions from Napoleon, says emphatically that the Emperor did not order Ney to occupy Quatre Bras; that his language was, "*Push the enemy !*" Not a word was said about the occupation of Quatre Bras.*

Marshal Soult, in 1829, told Ney's son and Colonel Heymes that the "Emperor had not the slightest idea of occupying Quatre Bras on the evening of the 15th, and gave no orders to that effect." Ney himself, in his letter to Fouché, says in substance that he had no orders to occupy Quatre Bras on the 15th. "On the 16th," he said, "I received orders to attack the English in their position at Quatre Bras." If he had received instructions of this kind on the 15th he would have said so.†

Ney "pushed" the enemy in accordance with the order which Bonaparte had given him, and on the evening of the 15th he drove the Prussians from Gosselies, Hépignies, Millet, and Frasnes. A portion of Ney's troops took up their quarters at Frasnes about eleven o'clock at night. Frasnes is but two and one half miles from Quatre Bras. Ney gained some important advantages by these vigorous and well-directed movements, and but for Napoleon's blind, unaccountable neglect, of which I have already spoken, the results would

---

* Capefigue says Bonaparte's only instructions to Ney on the 15th were, "Push the enemy !"

Quinet, an able and impartial historian, says emphatically that Ney never received orders to occupy Quatre Bras on the 15th.—"Histoire de la Campagne de 1815."

† Thiers labors hard to prove that Napoleon ordered Ney to occupy Quatre Bras on the evening of the 15th, but his arguments are exceedingly flimsy. Indeed, he answers himself before he gets through.

Hon. John C. Ropes ("Campaign of Waterloo," 1892) says in effect no one now *doubts* that Napoleon ordered Ney to occupy Quatre Bras on the evening of the 15th.

In 1888 (see *Scribner's Magazine*, "Campaign of Waterloo") Mr. Ropes uses this language: "That Ney received from the Emperor during the 15th or at the midnight conference orders to press on to Quatre Bras, no one now *believes.*"

I quote Mr. Ropes against Mr. Ropes.

Count de Flahaut sustains Colonel Heymes, Marshal Soult, and Edgar Quinet.

MARSHAL NEY.

(From an old Pen-and-Ink Sketch.)

have been much more valuable. Colonel J. F. Maurice, R. A., completely vindicates Ney from the charges of inefficiency and disobedience of orders which Napoleon brought against him at St. Helena. Colonel Maurice shows conclusively that whatever errors were committed on the 15th and 16th were directly traceable to Napoleon himself.*

On the 16th Ney attacked Wellington at Quatre Bras. It was a fierce and sanguinary encounter. Ney handled his troops perhaps better than any other man could have handled them, and the Iron Duke, notwithstanding his dogged resistance, would most certainly have been defeated if Napoleon had not at the critical moment deliberately taken away Ney's reserve of twenty thousand men, troops which Napoleon had given to Ney for the purpose of attacking the English Army.† It really seems (to say the least) that Napoleon was indifferent to Ney's success. As it was, Wellington was on the very brink of disaster. If Ney had had just one half of his reserve, Wellington would have suffered a serious reverse. No one can deny that.

At Waterloo Ney fought his last battle. It was worthy of his genius and his fame. He went down with the Old Guard, but he went down in a blaze of glory. Napoleon blamed Ney and Grouchy for his defeat, but he had no one to blame but himself. He never ordered Grouchy to come to Waterloo, and he didn't expect him to come. Most of Napoleon's St. Helena history is pure fiction. I have read his orders to Grouchy with a great deal of care, and in no instance did he command Grouchy to come to Waterloo. As Colonel Maurice says, "Napoleon, at St. Helena, invented orders which were never sent." ‡ As to Ney, it is sufficient to say that his

* See articles on Waterloo, *United Service Magazine*, 1890 and 1891. Every student of Napoleon's last campaign ought to read these articles. See, too, Siborne's " History of the War in France and Belgium in 1815," London, 1844, and " History of the Campaign of Waterloo," by Colonel Charras.

† Napoleon had also ordered Ney *to spare the guard*.

‡ *United Service Magazine*, 1890 and 1891. See also " The Campaign of Waterloo," Appendix A, John Codman Ropes, New York, 1892, and Vaulabelle, " Campaign and Battle of Waterloo," Paris, 1845.

great military qualities never shone with brighter lustre than on this terrible and fatal day. If Napoleon had done his part as well as Ney did his, the French army would not have been annihilated. Late in the afternoon Ney captured La Haye Sainte, a strongly fortified farm-house on the Brussels road. No one but Ney could have taken it; and Bonaparte well knew it. It was the key to the English centre, scarcely three hundred yards from Wellington's line of battle. The duke's position was extremely critical. He was, as is well known, in a state of intense anxiety; but Napoleon failed to support Ney, and he was eventually driven from this important point. The last charge of the Old Guard was terrific. Napoleon led them on for a short distance as if he were going to head the charge, but when he reached a hollow which in some degree shielded him from the English fire, he stopped, harangued his troops impetuously, gave the command to Ney, and remained in the hollow. Headley thinks Bonaparte was not lacking in personal courage.* He says:

"Bonaparte has been blamed for not heading this charge himself; but he knew he could not carry that guard so far, nor hold them so long before the artillery, as Ney. The moral power the latter carried with him was worth a whole division. . . . Bonaparte committed himself and France to Ney, and saw his Empire rest on a single charge. Ney felt the pressure of the immense responsibility on his brave heart, and resolved not to prove unworthy of the great trust committed to him. Nothing could be more imposing than the movement of that grand column to the assault. That guard had never yet recoiled before a human foe, and the allied forces beheld with awe its firm and terrible advance to the final charge. Rank after rank went down, yet they neither stopped nor faltered. Dissolving squadrons, and whole battalions disappearing one after another in the destructive fire, affected not their steady courage. The ranks closed up as before, and each treading over his fallen comrade, pressed firmly on. The horse which Ney rode fell under him, and he had scarcely

* Marshal Macdonald thinks he was. See "Recollections" of Macdonald, p. 246.

mounted another before it also sunk to the earth. Again and again did that unflinching man feel his steed sink down, till *five* had been shot under him. Then, with his uniform riddled with bullets, and his face singed and blackened with powder, he marched on foot with drawn sword at the head of his men. In vain did the artillery hurl its storm of fire and lead into that living mass. Up to the very muzzles they pressed, and driving the artillerymen from their own pieces, pushed through the English lines; but at that moment a file of soldiers who had lain flat on the ground behind a low ridge of earth suddenly rose and poured a volley in their very faces. Another and another and another followed, till one broad sheet of flame rolled on their bosoms, and in such a fierce and unexpected flow that human courage could not withstand it. They reeled, shook, staggered back, then turned and fled. Ney was borne back by the refluent tide and hurried over the field; but for the crowd of fugitives that forced him on, he would have stood alone, and fallen in his footsteps. As it was, disdaining to fly, though the whole army was flying, he formed his men into two immense squares, and endeavored to stem the terrific current, and would have done so had it not been for the thirty thousand fresh Prussians that pressed on his exhausted ranks. For a long time these squares stood, and let the artillery plough through them; but the fate of Napoleon was writ, and though Ney doubtless did what no other man in the army could have done, the decree could not be reversed. The star that had blazed so brightly over the world went down in blood, and the 'bravest of the brave' had fought his last battle. It was worthy of his great name, and the charge of the Old Guard at Waterloo, with him at their head, will be pointed to by remotest generations with a shudder." *

Ney remained upon the field a considerable time after Bonaparte had quitted it.† He was perhaps the last man to leave.

* " Napoleon and his Marshals."

† " I arrived at Marchiennes-au-pont at four o'clock in the morning (19th) alone, without any officers of my staff, ignorant of what had become of the Emperor, who, before the end of the battle, had entirely disap-

"I was constantly in the rear-guard," said he, "which I followed on foot."* The rout was complete. Bonaparte and his army and his empire perished in one day. Wellington and Blücher marched to Paris, and in a few days the city capitulated, and a new *régime* began. The king entered Paris on July 9th.

Ney, though protected by the capitulation, was wisely advised by Fouché and others to leave Paris for awhile, and to retire to some foreign country. Ney accordingly quitted Paris under an assumed name, furnished with a passport and perhaps money by the Duke of Otranto. He started to Switzerland, with the intention ultimately to escape to the United States; but when he reached the foot of the Alps he suddenly changed his mind, and took refuge with one of his wife's relatives at the château of Bessonis, in the mountains of Auvergne. Here he remained for several weeks, "when one of those acts of imprudence" (I quote from Lamartine) " which are the snares of security, excited a suspicion in the neighboring town of Aurillac that some illustrious outlaw had taken shelter in the château of Bessonis. The marshal had formerly received, as a present from Napoleon, a Turkish sabre, one of the Egyptian spoils, the peculiar form and rich decoration of which attracted every eye.† This weapon always accompanied him as a souvenir and a witness of his glory. Having one day exhibited it to the admiration of his hosts, he forgot to take it back to his chamber, and left it carelessly in the drawing-room. A country neighbor, on paying a visit at the château, perceived the weapon, and was

peared, and who, I was allowed to believe, might be either killed or taken prisoner."—Ney to Fouché.

* " Ney displayed unexampled heroism, and his bravery seemed to surpass the capabilities of mere man. He was the last that descended from the plateau of Mount St. Jean."—Thiers' " History of the Consulate and the Empire."

† Napoleon had presented the sabre to Ney at the time of the marshal's marriage, July 26th, 1802. It belonged to a Pacha who was killed at the battle of Aboukir.

" Cette arme, dont Ney jura de ne se séparer qu'avec la vie devait treize ans plus tard être l'indice fatal qui le livrerait à ses ennemis."—*Nouvelle Biographie Générale.*

struck by its magnificence. Without any idea of doing mischief he spoke of the Turkish sabre he had seen a few days after in the town of Aurillac, and described it minutely.

"One of the idlers who listened to him, and who had a taste for and a knowledge of handsome arms, exclaimed that there were only two such sabres in the world, those of Murat and of Marshal Ney. This conversation awoke conjectures in some who were present, which at length reached the ears of the prefect. This functionary, being acquainted with the relationship between the family of Bessonis and that of Ney, no longer entertained any doubt that the unknown guest of the château was the marshal himself. He therefore sent a detachment of gendarmes, under the command of an officer, to surprise the château, and to bring away the suspected stranger. At break of day the gendarmes surrounded the château ; the officer commanding the detachment and eighteen men of his brigade entered the court-yard. The tramping of the horses, the noise of arms, and the alarm of the people of the house awoke the marshal. He could still, however, fly by stealing into the woods through the gardens, but he was weary of opposing his destiny ; he appeared at the window, and addressing the commandant of the gendarmes, he loudly declared who he was, ordered the doors to be opened, and stepping from his chamber said to the gendarmes : 'I am Michel Ney,' and accompanied them without resistance to Aurillac. He was there treated with respect by the prefect. His guards were withdrawn, he was only required to give his word not to escape, and he was sent to Paris under the superintendence of two officers. In passing through the cantonments of the Army of the Loire, he might have allowed himself to be carried off by his soldiers. General Excelmans offered to deliver him, but he refused, that he might not forfeit his word." *

Ney was imprisoned within the damp and gloomy walls of the Conciergerie, and treated with great indignity. His trial for high treason began on November 7th. He was defended

* " History of the Restoration."

by Dupin and Berryer, two of the ablest lawyers in France. The court-martial before which he was brought was composed of seven members, among whom were Marshals Jourdan, Masséna, Augereau, and Mortier. Ney's counsel objected to the court as incompetent. Ney was a peer, and they contended that in accordance with the constitution he could be tried only by the Chamber of Peers. The court held that this objection was valid, and the case was accordingly transferred to the Chamber of Peers. The trial, or rather the mockery of a trial, began anew on November 21st. There was abundant evidence to show that Ney remained loyal to the king until March 14th, when, seeing the general defection around him, and feeling that further resistance was useless, he read that unfortunate proclamation, declaring that the cause of the Bourbons was irretrievably lost. The strongest point made by his counsel was that Ney was protected by the capitulation of Paris. This argument, indeed, was unanswerable. There was but one way to meet it, and that was to reject the evidence altogether. "We cannot allow it," said the President, Jeffreys II., "the capitulation is the work of foreigners. It can have no weight in a French court. I interdict the defenders of the accused from making any use of the *pretended convention* of July 3d."

Dupin, as a last resort, rose and said: "The marshal is not only under the protection of the French laws, but under the protection of the laws of nations. I speak not of the convention, but of the limits traced by the treaty of November 20th, which certainly is an act solemn and legal, which we may invoke, since it is to that we owe the happy peace we now enjoy. The treaty of November 20th, in tracing a new line around France, has left on the right Saar-Louis, the birthplace of the marshal. The marshal, therefore, Frenchman as he is in heart, is no longer a Frenchman since the treaty."

Marshal Ney here interrupted his counsel, and said with much emotion: "Yes, I am a Frenchman, and I will die a Frenchman. I thank my counsel for what they have done for me and are ready to do, but I forbid them from saying a word more, unless they are permitted to make use of all the means in their power. I had rather not be defended at all than have the mere shadow of a defence." These words produced a deep impression upon the auditors, and for some moments not a word was spoken by any member of the court.

At length M. Bellart, the prosecuting officer, rose and said, "We have a right, and it is our duty to refute the captious means which have been resorted to; but since the marshal renounces all further defence, we renounce the right of reply." He sat down. The farce was ended. Ney was convicted of high treason, and sentenced to the full punishment of death. Marshal Ney was not present when the sentence was pronounced, and the secretary, M. Cauchy, was instructed to notify him of it.

The following account of the marshal's last night in the Luxembourg prison is taken from the reports of the trial and execution, published at the time :* "The marshal, upon returning to his prison, while the peers were deliberating upon his fate, appeared to be sustained by a feeling of deep resolution. He asked for dinner, and ate with a good appetite. He thought that a small knife was the object of attention and uneasiness to the persons charged to guard him. 'Do you think,' said he, on looking at them, 'that I fear death?' and then threw the knife some distance from him. After dinner he smoked a cigar tranquilly, and then lay down and slept for a couple of hours. The marshal was in a sound sleep when M. Cauchy repaired to him to read his sentence. Before he proceeded to read it, he attempted to address some kind words to the marshal, to testify how painful it was to him to be forced to discharge so sad a duty. 'Sir,' said the marshal, stopping him, 'I am grateful to you, but do your duty; every one must do his duty—read.' Upon the preamble being read he said impatiently, 'To the fact, to the fact at once!' The secretary read on conscientiously, word for word, the long enumeration of the names, titles, rank, and dignities by which the sentence designated the condemned man. Ney again

* See also " Histoire Complète du Procès du Maréchal Ney," Dumoulin; "Vie du Maréchal Ney," Maiseau; and "Memoirs" of Count de Rochechouart.

stopped him. 'What good can this do? Say simply Michael Ney, and soon a little dust.' As the secretary was about to leave, the marshal asked him at what hour the execution was to take place. 'At nine o'clock to-morrow morning,' replied M. Cauchy, bowing, as if ashamed of the shortness of the time doled out to him for his preparation. 'And my wife and children, can I embrace them for the last time?' This M. Cauchy was authorized to promise him. 'Well, then, let them come at five o'clock, but do not speak of my condemnation. Let my wife learn it only from myself, who alone can soften its horrors to her.' M. Cauchy promised that this precaution should be taken with his family. He then retired, and the marshal, throwing himself in his clothes on the bed, wrapped his cloak around his head, and fell asleep, as if on the bivouac and ready for action. About five o'clock Madame Ney, with her four sons, and Madame Gamot, her sister, arrived at the prison. The marshal, who adored this young and charming companion of his happy days, received her fainting in his arms, and with difficulty restored her with his tears and kisses. Then, taking his four young sons upon his knees, and pressing them to his heart, he uttered to them in a low voice those last sad words by which a father transfuses the purest portion of his soul into the memory of his children.

"Madame Gamot prayed aloud, and endeavored to console by turns the father, the mother, and the children. The marshal, who had solaced his heart with the sight and farewell endearments of all that he loved upon earth, maintained sufficient coolness to deceive his wife and withdraw her from the agony of his last moments, by imparting a hope to her which he did not feel himself. He flattered her with the idea that the heart of the king might still be overcome by the sight of her grief and the energy of her prayers. He thus succeeded in withdrawing himself from her arms, and the suppliants were conducted amid the darkness to the gates of the palace, where the king and the Duchess of Angoulême were still sleeping. In vain. There was no hope. At ten o'clock the Duke de Duras informed Madame Ney that her husband had ceased to live. The marshal had not lain down again after the last embraces of his wife and the sobbing of his children. He had dried up his own tears that he might no longer think of anything but the dignity of his death. He wrote his will; then, rising from his chair, he walked about his chamber, exchanging with great composure a few words with his guardians. One of them, a grenadier of La Rochejaquelein, said to him, 'Marshal, in your situation, should you not think of God? I have seen many battles, and every time 1 could I confessed myself, and found myself always the better for it.' The marshal regarded him with interest for a few moments, and then said, 'Comrade, I believe you are right. I am no woman, but I believe in God and in another life. One should die as a Christian. I wish to see the curate of St. Sulpice.' The curate of St. Sulpice was immediately sent for. He responded to the summons at once, and remained with the marshal nearly three quarters of an hour." At nine o'clock Ney left his prison. At twenty minutes past nine o'clock (according to the accepted historical account) he was publicly executed, at the back of the Luxembourg gardens, as a traitor to his country and his king.

"A truer patriot," says Headley, "never shed his blood for his country. If France never has a worse traitor, the day of her betrayal will be far distant, and if she has no worse defender, disgrace will never visit her armies."

Says Colonel Napier, in speaking of Ney's death, "Thus he who had fought *five hundred battles* for France, not *one* against her, was shot as a traitor."*

BUT WAS MARSHAL NEY EXECUTED, as history states? I do not believe that he was. I shall now proceed to give the reasons for my belief.

* See also "Court and Camp of Bonaparte;" "Le Maréchal Ney, le Soldat," etc.; Alison's "History of Europe;" Capefigue, "Les Cent Jours;" Lamartine, "History of the Restoration."

THE EXECUTION OF MARSHAL NEY.
(From an old Woodcut.)

PART II.

WAS MARSHAL NEY EXECUTED?

CHAPTER I.

On the 15th day of November, 1846, in Rowan County, N. C., died Peter Stuart Ney. Many persons believed then, as many believe now, that he was Marshal Ney of France, who, through the aid of the soldiers detailed to execute him, escaped death and came to the United States. I myself believe that he was Marshal Ney. The circumstances attending his alleged execution (elsewhere narrated) strongly point to a probable escape. He had all the characteristics of Marshal Ney. He was a masterful man. Wherever he went he ruled as an uncrowned king. He was like Marshal Ney in person —in feature, in complexion, in voice, in expression, in carriage, in mind, in character, in habits, in taste, in temperament, in manner—in peculiarities of every kind. The handwriting of P. S. Ney is strikingly like that of Marshal Ney, and yet unlike it in the sense of deliberate imitation. He was recognized as Marshal Ney by several persons of character who had known, or had often seen, Marshal Ney in France or other portions of Europe. P. S. Ney himself, in seasons of great trouble and distress, solemnly declared to a few devoted friends, in whom he had the fullest confidence, that he was Marshal Ney. In his last illness, a few hours before his death, perfectly calm and rational, he said to his attending physician and others who had asked him to tell them who he was: "I am Marshal Ney of France."

And no man could be farther from crankiness or imposture.

Honest, manly, warm-hearted, clear-headed, plain, practical, he was loved and honored, nay, reverenced by all who knew him. He had but one vice—he sometimes drank to excess. But this bad habit never mastered him. It did not seriously interfere with his ordinary duties. It never in the slightest degree impaired the great, the almost boundless influence which he exercised over all persons who were brought into association with him. Occasionally, when stirred by intoxicants, he would publicly declare that he was Marshal Ney. Everything considered, we must attach much force to the old saying, "*In vino, veritas.*" On all other occasions he would repel with firmness and dignity, sometimes with severity, all who approached him upon the subject of his identity with Marshal Ney. His intimate knowledge of Napoleon—of his military operations, of his genius and talents, his character, his habits, his plans, his intentions, his private life—his boundless affection for Napoleon, his intimate knowledge of men and things in general connected with the Napoleonic era ; his keen and constant interest in everything that related to the life and character and fame of Marshal Ney—these prove that he was an officer of the highest rank, very near the person of Napoleon, and in all probability Marshal Ney himself. There are many other circumstances of a strongly corroborative character.

But history says that Marshal Ney was shot to death by French bullets. No fact appears to be more firmly established. If Marshal Ney was not shot, say the unbelieving critics, then all history must be a lie. No. *All* history is not a lie ; but very much of what is called history is the biggest sort of a lie. What is history ? It is said to be a record of past events. But who makes the record ? A few historians will honestly tell the truth, so far as they know it ; but it happens not seldom that it is impossible to discover the truth, even with the most painstaking investigation. Four out of five historians will consult their passions, their prejudices, their feelings, their wishes, their interests. Each one will give, with more or less coloring, that which makes for his side of the case, and distort or suppress everything that makes against it. Opinions, reports, hearsays, traditions, etc., are given as *facts*. They handle the truth " very carelessly and very sparingly." Others, again, will *invent* history, not hesitating to make the falsest statements provided their purposes can be served by such means, well knowing that a lie consistently stuck to will eventually pass for the truth.

These " historians" are for the most part blindly followed by succeeding historians, who are either unable or unwilling to investigate for themselves. And this is HISTORY!

" Don't read history to me," said Sir Robert Walpole, " for history must be false."* Charles Kingsley said that history was "largely a lie," and on this account he refused to teach it in the University of Oxford.

Who has not heard of Cambronne's heroic *mot* at the battle of Waterloo?—" The Guard dies; it does not surrender." Very beautiful, very touching. It is an article of faith with most Frenchmen. And yet there is not a word of truth in it. Cambronne said nothing of the kind; he didn't die; he was not wounded; he was not even with the Old Guard when it *surrendered*. He was taken prisoner some time before by Colonel Halkett, of the English army. Halkett singled him out, rode him down, and was about to sabre him when Cambronne cried out, " *I surrender!*" †

Not long ago a learned gentleman said to me, " Marshal Junot was a great general."

" Junot," said I, " was no marshal, and he was a very sorry general."

" What! I will wager one half of my estate that Junot was a marshal."

The following books were quickly taken from the well-filled

---

* "Walpoliana," vol. i.

† The wits of Paris got up a caricature with the superscription, " La vieille garde meurt, et ne se rend pas"—" last words of General Cambronne on *surrendering* his *sword.*"

Wellington used to say that a certain set of ladies at Brussels had got the nickname of " La vieille garde, qui meurt mais *ne se rend pas.*"

Vide as to Cambronne's *bravery*, " A Voice from Waterloo," Sergeant-Major Cotton, and " Life of Wellington," Colonel John Montmorency Tucker.

shelves: Horne's "Life of Napoleon," Clinton's "Peninsular War," Alison's "History of Europe," Watson's "Camp Fires of Napoleon," Lockhart's "Napoleon," Hazlitt's "Napoleon," Adams's "Great Military Commanders," Browne's "Life of Wellington," and Headley's "Napoleon and his Marshals."* Sure enough, Junot was spoken of as marshal in every one of these histories. Still, Junot was not a marshal. Napoleon knew him too well. He came near ruining Napoleon by sheer imbecility. He died in disgrace as *General Junot, Duke of Abrantes.*

The story of William Tell and his apple—sacred to every school-boy—is now known to be the cruellest of myths. The celebrated speech beginning, "The atrocious crime of being a young man," was never made by William Pitt—it is Dr. Johnson's child. The Abbé Edgeworth never said to Louis XVI., as he was about to be executed, "Son of St. Louis, ascend to heaven." An enterprising editor invented the words for him.† Leonidas never stopped Xerxes' army with three hundred Spartans, but with seven thousand or more. Nine histories out of ten will tell you that Wellington was surprised at Quatre Bras and Waterloo, because Fouché promised to give him prompt intelligence of Bonaparte's movements, and treacherously deceived the Duke. It is false. Wellington repeatedly denied the silly charge. In a letter to General Dumouriez ("Dispatches," vol. xii.) he says: "Before my arrival in Paris in July (1815) I had never seen Fouché, nor had any communication with him, nor with any one connected with him."

And yet Sir Walter Scott and Sir Archibald Alison, who wrote their histories within a stone's throw of the duke's residence, repeat the stale story with a childlike faith that is simply astounding.‡ Lamartine ("History of the Restora-

---
* In the Introduction only does Headley speak of Junot as marshal.
† See Lord Holland's "Foreign Reminiscences."—Appendix.
‡ Alison tries to wriggle out of his false position by a wordy argument of three pages, founded upon an utter misconception of Wellington's character. He makes the fate of Europe, perhaps the fate of the world, hinge upon the honor of *Fouché*, the biggest of all hypocrites, with the single exception of Louis Philippe.

tion") says that at Waterloo Wellington "ordered the curb chains to be taken off the horses and brandy to be distributed to the dragoons, to intoxicate the men with liquid fire, while the sound of the clarion should intoxicate the horses," and that Wellington had "*seven* horses worn out or killed under him."

Stuff! No curb chains were taken off the horses, no brandy distributed, and the duke's elegant charger, Copenhagen, bore him safely through the day.*

Alison's "History of Europe" contains so many errors that his friend Croker in mercy refused to review it. Thiers' "History of the Consulate and the Empire" is about one third fiction. The St. Helena history† is utterly unreliable. Bonaparte wrote to the Directory that he had taken Acre. "I have," said he, "razed the palace of Djezzar and the ramparts of Acre ; not a stone remains upon another."

"I confess," says Bourrienne, "that I experienced a painful sensation in writing, by his dictation, these official words, every one of which was false. It was difficult for me to refrain from making some observation. 'My dear fellow,' said Napoleon, 'you are a simpleton ; you do not understand this business.' And he observed, when signing the bulletin, that he would fill the world with admiration, and inspire historians and poets."‡

Indeed, Napoleon said that history was "nothing but fiction agreed to." So thought Voltaire. When asked for his authority for a certain historical statement which he had made, he smiled and answered, "I have no authority for it ; it is a mere freak of my brain." Rostopchin did not burn Moscow,§ though almost every history says that he did. Napoleon did not win

---

* "Copenhagen lived several years after the battle of Waterloo, and was an object of interest to every one who visited Strathfieldsaye." On one occasion the duke said to Croker, "I rode Copenhagen throughout the war, and mounted no other horse at Waterloo."—See Croker's "Correspondence and Diaries."

† By Las Cases, Montholon, Gourgaud, O'Meara, Antommarchi, Warden, Napoleon, etc.

‡ Bourrienne's "Memoirs."

§ Haydon's "Autobiography," vol. ii.

the famous prize offered by the Academy of Lyons for the best essay on the question, "Which are the most important truths and feelings to be inculcated in order to render mankind happy?" though Montholon, Talleyrand, Scott, and others give us feeling details of this *youthful victory*.*

In many paintings, and numberless woodcuts in histories, Napoleon is represented as riding over the Alps on a magnificent charger, though, in fact, he rode on a *mule*, and a very sorry-looking one at that. The original painting was executed by David, within the shadow of the Tuileries, undoubtedly with the full knowledge and consent of Napoleon himself.

Even our encyclopædias, where one would expect accuracy, contain a great many errors, some of which are of the most serious character, while others are sublimely absurd. A foreign encyclopædia of high pretensions gravely gives the following poetic account of social life in Albany, N. Y. :

"After dinner the gentlemen at the reception followed the ladies to the salon and lighted their cigars. Those who did not smoke, chewed, and spat quite recklessly on the floor. Many who did not use tobacco took small knives from their pockets (for an American gentleman always carries some kind of a knife) and carved or cut slivers from the chairs. Almost all of them put their feet on tables or chairs. This behavior, which would insult our German ladies, the many beautiful American ladies in the room regarded as a matter of course, much to the astonishment of the writer."

Here's *richness* for you ! I would like to know who was the writer's host, or, rather, *hostess*.

In the late war between the States you can scarcely find two of the real actors in the struggle who will agree as to the details or even the general conduct of any particular battle. Wellington said that he had never seen a correct account of the battle of Waterloo.† In this respect, Gettysburg, cer-

---

* See "Biographic Universelle."

† Nobody knows when the battle of Waterloo commenced. Wellington says it began at or about 10 o'clock ; Napoleon and General Drouot, at 12 ; General Alava, at 11.30 ; Marshal Ney and Colonel Heymes, at 1 ; General Hill, with two watches in his pocket and one a stop-watch, at 10 minutes

tainly one of the decisive battles of the world, is even more unfortunate than Waterloo. History has been so grossly perverted in the general accounts of this battle as to make it almost if not altogether impossible for any historian to arrive at the truth. Look at the Isidorean Decretals—an impudent and clumsy fraud—and yet for six hundred years they were unhesitatingly received by the whole civilized world as " true gospel history." Barère's " Memoirs" are a tissue of unblushing falsehoods. Macaulay says Barère was the biggest of all liars, ancient or modern. But the Rev. Joel T. Headley is a little ahead (historically) either of Isidore or Barère.*

I quote from his " Napoleon and his Marshals" :

" The French marshal" (Soult) " showed himself a match for Wellington at any time—nay, beat him oftener and longer than he was beaten."

Now, it is well known to every tyro in history that Wellington completely outgeneralled Soult ; that he whipped him badly on several occasions ; that he drove him in disgrace from his strongholds ; that Soult never gained a single victory over Wellington, and that Wellington never lost a battle or a gun in his life.

Historic cheek can go no further.† I tire.

The Chamber of Peers, at the time of Ney's trial, was composed of one hundred and sixty-one members. Of this

before 12 ; other officers, with watches in their hands, say the first gun was fired at 11 o'clock ; and Haydn's "Dictionary of *Dates*," which of course makes a special point of accuracy, says the battle began at *9 o'clock*. The same high authority further states that Wellington had but fifty-eight thousand men, and that Ney was shot *August 16*, 1815.

Byron's famous lines,

" Within a window'd niche of that high hall
Sate Brunswick's fated chieftain,"

have no foundation in fact. The Waterloo ball was held in a long, low, narrow room, which had been used as a *coach-builder's shop*. " The ball did not take place at the residence of my mother" (the Duchess of Richmond), "but in some sort of an *old barn* at the back or behind."—LORD WILLIAM PITT LENNOX.

* Tolstoï's *stuff* ("Napoleon and the Russian Campaign") does not deserve the name of history.

† Poe was *half* right. Headley is the "autocrat" of bold historians.

number one hundred and thirty-nine yielded to the clamor of the ultraists and voted for the marshal's death ; seventeen voted for exile, and five abstained from voting. The names of the seventeen peers who voted for exile (I shall do my part, however humble, toward making them immortal) are as follows : The Duke de Broglie,* one of the noblest of men ; the Duke de Montmorency, Berthollet, Chasseloup-Laubat, Cholet, Colaud, Fontanes, Gouvion, Herwyn, Klein, Lanjuinais, Lemercier, Lenoir-Laroche, Malleville, Richebourg, Curial, Lally-Tollendal.† The names of the five peers who refused to vote I shall not give. They are suspended between honor and dishonor. I leave them there.

But in justice to the one hundred and thirty-nine peers who bowed the knee to Louis XVIII. and the Duchess d'Angoulême (for she was the power behind the throne), it must be said that they were cruelly deceived. " The sentence of death was scarcely pronounced when the Duke de Richelieu, who attended this nocturnal sitting,‡ was surrounded by a great number of the voters," who openly declared they did not desire the marshal's death ; that they had voted for it in obedience to the royal wish, but under the tacit condition of a commutation of the penalty by the government.§ They therefore " conjured the prime-minister to solicit from the king *exile to America* for the condemned instead of the scaffold." The Duke de Richelieu, although he had demanded Ney's condemnation in the *name of Europe*,‖ was in the main a just

---

* " The Duke de Broglie claimed the right of sitting, from which he was dispensed by his youth" (he was but thirty years old), " in order to protest by his vote against a political immolation as contrary to the gratitude and the honor of his country."—Lamartine's " History of the Restoration," vol. iii., p. 317.

† " We record their names that public esteem may also have its tablets, in which history will find and award its meed of praise to those hearts which are inflexible to the passions or the calculation of parties."—Lamartine's "History of the Restoration," vol. iii., p. 318.

‡ The sentence was pronounced at 11.30 P.M., December 6th, 1815.

§ Vaulabelle's " Histoire des deux Restorations ;" Lamartine's " History of the Restoration ;" Lady Jackson's " Court of the Tuileries."

‖ A miserable pretext. Europe, as elsewhere shown, did not ask for Ney's " condemnation."

and merciful man. He did not desire Ney's death ; and the police reports, brought in every fifteen minutes to the quaking ministers, were of the most alarming character.

A Cabinet council was hastily summoned, at which it was unanimously resolved to petition the king for a commutation of the penalty. The Duke de Richelieu hastened to the royal apartments, and boldly "infringing the regulations of the palace," entered the king's chamber between one and two o'clock in the morning, and anxiously pleaded for mercy. The prime-minister kept back nothing. He frankly told the king that the situation was extremely critical ; that a large number of the peers, although they had condemned the marshal, were strongly opposed to his death ; that public sentiment was against it ; that a general uprising of the people was imminent, and that it was *necessary* to commute the sentence.*

The king indulged in a good deal of sentimental twaddle— "I pity Ney. I have no hatred against him. I would gladly preserve a father to his children, a hero to France," etc., but he doggedly refused to change the sentence of the court. Others—not a few of them known and honored throughout Europe—came to plead for the life of the great marshal ; but when they "arrived at the palace, his gracious majesty was going to bed, and would not even listen to a word they had to say. Waving his hand as he was wheeled away, he exclaimed : ' Let me hear when I awake that the traitor has paid the forfeit of his crime ! ' The people of indignant France uttered the word RESCUE."†

The last hope of royal clemency had fled, and the marshal doubtless found, as he had said to Lavalette in prison, that

---

* The Government officers were terribly frightened. They were evidently ready for any feasible solution of the difficulty which confronted them.

"The evening before the accused had been transferred from the Conciergerie to the Luxembourg with an escort and a precipitation which evinced the uneasiness of the government with respect to a rescue, or a rising of the people."—Lamartine's " History of the Restoration," vol. iii. ; Alison's " History of Europe ;" Craik and McFarlane's " History of England."

† " Court of the Tuileries," Lady Jackson.

"many friends were watching over him."* Outside of the few bloody ultraists it was difficult to find any one, even among the foreign soldiers, who really desired the death of the "bravest of the brave," while a very large number of Ney's friends, soldiers and citizens, had secretly sworn—many of them had publicly sworn—that he should not die by the hands of Frenchmen.†

Ney's popularity was almost boundless. He had brought more glory to the French arms than any other man of his age, Bonaparte not excepted. Great as a warrior, "wholly unrivalled on the embattled plain," ‡ he was yet greater as a patriot and as a man. Beneath that rugged exterior was a heart as true and tender as ever beat in the breast of man. The people *loved* him. The soldiers IDOLIZED him.§

Now, would French soldiers, and especially French veterans, have shot such a man as that? I do not believe it. For the honor of the French name, for the honor of human nature, I will not believe it. Would any Southern soldier have shot General Lee, or Stonewall Jackson under similar circumstances? There is not one worthy of the name who would have committed so foul a deed. Death would have been preferable to such sacrilege.

Every soldier, too, as well as many of the peers, felt that Ney was protected by the capitulation of Paris. And he undoubtedly was. The twelfth article of that capitulation states that "The inhabitants and all individuals who shall be in the capital shall continue to enjoy their rights and liberties without being disturbed or called to account either as to the situa-

---

* Lavalette's "Memoirs."

† "History of French Wars;" "Sketches of Napoleon and his Generals;" Anecdotes of "Napoleon," etc., W. H. Ireland; Private Letters.

‡ General Jomini.

§ " Ney was first brought to trial in the great Hall of the Palace of Justice. The concourse of persons assembled to hear the trial was prodigious. Almost all instantly rose to their feet as Ney entered. . . . His presence produced a lively sensation, and a short pause followed."—" Wars in Europe."

"There was but one way to destroy Ney's influence with his troops, and that was to *kill him*."—General Bourmont, at Ney's trial.

tions they hold or *may have held,* or as to their *conduct or political opinions.*" The fifteenth article states that "If difficulties arise in the execution of any one of the articles of the present convention, the *interpretation* of it shall be made *in favor of the French army* and the city of Paris."

Nothing, it would seem, could be clearer; and yet the Duke of Wellington positively refused to save, or, at any rate, openly to save, the life of Marshal Ney, stoutly maintaining that the convention was "exclusively military; that it touched nothing POLITICAL, and was not intended to bind and could not bind the hands of the King of France."*

Such sophistry was worthy only of a pettifogging lawyer. Was not Louis XVIII. an ally of the English and Prussian armies? Did he not act in concert with them? Did he not follow in the wake of the English army, timidly, obediently, almost slavishly, waiting for Wellington to open for him the gates of Paris? Did he not enter Paris and ascend the throne by virtue of this convention? Did he not threaten France, when he fled ignobly from it the preceding March, with three hundred thousand foreign bayonets? Can any one believe that one hundred and twenty thousand brave French soldiers surrendered to Wellington and Blücher (who were really afraid to attack them in their strong intrenchments),† with

---

* See "Wellington's Dispatches," vol. xii.; the duke's letter to Marshal Ney, November 14th, and the Duke's "Interview with Princess de la Moskowa."

Wellington did not have much respect for the king as an "independent monarch" when he sent his soldiers to the Louvre to bring away the paintings, etc., of the King of the Netherlands. Talleyrand protested; Denon protested in the king's name. Wellington replied that he would have the paintings at the point of the bayonet. He got them. But what a singular attitude did he put himself in! The king was an absolute sovereign so far as his people were concerned. He could bring them to trial, imprison, murder them, but he couldn't protect the public *property!* In this case, the greater does not embrace the less, but the less excludes the greater.

The fact is, that when Wellington wished to respect the king as an independent monarch, he did it, and when he didn't, he didn't. That is the long and short of the matter.

† See Wellington's letter to Blücher, dated Gonesse, July 2d, 1815; "Wellington's Dispatches," vol. xii., pp. 526, 527.

the understanding that they were to receive a temporary protection of two or three days, and then to be unconditionally surrendered to the French tyrant?

The thing is absurd. English precedent was against Wellington.* The common sense of mankind was against him. The fifteenth article does away with all possibility of misconstruction:

"If difficulties arise," etc. Now, every one knows that "difficulties" did arise in the execution of the twelfth article, and yet the interpretation of it was *not* made in favor of the French army and of the city of Paris.

Marshal Ney wrote a letter to the Duke of Wellington (November 13th), in which he says: "You cannot be ignorant of the gross violation which has taken place in my person of the Convention of Paris, on the faith of which the French army laid down its arms and I remained in France. It was on the following articles that I relied (twelfth and fifteenth), and without these terms is there a human being who believes I would not have died, sword in hand, joined and supported by all the brave and virtuous that remained in France?"

Marshal Davout, commander-in-chief of the French army, solemnly swore that he had "understood the Convention in the sense of a complete amnesty for all the acts of the interregnum; and that if the Convention had not had that signification in his mind, he would have fought, and might have conquered."

Count Guilleminot, one of the French commissioners, fully sustained Davout in this statement. He testified that he had received express orders from the French Government to break off the negotiation unless a complete amnesty were granted for *all* offences, military or political.†

---

* In Egypt, Naples, etc. In the case of Naples, Lord Nelson acted somewhat like Wellington, though he had firmer ground to stand upon; yet he was severely condemned by the public sentiment of England, and barely escaped parliamentary impeachment.

† "As chief of the staff, 1 was charged with stipulating for an amnesty in favor of all persons, whatever might be their opinions, their offices, or their conduct. This point was granted without any dispute. My orders

Many Englishmen,* too (Liberals and Tories), had grave doubts as to the correctness of Wellington's interpretation of the twelfth article, and freely expressed them. One of the English ministers wrote to Wellington, asking if the twelfth article did not grant a general amnesty to the inhabitants of Paris, etc.†

When Ney was executed, as was supposed, there was a burst of indignation in England which made Wellington feel that his conduct in this matter would be made the subject of parliamentary inquiry.‡

---

were to break off the conferences had any refusal been made."—Count Guilleminot, at the trial of Marshal Ney.

See also "Memorial" of Berryer and Dupin (Ney's counsel), addressed to Sir Charles Stuart; Lord Holland's letter on the capitulation; Marshal Ney's letter to the Duke d'Orleans; Circular distributed at Ney's trial; Madame Ney's letter to Sir Charles Stuart and the Prince Regent.

"How can Louis XVIII. attempt to violate this single article (most solemn of all), when in respect to the others, which are to the prejudice of France, he has been compelled to submit to their most rigorous execution? . . . Paris is still under the military dominion of the allies. The king has not a soldier at his command without the co-operation of the allies."— "Circular;" Madame Ney's letter.

"After three months the king feels unable to trust the security of his family and capital to anything but a foreign force. The general language of Paris is decidedly against the Bourbons. General officers and others of the most respectable description hold that language openly, and they say that were the foreign troops removed, the Bourbon government would not last ten days."—E. Cooke to Lord Liverpool, Paris, September 25th, 1815.

* Sir James Alexander, Earl Grey, Lord Kinnaird, Lord Holland, Duke of Sussex, Godwin, Thelwall, Dr. Parr, Hobhouse, Wright, Hume, Alison, Allen, Wilson, Bruce, Hutchinson, etc.

† Lord Liverpool. He "had been struck with the ambiguity of the terms of the capitulation," etc.—Crowe's "Life of Louis XVIII. and Charles X."

Vide also Lord Bathurst's letter to Wellington. Wellington didn't feel safe until he was propped up by the Prince Regent. Lord Bathurst in his letter gives us an insight (though unintentional on his part) into a very curious bit of contemporary history.

‡ See "Wellington's Dispatches," vol. xii.

"To have carried out the principle upon which Ney's sentence was based would have ended in a public massacre; . . . there never was a more flagrant violation of national honor. . . . The whole affair from beginning to end was a deliberate murder. . . . On Wellington's forehead is a spot that shall grow darker with time, and cause many a curse to be muttered over his grave."—Headley, "Napoleon and his Marshals."

With these facts before us, how is it possible for any one to believe that Ney's life and liberty were not shielded by the capitulation of Paris? For the first and only time in his life, Wellington completely lost his head. I honor the Iron Duke as few men honor him, but I must confess there is a *stain* upon that glorious forehead. It is not so dark as Headley, Abbott, and others would have us to believe, but it is *there* nevertheless. Still, we should not judge too harshly. Wellington's position as an English general—virtually as the generalissimo of the allied armies—was extremely delicate. The king was barely seated upon his worm-eaten throne. It was quivering beneath him day and night like an aspen leaf. The situation was critical. A single spark might set everything on fire. The safety of France and the peace of Europe, perhaps of the world, were at stake. We do not know, we cannot know what Wellington knew. We have reason to believe (from Wellington's own admissions) that he died with secrets locked up in his bosom which would have helped greatly to clear away this murky atmosphere.*

* " The proscription of Ney was opposed to every principle and word of the capitulation, an act as dishonorable to the French Government as it was opposed to and in violation of the faith and honor of the allies. It was mean and dastardly, after the ferment of men's passions was cooled, to pursue these men" (Ney, Labédoyère, Lavalette, etc.), " a paltry and despicable use of victory."—Sir James Alexander, " Life of Wellington."
See also Capefigue's " Histoire de la Restauration ;" Stocqueler's " Life of Wellington ;" Crowe's " History of France" and " Life of Louis XVIII. and Charles X. ;" Wright's " Life of Wellington."
" Marshal Ney was clearly included in the terms of Article 12. . . . Such a Machiavellian doctrine" (that the Convention was purely *military*) " is contrary to all reason, and such a principle once established might cover the earth with scaffolds.' —*Monthly* (English) *Magazine.*
" To deny the validity of the Convention because it was not formally accepted by the king was to add fraud to oppression ; for what can be a baser fraud than to accept the benefits of an agreement and to refuse its obligations ? The recollection of Ney's death was one of the principal causes of the unpopularity with the army which haunted the elder Bourbons, and fifteen years afterward, when in their utmost need they had to rely on the army for support, that recollection precipitated their downfall."—Senior's " Biographical Sketches."
* Wellington was magnanimity itself. He kept back for some time one volume of his famous " Dispatches," for fear he might injure the char-

Ney's letter to Wellington was, I think, unfortunate in its tone. It offended his *amour propre*. Madame Ney, too, was most unwise in publishing detached portions of her interview with the Duke of Wellington. Such things oftentimes have much weight—more than one is willing to acknowledge even to one's self. Wellington was an honest man, and his conduct in the case of Ney is the only blot * upon his private or public character. He erred, but it was an error of the head and not of the heart. Wellington really did not desire the death of his old antagonist in arms. He repeatedly told his friends that he would gladly save him if he could, but that he had no right to interfere with the acts of the Bourbons. Not a few of Wellington's personal friends were constantly pleading with him to save the hero's life. Ney was almost as popular with the English as he was with his own countrymen, for the English people, above all others, admire a brave and manly fighter.

"Madame Hutchinson, the wife of a member of Parliament, and a relation of the Duke of Wellington, who was then in Paris, and whose house was the hospitable rendezvous of the most liberal-minded officers of the English army, interceded in the most earnest manner with His Grace to obtain from him a decisive intervention for the salvation of Marshal

acter and fortunes of those who were living both in England and in France.

* "Wellington's greatest admirers wish that the recording angel had dropped a tear on this page of his life and blotted it out forever."—Wright's "Life of Wellington."

Wellington laid great stress upon the fact that Ney *fled*, and therefore could not think he was protected by the capitulation. This is absurd. As Bourrienne says, "Now, even before Ney knew of his exception from the amnesty, to appear in Paris would have been a foolish piece of bravado. Further, the royalist reaction was in full vigor; and when the royalist mobs, with the connivance of the authorities, were murdering Marshal Brune and attacking any prominent adherents of Napoleon, it was hardly the time for Ney to travel in full pomp."

Ney knew that on every account he ought to leave Paris; that his presence would greatly irritate the Bourbons, and might lead to the most serious consequences; that the assassin would be on his track; that Louis XVIII. would, if possible, wreak his vengeance upon him, capitulation or no capitulation.

Ney. She conjured him by his own glory and the glory of his country to avert by such a step the reproach which would rest on his memory if this odious sacrifice were accomplished under his eyes, and apparently with his moral participation. It is even said that, in her ardent and eloquent appeal to the magnanimity of the English general, Madame Hutchinson threw herself at the feet of the duke, to draw from him by her prayers what she could not obtain by higher considerations."*

The Duke of Wellington was deeply touched by these appeals, and he resolved to do everything in his power short of forcible interposition to save the life of Marshal Ney. And he did. He spoke his mind freely to the king, and especially to his ministers. The king became alarmed at his boldness, and at last grossly insulted him.

On the evening of Ney's condemnation the king held a reception.† Wellington was invited, and he went to the palace a short time after Ney was sentenced to be shot. His object was, as he afterward said to a few intimate friends, to ask the king to spare the life of Marshal Ney. The king saw him

---

* Lamartine's "History of the Restoration."
Madame Hutchinson and the Princess de Vaudemont (a Montmorency) contrived Lavalette's escape, and it is extremely probable were privy to Ney's escape.

The fiendish conduct of the ultra-royalists at the time of Ney's trial surpasses all belief. It was fully equal to that of the *sans-culottes* of the French Revolution. "In the saloons of the aristocracy," says Lamartine, "the king's ministers were actually mobbed and entreated to give his" (Ney's) "blood as a personal favor to the applicants. Ladies of the highest rank, young, beautiful, rich, loaded with gifts, favors, titles, and court dignities, forgot their families, their ease, and their amours, quitted their houses at daybreak, ran about all day, and intrigued all night to gain over a voice among the judges," etc.

No wonder that Wellington was "disgusted," and that he felt, with a very large majority of the people of France, of England, and, I believe, of Europe, that enough blood had been shed, and that it was time to call a halt.

† There is a "sound of revelry" in the Bourbon palace while the greatest soldier of France is being sentenced to an ignominious death.

"And Gallia's capital had gathered *then*,
Her beauty and her—CHIVALRY !!!"

coming and knew his object, and just before he reached the king the Count d'Artois darted between Wellington and His Majesty, as if he were afraid that Wellington wished to assassinate the king. The king at the same moment deliberately turned his back on Wellington in the presence of the whole court in the most marked and offensive manner. The duke felt this insult most keenly. He turned to the king's courtiers and said : " You forget that I commanded the armies which put your king on his throne. I will never again enter the royal presence."

Stung to the quick, his gray eyes flashing fire, so angry indeed that several suns go down upon his wrath,* the great duke instantly leaves the presence of the royal dotard and his fawning courtiers. The greatest captain of his age, or of any age, is compelled for the moment meanly to retreat before a cowardly and contemptible foe.† It was not in Wellington's nature to stand this unparalleled insult and humiliation. I cannot doubt that before Wellington left the palace, or very shortly afterward, the king, or his ministers, or both, were informed that Marshal Ney could not be shot.‡

* " After Marshal Ney was shot, the Count d'Artois called upon the duke and begged him, almost on his knees, to visit the king. The duke sternly refused. At length, possibly from political necessities, he consented to an interview with the king on business, . . . but I know that to the last he deeply felt the base requital which he had received at the hands of those to whom he had given a kingdom."—Sir William Fraser's " Words on Wellington."

† See " Correspondence of Prince Talleyrand and Louis XVIII. ;" *Army and Navy Gazette*, England ; " Journal" of Thomas Raikes ; Sir William Fraser's " Words on Wellington."

‡ Indeed, Wellington could not have acted otherwise. It was not simply a personal question. That, in all conscience, would have been bad enough. It would have justified Wellington in a quiet though forcible interference. But Wellington was insulted, not merely as a man, but as an Englishman, and as the general-in-chief of the English Army and virtually of the allied armies. His government was insulted ; all the allied governments were insulted ; Europe was insulted. It was not a mere personal issue.

It was raised far above that. It was a public question—a question of politics, of good government, of international comity, of the respect and consideration due from one government to another, and which, indeed, every State must exact from another, or lose its place among nations—a

Wellington was in command of all the troops in Paris. In one hour—aye, in thirty minutes—he could have had the king publicly executed. And Wellington would allow no man to insult him, or his army or his government through him. He was as firm as a rock, as open as day, and as high-mettled as any knight of the olden time. "He did not hesitate," says Napier, "to speak the truth at all times, even to kings. Monarchs have bowed and been abashed before him." Louis XVIII. in particular had bent before him as a reed bends before the gushing wind. Twice had Wellington put Louis on the throne of France—in 1814 and in 1815. Without Wellington the allied armies would have been as a rope of sand. They would have accomplished nothing but their own ruin. Wellington was at all times the head and the soul of the coalition. Louis XVIII. owed everything to Wellington, and yet, when the great duke goes to him to ask for the life of a gallant foe, he deliberately turns his back upon him. Can any one believe that Wellington quietly submitted to so great an indignity? If so, one must have very little knowledge of human nature, less still of Wellington's character.

I believe that Wellington saved Ney's life.* Wellington, in all probability, did not wish to interfere publicly and forcibly. He was a patriot, and, above all, a lover of peace. He well knew that any open rupture with the king in so grave and delicate a matter would be productive of evils the end of which no one could foresee. A mock execution would answer his purpose, everything considered, and Ney at the same time would be sufficiently punished.†

---

question of good order and discipline, of the peace and security of France, of the neighboring nations, of Europe.

The insult was public and premeditated; as cold and cruel and foul as an insult possibly could be. I say, Wellington *could not* have acted otherwise. Any *man* in Wellington's place would have saved Ney's life.

* Peter S. Ney told Dr. A. H. Graham, of Texas, a nephew of ex-Governor Graham, of North Carolina, and a few other intimate friends, that Wellington did save his life. See Testimony.

† Apart from the brutal insult, however, I do not believe that Wellington ever had the slightest idea that Ney would be shot. He thought Ney was guilty, and should be punished by trial, conviction, anxiety, suspense,

SKETCH OF DEATH OF MARSHAL NEY. BY GÉRÔME.

Marshal Ney was led out of his prison for execution on December 7th at nine o'clock in the morning.* Even nature frowned. A cold, clammy fog hung like a funeral pall over the murderous scene. The following account is taken chiefly from Lamartine's "History of the Restoration" and from several reports of Ney's trial and execution :

"His door opened. He understood the sign. He descended with a firm step, a serene brow, and a lofty look, his lips almost wearing a smile, but without any theatrical affectation, through the double ranks of the troops drawn up on the steps

etc., but that the king would pardon him. Indeed, I believe the king deceived Wellington. I have no doubt there was an understanding, expressed or implied, between Wellington and the king, or the king's ministers, acting for the king, that Ney should not be shot; or, if not, Wellington must have felt that the king would not and *could* not refuse to pardon Ney at his (Wellington's) request; or, lastly, Wellington knew that he had the *power* to save the marshal's life ; and I do not doubt that, in case of necessity, he fully intended to exercise that power. So great a man as Wellington could *not* have permitted the atrocious butchery of so great a hero as Ney, for he was a hero, say what you will about his disloyalty to the Bourbons.

"It was necessary," said Wellington afterward, "to give the king a great moral lesson," and he gave it.

The king certainly did deceive Wellington in the most outrageous manner as to the paintings in the Louvre, and Wellington was too magnanimous and too prudent to expose the king. See Stocqueler's "Life of Wellington."

During the preceding summer and autumn the king and his ministers had been growing more insolent toward the Duke of Wellington. The very fact that they were under boundless obligations to the Duke of Wellington made them more sensitive, more jealous, more suspicious, slyer and meaner.

The first Cabinet had been broken up and a new one had taken its place, which scarcely treated the duke with common civility. During Ney's trial the government officers spoke sneeringly of Wellington and Blücher as *foreigners* who had no right to make laws for the people of France, as *intruders upon its sacred soil*, etc. The last crowning insult at the Tuileries was more than Wellington could bear.

* "Never did execution succeed a sentence more rapidly. The king's ministers were in a state of extreme anxiety," etc.—Alison's "History of Europe."

The Government feared a general uprising of the people—no doubt about that—but this indecent and savage hurry could not have prevented it.

of the staircase and in the vestibule of the palace, like a man happy once more to see the uniform, the arms, and the troops —his old family.

"The carriage containing Ney, the curate of St. Sulpice, an officer, and two sub-officers, proceeded at a foot-pace through the broad alleys of the Luxembourg and between the silent ranks of the soldiers. It suddenly stopped midway between the railing of the Luxembourg and the Observatory, in front of a long wall of a black and fetid enclosure that bordered an alley leading out of the avenue.* Ney was astonished at this halt, halfway as he supposed, when the carriage door opened and he was requested to alight. He felt that he was never to return, and gave to the priest who accompanied him his snuff-box, to be delivered to Madame la Maréchale, and some pieces of gold which he had in his pocket to be distributed among the poor. He then embraced the priest and marched rapidly toward the place indicated by a picket of veterans, sixty strong, which had been on the ground since five o'clock in the morning.† He stopped about eight paces from the wall ; then turning round, he faced the platoon of veterans drawn up to execute him. The officer commanding the party advanced toward him and requested permission to bandage his eyes. Ney stopped him. 'Are you ignorant,'

* "The Government," says Lamartine, "was ill advised even in the choice of a place of execution."
"The Bourbons could not, dared not, attempt to carry out the sentence of the law with the forms of the law. The Government did not venture to let the *troops* or the *people* face the marshal."—BOURRIENNE.

† Why had these veterans been on the ground since five o'clock in the morning ?—four hours and twenty minutes before the alleged execution.
It was resolved, at the last night conclave of Louis XVIII. and his family, to *hasten the execution*, to shoot the marshal probably at or about five o'clock. Why was the hour changed ? And who changed it ?
See Craik and McFarlane's "History of England."
Blücher was very anxious to shoot Napoleon on the same spot where the Duke d'Enghien was shot, and at the same hour. The Bourbons doubtless thought that by murdering Ney at five o'clock in the morning in a clandestine manner, in a damp, secluded place, by yellowish, ghoulish torchlight, they would avenge the duke's death, and would at the same time (and this was their main object) prevent all possibility of Ney's escape. Wellington no doubt upset all these nice calculations.

said he, 'that for twenty-five years I have been accustomed to face both balls and bullets?' The officer, disturbed, hesitating, undecided, expecting perhaps a cry of pardon, or fearing to commit a sacrilege of glory by firing on his general, stood mute between the hero and his platoon. The marshal availed himself of this hesitation and of the immobility of the soldiers to cast a final reproach upon his destiny. 'I protest before God and my country,' he exclaimed, 'against the sentence which has condemned me. I appeal from it to man, to posterity, to God.' These words, and the countenance enshrined in their memory of the hero of the camp, shook the steadiness of the soldiers. 'Do your duty,' cried the commandant of Paris to the officer, who was more confused than the victim. Ney advanced a few paces; then, turning toward his unwilling executioners, he thus addressed them: 'My brave comrades, when I place my hand upon my breast, *fire*. See you take a sure aim at the heart.' Then, taking off his hat with one hand, he gave the command in a loud and strong voice: 'Soldiers, straight to the heart—fire!' striking his hand upon his heart as the last word was uttered. A single report was heard. Ney fell as if struck with a thunderbolt, without a convulsion and without a sigh. The soldiers, the officer, the spectators, turned away their eyes from the body as from the evidence of a crime. During the quarter of an hour which the military regulations required that the corpse should lie exposed upon the place of execution, no spectators except a few passers-by and some women from the neighboring houses looked upon the body, or mingled their tears with its blood. Some groups demanded with a low voice who the criminal was thus abandoned on the public highway, and shot to death by soldiers of the grand army. None had the courage to reply that it was the body of the 'bravest of the brave,' the hero of the Beresina. After the legal period of exposure, a cloth was thrown over the body, and it was carried on a litter to the coach, which immediately drove off to the Hospital for Foundlings. The Sisters of the hospital watched over the body during the night, and the next morning at 6.30 o'clock it was carried to the cemetery of Père la Chaise and buried without the slightest ceremony. The hearse was followed by three coaches containing distant relatives of Madame Ney. Madame Ney did not go."*

According to the *official report*,† Marshal Ney " fell dead instantly, without a struggle or a movement, pierced with twelve balls, nine in the breast and three in the head." The report continues : " Conformably to military regulations, the body remained exposed on the place of execution for a quarter of an hour. There were, however, but few persons present ; for the populace, believing that the execution would take place on the Place de Grenelle, had repaired thither. After remaining exposed a quarter of an hour, the body was placed upon a litter, covered with a cloth, and carried by the veterans to the Hospital for Foundlings. At 6.30 the next morning it was conveyed to the burying-ground of Père la Chaise in a hearse, followed by a mourning-coach and several other coaches. It had been enclosed in a leaden coffin within an oak one. During the whole night the *religieuses* of the hospital prayed near the body."

Sir William Fraser, author of " Words on Wellington," has furnished us in that excellent work with another account of Ney's execution—to wit :‡

" The late Quentin Dick, who sat in the Irish Parliament, and, after the Union, in the English Parliament for many years, whom I know well, saw Marshal Ney shot, and described the execution to me. The marshal was brought from the Luxembourg Palace in a *fiacre*, accompanied by an officer of gendarmerie and two sergeants. He was dressed in a dark-colored surtout, dark pantaloons, white neck-cloth, and round hat with crape ; he was in mourning at the time for (I think) his father-in-law. He wore no decoration. On his leaving the coach the picket at the gate of the Luxembourg Gardens

---

* See " Histoire Complète du procès du Maréchal Ney," Dumoulin ; " Report of Marshal Ney's Trial and Execution," London, 1816.

† See " Official Report" of Count de Rochechouart, and of Laisné, Inspector-General of Prisons.

‡ See also Sir William Fraser's letter to the editor of the London *Times*, 1884.

close by were beckoned to the spot; the men loaded and fired; the marshal fell on his face, and the body was at once replaced in the *fiacre*, which drove off—the whole transaction not occupying three minutes. It was all over before the nurses and the children—the only spectators—could realize what had happened."

Now, look at the facts: The execution is practically private—at the back of the Luxembourg Gardens—at an unfrequented spot—a dark, foul alley—at an early hour—very few persons present *—some children with their nurses are almost the only spectators—the soldiers load their own guns †—Ney walks several paces ‡ toward the wall, turns round, faces the soldiers—the officer advances to bandage his eyes—Ney stops him with a " proud interrogation"—the officer is confused, stammers, stumbles, falters—Ney speaks, declares before God and man that he has never betrayed his country—protests against the iniquity of his sentence—appeals to man, to posterity, to God—the soldiers are unnerved, they hesitate, they waver—the Commandant of Paris exhorts the officer to do his duty—Ney advances a few paces, addresses the soldiers, cautions them not to fire until he puts his hand on his heart—he raises his hand, gives a loud, slow, measured, deliberate command—the men fire—Ney falls on his face without a " movement or a sigh"—no examination is made by any surgeon— no *coup de grace* is given §—the soldiers immediately leave— they do not defile past the dead body, as is customary at executions of this character ‖—they (with the officers and spectators)

---

* The " populace" (more than ten thousand persons) " had gone out to the plain of Grenelle to witness the execution."

† In military executions the guns are loaded apart from the men by a non-commissioned officer, and one gun always contains a blank cartridge. It is a pleasant fiction. Each soldier is at liberty to think that he has the unloaded gun. The firing party was composed of *veterans*—perhaps of Ney's old soldiers whom he had often led to battle and to victory.

‡ At least forty.

§ " On voulut bien lui épargner ce qu'on appelle ' le coup de grace.' " " Le Maréchal Ney, 1815."—WELSCHINGER.

‖ " Ney fell forward, his face turned a little sideways. No one ventured to approach the body."—" Dictionnaire Universel."

" . . . . There was nothing of all this" (defiling past the body, "turn away their eyes as from the evidence of a crime"—the body is *instantly* placed on a litter, covered with a cloth, and carried by the veterans to the coach which had brought Ney from the Luxembourg prison. The "whole transaction," says Mr. Dick, "did not occupy *three minutes*." "It was all over" before the few spectators "could realize what had happened." And yet the official report states, and states *twice*, that conformably to military regulations, the body remained exposed on the place of execution *a quarter of an hour ! ! !*

I had the pleasure of meeting Sir William Fraser in London in 1891, and he told me that he had grave doubts as to the execution of Marshal Ney ; that the official account was evidently a fabrication ; that it carried the evidence of falsehood upon its face ; that Mr. Quentin Dick was a man of the very highest character,* and his word could not for a moment be doubted. "It is probable," added Sir William, "that Wellington saved Ney's life."

M. Claveau, Sr., of the Paris police, also saw Marshal Ney shot. He says : "I was present at the sad spectacle quite unexpectedly, and, I may say, unwillingly, for the authorities gave out that Marshal Ney was to be shot in the plain of Grenelle. Being in the Luxembourg quarter that morning, however, and seeing something unusual about to take place, I went along with a few others to the fatal spot. It may seem a trivial thing to notice, but I cannot help remarking a circumstance that I observed as being indicative of the character of our Britannic neighbors—that as soon as the marshal's body was taken up, an English gentleman suddenly advanced and gathered up several small stones that lay about the path and had received some sprinklings of the victim's blood.

etc.) "in the execution of Ney."—Bourrienne's "Memoirs of Napoleon."

Colonel Knollys, of the Scotch Guards, says that he "was on duty near the Luxembourg when Ney was shot, and was surprised to see that the murder created so little sensation. There was no assemblage, no excitement of any kind."

* Napier, in his "History of the Peninsular War," alludes to Quentin Dick in most honorable terms.—See Appendix, "Controversial Pieces."

These he carefully wrapped up, and precipitately walked away. These will doubtless be found deposited in some collection of curiosities, public or private, over the Channel."

Mr. W. H. Ireland, in a work entitled "Anecdotes of Napoleon," etc., says : "At the Hospital of the Maternité the body was laid out, being stripped of the coat and neckerchief. Independent of the physiognomy, which was not handsome (as the marshal was rather hard-featured), the body and the limbs presented the most striking symmetry it is possible to conceive, the leg in particular being a perfect mode. A smile of the most winning placidity still seemed to play upon the countenance of the defunct. Under the roof of this hospital the corpse continued until the will of the government was made known, by which the body was ordered to be consigned to the relatives of the departed. During the time the body lay exposed at the hospital an officer who was on duty commanding the escort of horse that attended the marshal to his fate, made a correct design of Ney, precisely as he appeared, from which a very beautiful engraving was executed, but only distributed privately, as the police would destroy the plate and every impression in case the same could be traced by any of its *mouchards* or emissaries. The next morning the body of Ney was conveyed, with as much privacy as possible, to the cemetery of Père la Chaise. Such was the secrecy and expedition practised upon the occasion of Ney's execution that his unfortunate widow, wholly unconscious of the tragical event, repaired to the Tuileries for the purpose of presenting a petition to the king, when she learned from the Duke de Duras that the marshal had ceased to exist."

The Hospital of the Maternité, to which the body of the marshal was carried, was about two hundred yards from the spot where Ney was supposed to be shot. It was a queer-looking building, of funereal aspect, surrounded by high, massive walls, carefully guarded, and from its very character free from the prying eyes of the public or from intrusion of any kind. At this place " the body is laid out, being stripped of the coat and neckerchief" (a very curious *laying out*)—" the body and the limbs present the most striking symmetry it is possible to conceive, the leg in particular being a perfect mode" (nothing is said about the wounds) ; "the marshal's physiognomy is not handsome," simply because "the marshal is rather hard-featured." That is all—there is no disfigurement by French bullets.

Now, here is a man with (historically) twelve balls in his body—Lamartine says thirteen—nine in the breast, and three in the head—necessarily in the *face*—not only shot to death, but shot to pieces—a ghastly spectacle ; * and yet a smile, and a smile, too, of the most winning placidity, seems to play upon his countenance !

A MIRACLE !

Again, " an officer who was on duty commanding the escort of horse that attended the marshal to his fate draws *a beautiful picture* of this same horribly mangled man, from which engravings are made, but distributed privately by Ney's friends lest the " government spies" should find them out and " punish them." Strange.

The picture of a man shot to death for high treason would have had a tendency to strike terror into the hearts of malcontents and criminals. Why, then, should the government have wished to punish people for circulating such pictures ? Who was the officer that " made a correct design of Ney precisely as he appeared," with that "smile of the most winning placidity playing upon his countenance" ? He was in the king's service, yet undoubtedly a friend of Ney, † as the engravings were " distributed privately by Ney's friends."

The government ordered that the body of the marshal should be given to Madame Ney for interment in the cemetery of Père la Chaise.‡ It remained in the hospital until

---

* His *face*, too, was *bruised* and *battered* by the *fall*. He fell on his face.

† Was it La Rochejaquelein, Colonel of Grenadiers ? He " was on duty, commanding the escort of horse that attended the marshal to his fate." He had served in the Napoleonic wars, and was badly wounded at the battle of the Moskowa, where Ney particularly distinguished himself. He probably served in Ney's command. It is known that he was opposed to the execution of Ney.—See " Memoirs of Count de Rochechouart."

‡ The government all of a sudden becomes very kind, very considerate, very merciful.

daybreak the next morning. It was then "conveyed with as much secrecy as possible to the cemetery of Père la Chaise and buried without the slightest ceremony of any kind whatever. Why did not Ney's relatives, on this cold December morning, wait for a more convenient, a more fitting, a more decent hour? Why this haste, this secrecy, this unceremonious, this unchristian, this inhuman burial? The night has many mysteries. It favors disguises of all kinds. Ney could have escaped without the slightest difficulty, and the body of another man, even with the twelve historic balls in breast and head, could with the utmost ease have been substituted for that of Ney; or an empty coffin, especially a leaden coffin enclosed within an oak one, might have answered the purpose; though I think it probable the body of another man was substituted for that of the marshal.

I do not know who the English gentleman was of whom M. Claveau speaks. Of one thing, however, I am quite sure —he was no relic fiend, no curiosity-hunter. Englishmen are not cast in that kind of mould. But the *fact* of which M. Claveau speaks is very remarkable. "As soon as Ney's body was taken up, an Englishman suddenly advanced and gathered up several small stones that lay about the path and had received some sprinkling of the victim's blood. These he carefully wrapped up and precipitately walked away."

Did Wellington send him there? Did he wish to assure himself of the marshal's safety? Did he distrust the Bourbon government? Was there any blood upon the stones, or the appearance of blood?* M. Claveau of course could not tell as to the blood with any degree of certainty. It is well known that several Englishmen—Sir Robert Wilson, Mr. Crawford Bruce, Captain Hutchinson, and others—did attempt to save Ney's life. They even went so far as to contrive a plot for his escape from prison, but they failed to accomplish

---

* See testimony of Dr. J. M. Spainhour, of Valentine Stirewalt, and of Robert A. Henderson. Mr. Henderson's testimony is especially important. His grandfather was sent by Wellington to witness the so-called execution of Marshal Ney. He reported that *Ney was not shot.*

their object.* There were many Englishmen in Paris who would have gone every possible length to rescue Marshal Ney from the clutches of the Bourbon government, feeling, as they did, that every sentiment of honor and humanity demanded it. Not one month after this alleged execution, four Englishmen—Sir Robert Wilson ; Captain Hutchinson, of the English Guards ; Mr. Crawford Bruce, and Sergeant Ellister, of the Fifth Regiment of English Guards—assisted in the escape of another condemned man—General Lavalette, of Napoleon's army. These gentlemen were prosecuted by the French Government, but the trial was a mere farce. The lightest possible punishment was inflicted upon them—just enough to save appearances.† In his defence Sir Robert Wilson declared

---

*Lavalette's "Memoirs," Appendix ; Bourrienne's "Memoirs of Napoleon."

† The king even declared that in rescuing Lavalette the English officers had done him a great service ! although he had refused the last request of Lavalette and his friends, "that Lavalette might be shot instead of guillotined." The fact is, the king and his friends were scared almost out of their wits when Lavalette escaped. "There was no sleep at the Tuileries that night," said an officer of the law to Lavalette not long after his escape. "You can form no idea of the alarm and consternation that now fill the minds of all persons at court. They are convinced that your escape is the result of a great plot that is going to burst over them ; they see you already at the head of the old (Bonapartist) army marching against the Tuileries." "The joy of the whole capital in witnessing the despair of the police in their efforts to find Lavalette was inexpressible." Wherever the telegraph announced his escape, acclamations and *vivas* attested the delight of the people."—"Memoirs of Lavalette," vol. ii., "The Court of the Tuileries."

Lamartine says that the prime minister, the Duke de Richelieu, was privy to Lavalette's escape. "He" (Lavalette) "was conducted to the office of Foreign Affairs, where the Duke de Richelieu had prepared an asylum for him with one of the principal officers of his department. Lavalette was thus protected by those very persons who were directing a search to be made for him."—"History of the Restoration," vol. iii.

The Duke de Richelieu was also opposed to Ney's death. He said to a friend : "Time may acquit Marshal Ney of the charge of treason."

Sir Robert and Captain Hutchinson were *not court-martialed*. Wellington got out of the difficulty in the neatest possible manner. They were reprimanded by the Prince Regent, but the reprimand was so exceedingly mild that it really amounted to an approval of their conduct. It greatly offended the Bourbons.

that his conduct was perfectly justifiable. "There existed," said he, "a convention—the Convention of Paris—signed by an English general and ratified by the English Government, and the trial of Lavalette I hold to be a manifest violation of the twelfth article of that convention, and relieving him from the effects of that trial was discharging a debt due by Englishmen." In writing to Earl Grey, he used still stronger language: "Acknowledged as the victim of breach of faith with my country, he" (Lavalette) "had claims to my personal efforts, even at the foot of the scaffold. . . . It was for me to decide whether rage or vengeance should be satisfied . . . whether England should escape from the shame of again participating in a murder. . . . The secret had been entrusted first to young Bruce, who had been authorized to communicate it to me. It was, however, necessary to find some persons of trust who might facilitate the necessary dispositions, and our choice fell upon Ellister, of the Fifth Regiment of the Guards, and John Hutchinson, as well on account of the confidence we placed in their honor as because we knew that they had been already, once before, engaged in a business of the same nature. . . . I have learned most interesting particulars, but must wait to communicate them until I can write by some safe opportunity. I shall put Marshal Soult on his guard." * If these men did so much to save the life of Lavalette, it is extremely probable that they did much more to save the life of Ney.†

Ney, it is true, had dealt the English some heavy blows; but they liked him all the better for that. He was a noble and generous enemy. His was a great life, not free from faults (whose life is?), but still a glorious life, the most heroic of all lives. There was not an Englishman with a spark of honor or feeling in his bosom that did not shudder at the bare thought of the execution of such a man.

The English "public almost universally commended Sir Robert and his friends."—Walpole's "History of England;" Craik and McFarlane's "History of England."

* Lavalette's "Memoirs," Appendix.

† Sir Robert Wilson greatly admired Marshal Ney, although Ney had defeated him in the Peninsular War. Sir Robert was indeed a knightly foe.

What was the *business* to which Sir Robert Wilson alludes in his letter to Earl Grey? "Our choice fell upon Ellister, of the Fifth Regiment, and John Hutchinson . . . because we knew they had been already, once before, engaged in a *business of the same nature.*"

Did not Sir Robert refer to Ney's escape? I think it very probable. Captain Hutchinson was deeply interested in Ney's fate. He was intimately connected with Madame Hutchinson, who had pleaded so earnestly with the duke in behalf of Ney. He and Ellister were the very men to undertake that kind of "business." Chivalrous, cool, brave, exhaustless in resources, they were ready to do and dare everything to vindicate the national honor and to save a man like Ney. Sir Robert Wilson and Mr. Bruce were men of the same stamp.* The letter of Marshal Moncey, in which he gives his reasons for refusing to sit on Ney's trial, is a model of its kind.† It made a deep and lasting impression upon the public mind. It touched a popular chord everywhere, and made him a great

---

* It is true Sir Robert Wilson, Hutchinson, and Bruce declared before the court which tried them for aiding Lavalette that they had not the slightest knowledge of any plots for Ney's escape; that they had never believed it possible for Ney to escape, etc.; but the very boldness and vehemence of their denials are calculated to excite, and did excite at the time, the gravest suspicion as to the truth of their statements. If they had had any knowledge of or been concerned in any plots for Ney's escape, they would have been the veriest fools to admit it on the stand or anywhere else. See "Wars of the French Revolution," etc.

† "I do not enter into the question of the guilt or innocence of Marshal Ney. Your justice and the equity of his judges must answer for that to posterity, which weighs in the same balance kings and their subjects. . . . My life, my fortune, all that I hold most dear, belongs to my king and my country; but my honor is my own, and no power can rob me of it. What! shall I pronounce upon the fate of Marshal Ney? Permit me, sire, to ask your majesty where were these accusers when Ney was marching over the field of battle? . . . Can France forget the hero of the Beresina? Shall I send to death one to whom France owes her life, her families, their children, their husbands and parents? Ah, if the unhappy Ney had accomplished at Waterloo what he had so often done before, perhaps those who to-day demand his death would have implored his protection. It is very dangerous to push brave men to despair. Reflect, sire; it is perhaps the last time that truth shall come near your throne."—Letter of Marshal Moncey to Louis XVIII.

hero, not only in France and in Europe, but in every part of the world. True, it incensed the Bourbons, but it encouraged Ney's friends, and, in the estimation of every high-minded and generous person, did Moncey more credit than all the victories he ever gained.

It was not true, as the Duke de Richelieu said, that Europe demanded the death of Ney. England certainly did not demand it. Russia did not demand it. Austria did not demand it. Wellington did not wish it. The Emperor Alexander said on several occasions, even to the king and his ministers, that he was opposed to these military executions; that they could do no good, and would probably do much harm. "Clemency," he declared to the bloodthirsty Duchess d'Angoulême, "will gain hearts and will subdue them; severity will bring you countless evils." The Emperor of Austria entertained the same sentiments.* General Jomini, of the Russian army, very near the person of Alexander, pleaded Ney's cause with a generous earnestness which did him much credit. Europe demanded no such "reparation," and the Duke de Richelieu well knew it. It was a fiction invented for "reasons of state."† Indeed, these state fictions were as thick as forest leaves. "Convict Ney," said the king's representatives, "and the king will pardon him. This act of clemency will greatly strengthen the king's government." "Give a verdict against Lavalette and his life shall be spared, while justice will be satisfied, society avenged, and the king's bounty will shine in all its splendor," etc.‡ Louis XVIII. pretended to be a "father" to his people, and he was the cruellest of masters, the Pharaoh of Pharaohs. His "God-given" charter was scarcely worth the paper upon which it was written.

When everything had been arranged for Lavalette's departure, Bruce took leave of Lavalette, Captain Hutchinson, and

* The King of Bavaria wrote a letter to Louis XVIII. in which he told him that these military executions were simply shameful.

† The tyrant's plea always. "Convict Moreau for reasons of state," said Bonaparte's pliant tools, "and the First Consul will pardon him." See "Last Days of the Consulate," Fauriel.

‡ "Memoirs" of Lavalette; Lamartine's "History of the Restoration;" "Court of the Tuileries."

Sir Robert Wilson, saying, "I am going to spend three days at the country-seat of the Princess de la Moskowa—for you will not want me any longer." *

This, it seems to me, is a significant circumstance. Why should Bruce have taken so much interest in the Princess de la Moskowa? He was "going to spend three days at her country-seat." † Where were Ney's friends, devoted and numerous, at the time of the alleged execution? They were watchful and determined. They were acquainted with every move in the game that his enemies were playing. They feared treachery. They had spies everywhere—in the chamber of peers, in the Luxembourg prison, in the Bourbon palace, among the police (still controlled in great part by Fouché, one of Ney's strongest friends), among the soldiers, on the streets—spies everywhere. Even the very guards who were more immediately about Ney's person in the Luxembourg prison, some of whom were chosen with especial reference to their devotion to the royal cause—men, for the most part, of gentle birth—were opposed to the execution of Ney. They treated him with great tenderness and consideration, and did not hesitate to denounce, in no measured terms, those madmen who thirsted for Ney's blood. In less than one hour after Ney's condemnation the *fact* was known in every part of Paris. Ney's friends were now especially vigilant. They could not be deceived. They knew, or the leaders knew, that Ney would not be shot on the plain of Grenelle. Where were they, then, on the morning of December 7th? Why were they conspicuously absent from the so-called place of execution? Ney was but indifferently guarded. There were no English soldiers,‡ no Prussian soldiers, only a few French soldiers whose hearts were not in the infamous work they were

---

* "Memoirs" of Lavalette.
† Coudreaux, near Chateaudun.
‡ "The English army were not all satisfied at being employed to keep the French quiet while the men who had fled at the sight of Napoleon butchered the soldiers who had faced every army in Europe. . . . A scheme which had been prepared to rescue Ney was now directed to save Lavalette."—Bourrienne's "Memoirs," new edition, edited by Colonel R. W. Phipps.

called upon to do. Ney's friends, a hundred times as numerous, and ready to die for him at any moment, could easily have overpowered them, especially as a very large majority of them —possibly every man—wished to be overpowered.

The marshal's friends had heard of the atrocious insult which Wellington had received the night before. They knew that the king was powerless * without the duke's support, and that Wellington would under no circumstances assist the king in the execution of Ney.†

In any case, would Ney's friends—than whom no man ever had warmer or braver—have basely deserted him at this trying moment ? Would they not have been present to testify, silently at least, their boundless affection for him ?

No one at the execution ! No one, not even a clergyman, at the unceremonious, brutal burial at the heathenish hour of six and a half o'clock on a December morning ! No sign of grief or indignation anywhere ! Had human nature sunk so low ?

Why did not Madame Ney erect a monument to the memory of her husband ? She doubtless could have done so after the revolution of 1830. Louis Philippe gave her a pension of twenty-five thousand francs, and permitted her to place a handsome bust of the marshal in the museum at Versailles. Her eldest son, the Prince de la Moskowa, married in 1828 the daughter of Laffitte, the rich banker, and was afterward an aide-de-camp of Louis Philippe. Laffitte himself was for a

* " If the allies had evacuated France, Louis le Désiré would have ordered his carriage and have been at the frontier before they had reached it."— Bourrienne's " Memoirs of Napoleon."

† The Duke de Feltre (General Clarke), an old officer of the empire, was *War Minister*. The Duke de Fezensac, who loved and adored Ney, had married Clarke's daughter, and exercised a powerful influence over his father-in-law. M. de Cazes was *Minister of Police*, and Queen Hortense, devoted to Ney, had the duke completely under her thumb, though he seemed to be loyal to the king. He did whatever she told him to do. See Lamartine's " History of the Restoration."

Both Talleyrand and Fouché were anxious to save Ney, especially Fouché. They were skilled in plots of all kinds, and though out of office, had more real power over the French people than any two men in France —perhaps than any ten men.

short time a member of the king's cabinet. So was Dupin, one of Ney's counsel. The king could not have objected to the erection of a simple monument at Ney's grave in Père la Chaise.

In 1848 Louis Napoleon came into power, and then certainly Madame Ney could have erected the most costly, the most imposing monument. But she did nothing of the kind. She paid no attention to the *grave* of her husband. In 1853 the French Government erected a statue of the marshal on the spot where he was supposed to be executed, but his *grave* —the most sacred of places—was utterly neglected alike by the government and by his family.

Madame Ney died in July, 1854. She never married a second time, though she was a most beautiful and accomplished woman, and in 1815 was but thirty-three years of age. She loved the marshal with deathless affection, and her whole life, especially after the July revolution of 1830, was sacredly devoted to a formal rehabilitation of her husband's memory. Her children aided her in every possible way, and proved themselves worthy to bear the name of NEY.

In 1891 I visited Ney's grave, so-called, in the cemetery of Père la Chaise. There is nothing whatever to mark the spot. The ground is perfectly flat, and there is no headstone, no footstone, no memorial of any kind. Underneath the rusty iron gate is a small, narrow stone slab, and on this slab is roughly carved or cut by some unknown hand the one word "NEY." *

---

* "The body of the marshal," says Welschinger ("Le Maréchal Ney, 1815"), "was buried in the family vault. Eleven months afterward the Minister of Police gave La Maréchale Ney permission to construct in the cemetery of Père la Chaise a special vault or tomb in which to deposit the remains of her husband." In removing the body, "on ne travailla que la nuit et l'on plaça le corps dans le caveau, au lever du jour, à huis clos." Why this secrecy, this mystery eleven months after the burial? They worked "all night," and ceased operations only at "break of day." As Louis Philippe once said, "Some other man may have filled Ney's grave." Doubtless Madame Ney did not wish that the body of another man should lie in the grave that was supposed to be her husband's. She had previously applied for permission to remove the body of the marshal, but her request was not granted. Was an empty coffin buried in the *new caveau?*

I think that I have now established a case of *very great probability* as to Ney's escape. Those who do not agree with me must prove that Marshal Ney was executed. The *onus probandi* is transferred to history. And if Ney escaped, it is almost certain that he came to the United States. Before he was tried, even before he was arrested, his thoughts had turned to this country as a place of refuge from the Bourbon storm. Smarting under Napoleon's unjust charges (for Napoleon had thrown the blame of his defeat at Waterloo upon Marshal Ney), and disgusted with the emperor's unsoldierly, cowardly flight from his last battle-field, Ney appeared before the Chamber of Peers four days after the battle and made the following speech : " The army is destroyed. You must recall the Bourbons. As for me, I will retire to the United States."*
And so, during his trial, he said to his counsel, " I do not fear death ; I have beheld it a thousand times under every aspect in the field of battle and amid the snows of Russia, yet I confess to you that I wish to live. I have a young and handsome wife whom I love with all the tenderness of our first happy days ; I have children scarcely out of the cradle to love, to bring up, to protect : these things bind me to exist-

At first it was necessary to keep up appearances, to remove all suspicion to kill all reports as to Ney's escape ; for it was reported that he had escaped. The official report and all the histories that I have ever seen state that Ney died instantly, as if struck with a thunderbolt ; but one of the marshal's relatives, now living, informs me that the marshal did not die instantly, that he lived several hours after he was shot (though without regaining consciousness), and that this fact gave rise to the report that he had escaped and had gone to St. Helena to rejoin the emperor. See also Bourrienne's " Memoirs," revised edition, as to reports of Ney's escape. It was said, apparently by authority, at the time of the disinterment, that the " bullet-holes in Ney's forehead were distinctly visible." Possibly there were bullet-holes in the exhumed skull. But whose skull was it ? See Bourrienne's " Memoirs of Napoleon," revised edition, and " A Faggot," etc., by the author of " Bubbles from the Brunnen of Nassau," London, 1852.

The Princess de la Moskowa was not buried by the side of her husband. Why ? The grave of Marshal Lefebvre is in the cemetery of Père la Chaise, not far from the so-called grave of Ney, and Madame Lefebvre is buried by his side.

* It will be remembered that when he fled into Switzerland his intention was to escape to the United States.

ence. And who knows if, after a retirement and an expiation of some years, the course of events, my country, the king himself, revolutions, or war, may not recall me to the assistance of France, and give me an opportunity of one of those acts of devotion and for one of those victories which redeem in the life of a soldier, as in that of Turenne and of Condé, faults and errors which are blotted out forever by the immensity of the service? To live still to find again one of those opportunities of redeeming my life would be to live twice."

He condemned himself. He felt that banishment would be a just punishment. His best friends would have acquiesced in that verdict. One of them said, "We would hail banishment to America with transports of joy."

I can find no trace of Peter S. Ney in the United States prior to the year 1819. Chapman Levy, a distinguished lawyer of South Carolina, said that he was told by some French refugees that they saw P. S. Ney in Georgetown, S. C., in the early part of the fall of 1819, and recognized him as Marshal Ney, whom they had frequently seen in France; that when P. S. Ney heard of this recognition he left Georgetown, and no one knew where he went.* In September or October, 1819, Colonel Benjamin Rogers, of Brownsville, S. C., saw P. S. Ney at a hotel in Cheraw, S. C., and engaged him to teach the village school. He taught in Brownsville about three years, and then went to Mocksville, N. C.† He taught in Mocksville, in Iredell County, and in other portions of Western North Carolina until 1828. In that year he went to Mecklenburg County, Va., where he taught about two years. He returned to North Carolina about January 1st, 1830. From that time he was engaged in teaching in various parts of the State, chiefly in Lincoln, Iredell, Davie, Cabarrus, and Rowan counties until August, 1844. During the fall of 1844 and the winter of 1844-45 he taught in Darlington District, S. C.

---

* See testimony of Captain F. M. Rogers.
† See testimony of Colonel John A. Rogers.

He then returned to North Carolina, and taught in Lincoln and Rowan counties until his death in 1846.*

Now, if P. S. Ney were Marshal Ney, how did he escape from France, and where was he from the time of his landing in this country until the fall of 1819 ? Mrs. Mary C. Dalton, of Iredell County, N. C., says : "I was a pupil of P. S. Ney for several years. He taught near the residence of my father, Colonel Placebo Houston, with whom he boarded. I knew him well. He told me twice, when perfectly sober, how he escaped, and how he spent the first few years of his life in the United States. He said : 'My name is not Peter Stuart Ney. I am Marshal Ney. History states that I was executed, but I escaped death through the aid of my friends and others. On the day appointed for the execution I was told that my life was to be spared. I was instructed to give the command to fire, and to fall while giving it, so that the balls might pass over me. I carried out my instructions. In battle I never knew what fear was, but when I took my position in front of the soldiers, and gave the command to fire, *bedoust*'—that was the very word he used—'I was almost frightened to death. I was taken up by the soldiers'—I think he said they belonged to his old command—'and carried to the hospital. That night I was disguised, and went to Bordeaux. From that place I sailed to the United States, landing in Charleston the latter part of January, 1816. The next few years I spent in seclusion, and prepared myself for teaching by studying the classics and the higher mathematics.' He said he thought every one ought to have a visible means of support, and that he chose the profession of teaching, because it was in many respects like the military profession, to which he had been accustomed all his life. He could not bear the thought of engaging in any occupation where he would be commanded or controlled by others whom he might regard as his inferiors. In the school-room he would be supreme ; hence he remained in seclusion three or four years

---

* Testimony of Burgess Gaither, Mrs. Clement, Mrs. Dalton, and Mrs. Hughes.—P. S. Ney's "School Register."

—I forget the exact time—in order to qualify himself for his new profession."*

But there were probably other and weightier reasons for so long a concealment. He doubtless thought that in three years and a half the reports of his escape† would be forgotten, or, at any rate, would pass out of the public mind. The danger of recognition would be greatly lessened, and in case of recognition, the statements of those who had identified him as Marshal Ney would be generally discredited. People would ridicule the idea of Ney being alive in the United States, and his alleged execution would become an accepted historical fact.‡

* Mrs. Dalton is a remarkably intelligent woman, of high social position, and an unimpeachable witness in every respect.

Colonel Thomas F. Houston, of Missouri, a brother of Mrs. Dalton, says that P. S. Ney told him that as he passed the file of soldiers drawn up to execute him, he whispered, "Aim high!" that his command in battle had always been, "Aim low!" Colonel Houston. thinks P. S. Ney said that he landed at Charleston, January 29th, 1816. See testimony of Mrs. Dalton and Colonel Houston.

† "It was impossible to get the public to believe that Ney had really been killed in this manner, and nearly to this day we have had fresh stories recurring of the real Ney being discovered in America."—Bourrienne's "Memoirs of Napoleon," revised edition. See also statement of one of the marshal's relatives, already given.

‡ Welschinger ("Le Maréchal Ney, 1815") says the firing party was composed of "twelve men—four sergeants, four corporals, four fusileers—all veterans. They were in two ranks. The marshal was killed instantly, having received eleven balls out of the twelve : one in the right arm, one in the neck, three in the head, and six in the breast. Some days after the execution an officer of the Fifth Hussars visited the place where Ney had fallen. They had taken away the earth, he said, so as entirely to destroy all traces of his blood. The officer saw on the wall six traces or marks of balls, one of which was at the top." How, then, did eleven balls strike the marshal? One ball was at the top of the wall. Welschinger says one soldier was agitated, and missed the Marshal. One gun contained a blank cartridge. *Ten* balls only could have struck the Marshal. Welschinger has a bad memory. All those who were in any way connected with the supposed execution—Count de Rochechouart, who was appointed to "make the necessary dispositions for carrying into effect the sentence of the court;" La Rochejaquelein, who commanded the Grenadiers ; Laisné, Inspector-General of Prisons ; Adjutant St. Bias, who was struck dumb ; the veterans detailed for the execution, even the soldier who drove the horses of the coach containing the marshal—all were friends of Ney, and bitterly opposed to his execution.—Welschinger ; "Memoirs of Count de Rochechouart ;" Lamartine's "History of the Restoration."

THE EARL OF ELGIN.

(This Portrait bears a striking resemblance to Peter S. Ney. See note on opposite page.)

NOTE.

OPINIONS of witnesses who were personally acquainted with P. S. Ney on the portrait of the Earl of Elgin:

Dr. A. H. Graham: "The portrait of the Earl of Elgin is a fair likeness of P. S. Ney in size and feature. Ney's eyebrows heavier, eyes more sunken, mouth and chin indicated more firmness, as did the whole expression of his face."

Rev. Dr. Basil G. Jones: "Elgin's head, neck, shoulders, and breast like P. S. Ney's; also face and general appearance. When I first looked at the engraving I thought it was P. S. Ney's picture."

Mrs. Dalton, and N. L. Clarke (Decatur, Miss.): "Elgin's face shorter than P. S. Ney's. Ney's forehead higher. Top of Ney's head more flat, and longer from front to back; nose longer and more round at the end; a good likeness in general, but proportions not accurate; and Elgin lacks Ney's stern and commanding appearance."

H. C. Hamilton, Hickory, N. C.: "A fair likeness of P. S. Ney. Nose and forehead resemble Ney's. Ney's mouth firmer, and indicated more determination; lips rather thick, but closely compressed. Ney's eyebrows more heavy and full."

P. H. Cain: "Not an exact likeness of Ney, but nearer to it than anything I have ever seen."

Mrs. Elizabeth P. Sloan: "A striking resemblance to P. S. Ney; was startled when I looked at it."

Rev. Dr. R. B. Anderson: "A fair likeness of P. S. Ney. Ney had a higher forehead and a quicker play of expression."

Dr. D. B. Wood: "P. S. Ney's head and face more massive; forehead higher and larger."

Valentine Stirewalt: "A tolerably correct likeness. Ney's eyes were keener, and his mouth did not turn down at the corners like Elgin's. Ney had a straight mouth."

Harrison Cook: "Elgin portrait resembles P. S. Ney. Ney had a higher forehead and a sterner, more determined expression."

CHAPTER II.

TESTIMONY.*

COLONEL JOHN A. ROGERS, Florence, S. C. (September, 1888): "I first saw Peter S. Ney at my home in Brownsville, Marlborough County, S. C., in the fall of 1819. My father, Colonel Benjamin Rogers, met him at a hotel in Cheraw in September or October (1819), and engaged him as a teacher. He taught with great success about three years, and then went to North Carolina (in 1822 or 1823), where he taught for several years. I saw him often afterward, for he made occasional visits to his friends in South Carolina, and taught again in the State about 1844. He told my father that he was a French refugee; that he had left France for political reasons, but would give no further account of his life. He was a man of remarkably fine presence, and would arrest attention anywhere. No stranger could meet him without asking the first individual that he saw, Who is that man? He was tall—I suppose about six feet high—large, not corpulent, but muscular; a little round-shouldered, though otherwise erect, with fine military form and carriage. He looked every inch the soldier, even when he was quite an old man. His head was slightly bald on top. His hair was not a decided auburn, but was what might be called a reddish-blonde. His complexion was fair and ruddy; chin round; mouth tolerably large; lips compressed; nose high and large; eyebrows heavy and full; forehead broad, high, and massive. His eyes are hard to describe. They were a dark blue, verging on gray, with remarkably large pupils. When quiet, they had the mildest expression, but when excited, they were terrible—an eagle would dart from them in sheer envy. He spoke English well, though with a slightly foreign accent.

* For a list of witnesses, see Appendix C.

He appeared to be more of a Scotchman than a Frenchman. He was very neat in his person and dress. He always wore a long blue coat, cut in a semi-military style. He was very reserved in his manners, and would allow no one to take the slightest liberty with him. I was in the school-room in 1821 when a newspaper was brought to him by one of the boys containing the announcement of Napoleon's death at St. Helena. He read it, turned deathly pale, fainted, and fell to the floor, exactly as if he had been shot. Some of the older scholars threw water on his face, which soon revived him. He dismissed his school, went to his room, and shut himself up for the balance of the day. He burnt a large quantity of his papers—perhaps everything that he thought might lead to his identity. Among other things burnt was a very exact likeness of the Emperor Napoleon. The next morning Mr. Ney did not make his appearance as usual, and my father went to look after him. He found him with his throat cut.* The blade of the knife that did the work was broken in the wound. This probably saved his life.

"In the absence of the family physician, my father and Mr. Julius Poellnitz, son of Baron Poellnitz, a Polish exile, constituted themselves surgeons, and sewed up the wound. When my father reproved Mr. Ney for this extraordinary account, he gently took hold of his arm, and said with deep emotion, 'Oh, colonel, colonel, with the death of Napoleon my last hope is gone.'

"Some time afterward he went with two of my brothers to Columbia. While there a general military review took place. Mr. Ney made his appearance on the field mounted. So splendid was his horsemanship, and so magnificent his bearing every way, that he attracted universal attention. There were several foreigners in Columbia at the time, and they declared in the most positive manner that this man was Marshal Ney. They said they had seen Marshal Ney many

---

* "From the time of that unhappy proclamation life was a burden to me. I wished for nothing but death. A hundred times I was on the point of blowing out my brains."—Marshal Ney's "Histoire complète du procès du Maréchal Ney."—DUMOULIN.

a time in Europe, and that they could not be mistaken. When Mr. Ney heard this he rode immediately off the field, went to his hotel, and stayed in his room during the remainder of the day. That night he told the boys that they must start home very early the next morning. The boys were astonished, as they expected to remain two or three days longer, and begged Mr. Ney earnestly to change his mind. 'No, no,' said he, without offering any explanation, 'we must go.' They left at daybreak the next morning. The boys (Benjamin and Frank Rogers) were twin brothers, and about eighteen years old.

"Mr. Ney was a perfect master of fence. No one in this country could equal him, especially with the broadsword. One day he entered my room, and picking up my sword, which was lying on the table, surveyed it a moment and said, 'Why, John, this is only a baby to the sword which I carried in battle. I could cut off a man's head at a single blow, and my horse was trained to ride to the cannon's mouth.' He had a long and deep scar on the left side of his head, which he told me, I think, he received in battle. He complained greatly at times of a wound in the thigh. He had a remarkably good set of teeth. I have seen him crack the hardest hickory nuts with his teeth and suffer no injury from it.

"He drank wine, and sometimes, though not often, to excess. That was his only fault. He was very methodical in his habits, and retiring in his disposition. He avoided company for the most part, but was kind and obliging to his friends. My father was very hospitable, and entertained a great deal of company. On one occasion, when he had as his guests some of the most distinguished men of the State, the conversation turned in the course of the evening upon military subjects. The discussion waxed warm, every one held to his opinion, and finally my father appealed to Mr. Ney, who had been an attentive listener, to give his opinion upon the subject. Mr. Ney gave his views in the simplest, clearest, and most forcible manner, entering fully into the details of the question, and explaining them to the satisfaction of every one present. When he concluded there was a profound silence. Every one looked at Mr. Ney in astonishment. In a little while Mr. Ney rose and went to his room. One of the gentlemen turned to my father and said, 'Colonel Rogers, your friend, Mr. Ney, must be Marshal Ney. True, Marshal Ney was shot, but he must have risen from the dead. No one but Marshal Ney could have talked like that.'

"During the exciting tariff discussion, Mr. Ney said to me one day, 'O John, the tariff won't hurt you; it's the *black spot*'—alluding to the negro—'that is going to ruin you.' He had a way of going straight to the heart of any question, stripping it of superfluities, and laying it bare before you. He was a man of the highest character, and though a little rough and blunt in his manners and ways, was very tender-hearted and charitable, and entirely above everything that was dishonest, mean, or little. As a teacher he was surpassed by none and equalled by few. There was something about the man that drew all hearts to him. My father was devotedly attached to him, and his students fairly idolized him. He was certainly one of the most extraordinary men that I have ever known."

Charles A. Poellnitz, Rembert, Marengo County, Ala. (1887): "I knew P. S. Ney well. I was a pupil of his when he taught at Brownsville, S. C., from the fall of 1819 to 1821 or 1822. He was, without doubt, one of the best teachers that ever lived. I laid the foundation under him for all I know. He taught Latin and Greek in addition to the ordinary English branches. He sometimes delivered lectures. If not an eloquent orator, he was at all times a forcible and impressive speaker. He had a very distinct Scotch-Irish brogue. He was a very large, well-built, fine-looking man. His head was large and round and bald, complexion fair, eyes gray, teeth good. At the time of Napoleon's death, in 1821, he burned up valuable papers, relics of royalty and high military position, badges of honor, etc. The general belief then was that he was Marshal Ney. I remember it well. It was said that the guns of the soldiers detailed to shoot him were loaded with blank cartridges. He tried to cut his throat when Napoleon died. My father sent for Dr. Nicholson, who dressed the wounds. Mr. Ney sometimes drank to excess, but he never became intemperate until after Napoleon's death. He was a good marksman ; taught me how to shoot a rifle. In the school-room he paid much attention to the derivation of words from Latin and Greek. He was rough, sometimes severe, but his heart was good, and he was beloved and honored by every one."

Mrs. Clement, Mocksville, N. C. (1888) : " Peter S. Ney taught school in Mocksville in 1822 or 1823. I cannot remember the exact year when he began to teach. He taught a few years and then went, I think, to Iredell County. I was his pupil for some time—I think in 1823. I was quite young, and do not remember much about him, except that he was a very large, bald-headed man, with sharp eyes, bushy eyebrows, and a florid complexion. His pupils were somewhat afraid of him, but they all loved him."

Burgess Gaither, Farmington, Davie County, N. C. (1883) : " Peter S. Ney taught school on one of my father's plantations in 1832. I was his pupil at that time, and became very much attached to him. I was his pupil again in 1834–35, when he taught south of Mocksville. I will answer your questions in regular order :

" 1. I do not know when Peter S. Ney came to Mocksville. I suppose, from what I have heard, somewhere about 1820. A gentleman in whose word I can place the fullest confidence relates the following incident : ' One day in 1820 (it may have been later), during a heated political campaign, a party of men met in Mocksville (then consisting of but a few houses) to drink whiskey and to talk politics. One of the men was Dr. Schools, an educated gentleman, who had some years before come from Ireland, and settled in Mocksville. Words ran high, and at length one of the crowd used language which Dr. Schools deemed personally insulting. He demanded an apology. His opponent refused to make any. Thereupon the doctor drew his dagger, seized his adversary by the collar, and swore he must retract or he would thrust him through. No one would interfere, as most of the crowd were the doctor's friends. Just at that moment a stranger stepped up, and taking hold of the doctor's arm, remarked, "What! kill a man unarmed, with no chance to defend himself?" Dr. Schools turned quickly around, and looked the stranger full in the face. He immediately dropped his arm, and put his dagger in his pocket. The stranger was at once the hero of the hour. Dr. Schools shook him warmly by the hand, and to the day of his death Peter S. Ney (for he was the stranger) had no warmer, truer friend than this gallant, open-hearted Irishman. Mr. Ney needed no formal introduction to that crowd. He told them his name, and that he was a French refugee looking for a school. That was just what the people wanted. They gathered around him, and begged him to remain with them and teach their children. He did so. He taught in this county and in the adjoining counties for several years, acquiring a reputation as a teacher which, I think, has never been equalled, certainly never surpassed in the entire State.'

"2. He was a fine scholar. Those who were capable of judging say he could speak with ease and fluency the French, Latin, Greek, and Hebrew languages. He was a splendid mathematician. He seemed never to grow weary of solving hard and intricate problems. His mind was strong and vigorous, and seemed to be capable of grasping any subject.

"3. Mr. Ney was a large, heavy-built man, but not corpulent, with a round body and an erect figure. He would weigh, I suppose, over two hundred pounds. He had powerful muscles, and was remarkably quick and active for a man of his age. His person appeared to be uniformly straight from his hips up. He had a robust constitution, and could stand any amount of exposure. He was little affected either by heat or cold. It was a rare thing to see him near the fire, even in the coldest weather. He was about five feet ten and one half or eleven inches high, and very graceful, though simple and unaffected in all his movements. His head was large, round, and well shaped. It was nearly bald. There was a little hair on the back and sides of his head. His forehead was broad and full; his eyes were of a light blue color, keen and full of intelligence, and at times very fiery and piercing; his nose was prominent, broad at the base, and a little tipped at the point; mouth of medium size, with thin lips; chin round, prominent, and on the thin order; complexion fair, and face dotted from small-pox. He walked rather rapidly, except when in deep thought, and was quick and sprightly in all his actions. His feet were of medium size, rather thin and flat; his hands, small for a man of his size and well shaped; fingers rather short.

"4. He spoke English as well as any Englishman. I suppose he was familiar with the language when he came to this country, for he spoke it when he first came to Mocksville. He spoke French as if it were his mother tongue. I have heard him speak of his family. He told me that he had a wife and children in France, but did not say how many children. He said that his mother had Irish blood in her veins, and from her he inherited his impetuous temper.

"5. I do not know his exact age. I heard him say, in 1832, that he was over sixty years old, but that the people in France looked upon him as a dead man.

"6. He had the highest opinion of Napoleon Bonaparte. He thought him the greatest man that ever lived. If you wished to rouse up the old man, you had but to watch your chance and ask him of Napoleon or his battles. I have listened to him with inexpressible delight when I could draw him out on these subjects, but I was too young to remember or to comprehend all that he said. He told me about the Russian campaign, giving the names of persons and places, the details of battles fought, etc. I remember that he spoke with much feeling about the French soldiers attempting to cross a river on the ice, but too many crowding on it at once, the ice gave way, and a great many of the poor fellows were drowned in his sight, and he was unable to help them.* I

---

* "Their leader" (Ney at the passage of the Dnieper) " at length determined to attempt the passage of several wagons loaded with these poor creatures" (the sick, wounded, etc.), " but in the middle of the stream the ice sank down and separated. Then were heard proceeding from the gulf first cries of anguish, long and piercing, then stifled and feeble

have heard him speak of the Junior Reserves when called out (I suppose), in the campaign of 1813, how they would dread to go into the heat of the action, how sorry he would be for them, how after a few rounds he would send them to the rear, and how after a few trials they would become sturdy and fight like veterans.* He often alluded to Waterloo, and sometimes to Elba and St. Helena, but the mention of these places always appeared sadly to trouble him. He sometimes spoke of Wellington. He said that at Waterloo Wellington was so hard pressed that he looked at his watch, and murmured, 'Oh, that night or Blücher would come!' To show how great events oftentimes spring from small causes, he said that Blücher's horse was killed at the battle of Ligny, that Blücher was so badly hurt by the fall he could not get up, and that the French troops marched over him and then back again without discovering who it was; but had they discovered him, the Prussians would not have reached Waterloo, and that before night Napoleon would have annihilated Wellington's army, and perhaps have changed the fate of Europe. It always pained him deeply to say anything about the reverses of Napoleon. He seldom referred to Louis XVIII. When he did, it was with the utmost contempt. Mr. Ney was a

groans, quickly succeeded by an awful silence. All had disappeared. ... The narrators appeared to shudder again at the recollection of the horrible sight. ... Ney was looking steadfastly at the abyss with an air of consternation" etc.—" Napoleon's Expedition to Russia," SÉGUR.

* " I went to pay my respects to Marshal Ney, who, having received a severe contusion in the leg" (at the battle of Lutzen), " had not been able to march with his corps. He was so good as to explain to me his manœuvres and his reiterated attacks, which had decided the success of the day. He said, ' I had only battalions of conscripts, and I have reason to congratulate myself on it; I doubt whether I could have done the same thing with the old grenadiers of the Guard. I had before me the best of the enemy's troops, the whole of the Prussian Guards; our bravest grenadiers, after having twice failed, would perhaps not have carried the village, but I led these brave children *five* times to the charge, and their docility, perhaps, too, their inexperience, served me better than veteran courage; the French infantry is never too young."—Lieutenant-General Count Dumas' " Memoirs of the Revolution, the Empire, and the Restoration."

" These children are heroes; I shall accomplish with them whatever you please."—Ney to Napoleon.

splendid swordsman. I have heard him speak of fencing contests between him and Murat. He said they never could decide which was the better fencer. Sometimes in presence of Napoleon they would be trying their skill, and, both being high-tempered and impetuous, they would get their mettle up and become too much excited, when Napoleon would say, 'Come, come, that will do,' and put a stop to the fun.* That he was firmly attached to Napoleon you may judge from the fact that he wore the same style of coat that Napoleon used to wear. It was long, almost touching his ankles, generally of bluish-black broadcloth, and without lapels.

"7. He had a notable wound on the left side of his head. It was a sabre cut directly above the left eye, three or four inches long and about two and one half inches broad. It appeared to have been produced by a glancing stroke which cut up the scalp, but did not entirely separate it from the bone. The skin was sewed back, but rather unevenly, as every stitch was distinctly visible. He had another wound in the calf of his leg, produced by a musket ball. The ball, I think, was still in his leg, and pained him at times, especially when he walked. These are the only wounds that I have any personal knowledge of. He told me in what battle he received the sabre cut, but I have forgotten the name. He said he was on horseback at the time, in a hand-to-hand encounter; that he cut down a man from his horse just in front of him, but before he could recover, another man struck him from his horse; that his head would have been split open but for one of his friends on the right, who saw the danger, and threw up his sword to defend him, but was too far off entirely to avert the blow. He turned the sabre, however, and caused only a glancing stroke. He said it was like a flash of lightning, and that he knew nothing for some time afterward.

"8. He was anxious to get back to France—to his family and home and country. That seemed to be the absorbing

* Ney and Murat were the best fencers in Europe, and it is quite probable that they engaged in the friendly contests of which P. S. Ney speaks in the presence of their emperor.

object of his life. One Monday morning in the year 1832 Mr. Ney came to school feeling somewhat unwell from the effects of a little spree on the Saturday previous. He told his pupils there would be no school that day, but to come back the next day, Tuesday. 'If, however,' said he, 'any of you choose to remain, I will instruct you, but there will be no regular school.' I stayed and went on with my studies, as usual. Some time in the day Mr. Ney told me that he was suffering a good deal, and asked me to get him some brandy from my father's house, which was not far off. I did so. He drank it off, and said it gave him great relief. He then remarked that I had always been very kind to him, and he would be glad to reward me when in a position to do so. 'People here,' said he, 'call me old Ney, but they do not know who I am. Young Napoleon will soon be of age, and then the French people will put him on the throne, and I shall go back to France, and have rank and position and influence. I am not what I seem to be. I am Marshal Ney, of France.' He then told me how he escaped. He said he was tried and condemned to be shot, and was apparently shot, and that his countrymen thought he was a dead man. 'Louis XVIII.,' said he, 'was full of revenge. He ordered that some of my old soldiers, whom I had often led into battle, should be my executioners. The thing was so revolting to Frenchmen that a plan was formed for my escape. The officer appointed to superintend my execution told one of my friends to apply to the king for my body for interment. He did so, and the necessary permission was granted. I was told to give the command *fire*, and to fall as I gave it. I did so. The soldiers, who had previously been instructed, fired almost instantly, the balls passing over my head and striking the planks or wall behind. I was pronounced dead, hastily taken up, put into a carriage, and driven off to a neighboring hospital. That night I was disguised and left for America.' If he gave the names of any persons concerned in the plot, I do not recollect them, but I think he gave no names. In October, 1832, while sitting calmly at his desk in the schoolroom, one of the pupils brought him his papers. In a few minutes he threw down the paper which he had been reading, and began walking the floor in great excitement. As soon as I got to the door I saw that he was greatly troubled, and I felt very sorry for him. He turned to me, his eyes wildly glaring, the deepest agony depicted in his looks, his powerful frame convulsed with emotion. He pointed to a pair of andirons in the fireplace, and said to me, ' Little fellow, can you eat those *dogirons ?* ' I said that I could not. ' Well, then,' he replied, ' I have a harder task than that. Young Napoleon is dead, and with him dies all hope of ever going back to France, of again seeing wife and children and home and friends.' He then walked the floor, and in the most pathetic terms bewailed his unhappy lot. I never saw such grief. All of his scholars were deeply affected, for they almost worshipped the man. In a few minutes he dismissed his school, and went to Mr. Thomas Foster's, where he was boarding. The next morning, being anxious to hear from him, I went up to Mr. Foster's and saw Wiley Ellis, a student who boarded with Mr. Foster, and he told me that Mr. Ney took a large roll of manuscript from his trunk and burnt it, and that he had been so wild and restless that Mr. Foster had had him watched all night, fearing he might commit suicide. I had seen the manuscript to which Wiley Ellis alluded. Mr. Ney showed it to me one day, and said that it contained an account of his life, and that if he should die before he got back to France, his full history would be known. There was quite a large quantity of the manuscript, and Mr. Ney always kept it locked up in his trunk. It was several days before Mr. Ney's friends could induce him to resume his school. From that time on he was a changed man. He never spoke again, so far as I know, of going back to France.

" 9. Mr. Ney was entirely free from hobbies or idiosyncrasies of any kind. His mind was clear on all subjects, and he was thoroughly practical in every thing that he did. He was plain in his ways, outspoken on all subjects, sometimes rough and apparently severe, but always just and generous and merciful. If he wounded or hurt anybody by word or deed, he was quick to apologize, and to repair, to the fullest

extent, any wrong which he may have committed. As a
teacher he seemed to know exactly what each pupil could
accomplish; that much he required, and nothing more. If a
pupil was obedient and studious, he was gentle and indulgent;
but if disobedient and idle, he was very strict and rigid. I
have seen grown-up young men, who had been spoilt at home,
and who openly declared they intended to do as they pleased
in school, cower before him in perfect submission to his will.

"10. Mr. Ney's character as a man and citizen was above
all reproach. He was quiet, orderly, industrious, public-spir-
ited, and honorable in all the relations of life. Nothing could
be said against the man except his habit of drinking too much
at certain times; but even then he was guilty of no disorder,
or rude and improper conduct of any kind. You never saw
him in a grog-shop or drinking-saloon, or mixing in with a
drinking crowd. He was talkative and communicative when
drinking, but careful to say nothing offensive or to give
trouble to any one about the house. He was not only kind-
hearted, but benevolent. He gave a great many poor orphan
children their tuition free. He was polite and gentlemanly
in his manners, but quick to resent an insult. In 1835 he
was teaching a few miles south of Mocksville, and boarding
with a gentleman whose sons were Mr. Ney's pupils. At
one time two clergymen were on a visit to this gentleman.
When dinner came Mr. Ney, being a little tipsy, made some
witty but inoffensive remark to one of the ministers. Mr.
—— fearing Mr. Ney might be tempted to divert the conversation into unclerical channels, said to him rather pleasantly,
'Mr. Ney, you are at my table.' Mr. Ney instantly replied,
'Do you suppose I do not know what is due a gentleman?'
quit the table and never returned. I never saw him drunk
enough to stagger, though I have heard that he was occasionally in that condition. It has been said that he used profane language when he heard of the death of young Napoleon. I do not think he did. He was too refined and well-
bred to use profane language in presence of his pupils. I
certainly never heard him do so, though in this case he may
have been carried away by his feelings. The only expression

like an oath that I ever heard him use was 'By Jove!' He was remarkably modest and unobtrusive in his general deportment. There was no bluster or brag or affectation about him. He lived entirely in the country, always boarding with the best people, and seldom went to town. He avoided large crowds and public places, and spent much of his time in reading and writing. He wrote for several newspapers. As a rule, he would not talk about himself, even to his intimate friends. If you interrogated him about his history, you would be almost sure to get a rebuff. I think he left no likeness of himself. If he had pictures of Napoleon and Josephine, I never saw them. I do not think he ever wrote letters to France. I used to take letters for him to the post-office, but I do not remember that he ever sent any to or received any from France or any other portion of Europe. He died beloved and lamented by all who knew him. Peace to his ashes."

Colonel Thomas F. Houston, Houstonia, Mo., formerly of Iredell County, N. C. (1877) : " About 1826 (fifty-one years ago) my uncle, Colonel Francis Young, of Iredell County, N. C., engaged P. S. Ney to teach the languages to his sons at Oak Hill Academy. I was too young at that time to attend school, but in January, 1830, I became his pupil, and continued so most of the time until 1838. Mr. Ney was about five feet eleven inches high, of fine physique and muscular power, and would weigh about two hundred pounds. His head was large—so large, in fact, that it was necessary to send away to have his hats made. His head was bald, save at the sides and back, and there was but a slight fringe of hair there, though it grew long and was combed over the top of his head partially to hide his baldness. On one side of his head—the left, I think—there was a scar about two and one half inches in length, which he told me was a sabre cut received in battle. It was healed, but there was an indenture in which a quill could have been placed. He told me, I think, that he had been 'trepanned.' On one occasion he opened his shirt-bosom and showed me scars upon his body, inflicted at the same time that he received the wound described above, by the shoes of the cavalry horses charging over him. While I was his pupil he boarded a great part of the time with my father (Placebo Houston), and a strong attachment was formed between us, at least on my part. During the life of Napoleon's son—the Duke of Reichstadt—he frequently told me of his intention to return to France, and asked me to go with him. Many times he reverted to the subject, always asking me if I would accompany him. Assuring him that I would, he said, ' I'll make a man of you.' I was not a student of his at the time of the death of Napoleon's son (1832), but never after that event, to my knowledge, though his pupil for several years after, did he speak of returning to France. Young Napoleon's death seemed to have blasted all his hopes. When he heard this sad news he trembled, turned very pale, dismissed his school for several days, destroyed many of his private papers, and his grief was so great that fears were entertained that his reason might be dethroned, and that he might commit suicide.

" Mr. Ney was an expert stenographer, and at the time of his death he had a large volume of manuscript (in short-hand) which I have frequently seen, and which contained an account of his life. Mr. Lucius Q. C. Butler, of Davie County, N. C., told me in 1875 that Ney, a few years before his death, pointing to the desk which contained the document, said to him, ' I expect to die in this section of the country. There is something in that desk which will astonish the world. Get it and translate it, or have it translated.'

"Soon after Ney's death I was written to by General Young, of Charlotte, N. C., asking me to take the volume and translate it. Thinking it would be a tedious and troublesome task, and that some other pupil in North Carolina would perform that service, I declined to do so, which I now very much regret. The manuscript was subsequently obtained from Mr. Osborne G. Foard, Ney's administrator, by Pliny Miles, of New York.* Mr. Miles promised that he would have the document translated, and would return it with the

---

* At that time Mr. L. Q. C. Butler had not heard of Ney's death.

translation to Mr. Foard ; but nothing more was ever heard of it. Mr. Ney was a good Latin and Greek scholar, and a splendid mathematician. He was the best of teachers, and gave universal satisfaction. He had a rare faculty for imparting instruction. He would at once seize the vital points of a question, and make it plain to the dullest understanding. He taught more for the pleasure and employment which it afforded him than for the profit, as he asked only his board and $200 per annum. He preserved the strictest order and discipline in his school. His scholars feared him, but loved him. Indeed, no one could help loving him. Mr. Ney was a man of martial appearance, the finest specimen of manhood I ever saw. He showed his military training in his step and bearing. His countenance was open and noble. His eyes were of a bluish-gray color, and in repose they had an exceedingly gentle and even tender expression; but when he was thoroughly aroused upon any subject, they were indescribably keen and piercing. He seemed to look down into the inmost depths of your soul. He ruled men—all classes of people— as Marshal Ney is known to have ruled his soldiers. I do not hesitate to avow my belief that he was Marshal Ney. He was always reticent when with strangers, and rarely spoke of himself and his connection with the French Army, even to his intimate friends, unless the hinges of his tongue were loosened by an extra glass of wine or brandy, and his characteristic reserve thrown off. Then he never manifested any boastful disposition, but sometimes spoke of his connection with the army and the part he had borne in its campaigns.

"On one occasion Ney, while intoxicated, lay down in the snow near my father's house. General John A. Young, of Charlotte, N. C., a cousin of mine and a pupil of Ney, then a boy, saw him and told my father. Father sent several negro men with a horse to bring Ney to the house. I accompanied the negroes, and found him asleep. Repeated efforts to arouse him proving ineffectual, I concluded to have him placed on the horse and taken to the house. One of the negroes mounted the horse, when the others lifted Ney and placed him across the horse's shoulders. In that act the old man was awakened, and his first words were, 'What! put the Duke of Elchingen on a horse like a sack! Let me down.' He struck one of the negroes, and they let him down. He walked with military tread a few steps to the fence, and placing his elbows thereon, wept at the indignity which had been offered him. One of the negroes, addressing him, said, 'Mr. Ney, can you ride?' 'Yes, I could ride into battle.' He mounted the horse and rode to the house without reeling, sitting erect and dignified in the saddle. I told father what Ney had said, and he told me that Marshal Ney was Duke of Elchingen, which was my first information upon the subject, as I did not understand Ney's meaning. This affair was never mentioned to or by Ney afterward. Mr. Ney liked his glass, but he rarely drank to excess. He said that trouble made him drink. He once related to me, when we were alone in his room, the circumstances of his escape. 'Much of history,' said he, 'is false. History says that Marshal Ney was executed, but it is not true. I was sentenced to be executed, and was marched out for that purpose, but the soldiers detailed to do the work were veterans, and '—I think he said—' belonged to my old command. As I walked by the file of soldiers I whispered, " Aim high !" My old command in war had always been, " Aim low—at the heart !" As I took my position in front of the file, refusing to have my eyes bandaged, I raised my hand and gave the command, *Fire!* They fired. I was pronounced dead, and my body was delivered to my friends for interment. I was secretly conveyed to Bordeaux, from which place I sailed to America, landing in Charleston, S. C.'—I think he said—'January 29th, 1816.'

"Mr. Ney also gave me an account of his famous retreat from Moscow, amid the snows and across the rivers upon ice ; how the ice bridge gave way under his army and drowned many of them ; how they perished from hunger and cold ; how the Cossacks hung upon his rear and flanks, cutting off his men, and slaughtering those who from cold and exhaustion straggled, and lay down in the snow to die ; how he marched on foot with his men, and finally brought up the rear-guard of a few hundred soldiers; and how Napoleon embraced him and called him the 'bravest of the brave.' In the fall of 1874 (if not mistaken as to the date) I read in the *Dayton* (O.) *Journal* the account of an interview between the *Journal* reporter and an old French soldier named Philip Petrie, who once belonged to Marshal Ney's command. He stated to the reporter that after the fall of Napoleon and capture of Ney he deserted from the French Army, and in December, 1815, shipped as a seaman on board a vessel bound from Bordeaux, France, to Charleston, S. C., landing in Charleston, January 29th, 1816. He noticed after sailing a man whose appearance struck him very forcibly as some one whom he ought to know. He tried for several days to remember who it could be. At last it flashed across his mind that it was his old commander, Marshal Ney.

"He sought the first opportunity to satisfy himself, and the next time the mysterious personage appeared on deck Petrie approached him, and told him he thought he knew him. He replied, 'Who do you think I am?' Petrie answered, 'My old commander, Marshal Ney.' In a gruff tone he responded, 'Marshal Ney was executed two weeks ago in Paris!' and turning round walked directly to the cabin, and was not seen on deck again during the voyage, though they were thirty-five days in reaching Charleston. Petrie said he knew Marshal Ney was not executed, but escaped to America. This corroborative statement was made by Petrie prior to the discussion of the question as to the identity of P. S. Ney with Marshal Ney, which has been so extensively commented upon by the public press, and almost surely without any knowledge of the whereabouts and occupation of P. S. Ney in the Carolinas and Virginia. Petrie, if living, is, I believe, an inmate of the Soldiers' Home at Evanston, Ill., Detroit, Mich., or Milwaukee, Wis. Ney was a splendid swordsman, and taught me how to fence, at first using wooden swords. At length we had an encounter with two real swords. One of these swords was my father's, and the other belonged to my uncle, Samuel Houston, who carried it in the War of 1812. I was, of course, no match for Ney, and he could easily have cut me down had he so desired. I have his old Latin grammar, published in 1818, in which are inserted a large number of Latin and Greek exercises in his handwriting, such exercises as he used in instructing his pupils. In that grammar were many of his autographic signatures, which were fac-similes of the signature under the portrait of Ney in the history of ' Napoleon and his Marshals.' These have been taken out by persons to whom the book was loaned, or sent to friends as souvenirs. This grammar was given me by Ney in 1838, and I treasure it as a memento from one to whom I was deeply attached. My affection was not lessened by a thrashing he gave me because of continued improper recitations in conjugating the moods of the verb *amo*. Ney labored faithfully with me, but my contrariness was so great that he detected it. With the remark, ' I'll make you say it ; you are perverse,' he vigorously applied a hickory switch. It took a second application to conquer me ; but this is another reason why I treasure the grammar. I have a pair of glasses given my mother by Ney, and which came into my possession at her death. The glasses show their age from the peculiar style of the frame, that portion of it containing the glasses working on tiny hinges, so they can be shut up or opened out, while the remainder of the frame on either side is made in two sections, that they may be closed up and put in the case. These sections are wide, thin, and flat, sliding in and out like a gold pen or pencil from the holder. They are kept in the same case which Ney used, but which is now partially destroyed. It is made of plain, common pasteboard, and has a piece of paper pasted upon it on which is written the single word, ' Ney.' * In speaking of his family, P. S. Ney, according to my recollection, told me that his father was a Frenchman named Peter, and his mother was a Scotchwoman of the Stuart family. In the prominence of his cheeks and the general expression of his face, as well as in his general appearance, he resembled the Scotch more than the French. He spent his leisure hours chiefly in reading and writing. He

* I have no doubt these were Marshal Ney's glasses, which he had often used on the field of battle.

read the newspapers attentively, and occasionally wrote for the *National Intelligencer*, Washington City, and for the *Carolina Watchman*, published at Salisbury, N. C. It was his custom to sit up very late at night, only sleeping from four to six hours in the twenty-four. He said that was a habit contracted in camp while in the army. He was a great admirer of Napoleon Bonaparte, and always spoke of him in terms of the highest admiration. It was evident to every one who knew Mr. Ney that he was a man of genius, and must have been a soldier of the highest rank. It was generally believed by those who knew him best that he was Marshal Ney. I have studied the subject in all its bearings for upward of forty years, and I repeat my conviction, long since entertained, that he was the great marshal of France."

Mrs. Mary C. Dalton,* Houstonville, Iredell County, N. C. (1885) : ". . . Most of the facts related in the testimony of my brother, Colonel Houston, are well known to me, and I need not repeat them. His description of the person, character, habits, etc., of P. S. Ney is very accurate. Perhaps I knew Mr. Ney as well as any person in this country. I had every opportunity to learn his real worth, and I assure you that I never knew any person who was governed by higher principles, who possessed more sterling merit in every relation of life. There was nothing dishonest, low, little, or vulgar about him. He sometimes offended people by his abrupt manner and his plainness of speech on all subjects, but he never failed to apologize and make full reparation for any wrong that he may have done. He was a giant intellectually ; could master any subject that was brought to his attention. On one occasion Judge Pearson said to me : ' Nature has done much for Mr. Ney ; he possesses a very clear and vigorous mind, but I do not believe he is Marshal Ney.' Some years afterward, when Judge Pearson had become better acquainted with Mr. Ney, he said to me in substance : ' I have made a special study of your friend, Peter S. Ney. He is one of the strongest-minded men I have ever met, he has all

---

* A portion of Mrs. Dalton's testimony has already been given.

the qualities ascribed to the great marshal, and the resemblance is so striking in other respects that in spite of history I cannot doubt that he is Marshal Ney himself.' I have often heard Mr. Ney speak of his mother—seldom alluded to his father; he seemed to think that his mother was perfect. He said that he was not a native Frenchman; pointed out in Cummings' atlas the place (Lorraine) where he was born; said he had to change his name after coming over here, but he could not give up the name of Ney. One day, about dark, a stranger rode up to our gate and asked father if he could stop with him that night. We had a good deal of company at the time, and every room was occupied. My father told him that he was sorry he could not accommodate him, but the young man insisted, and said he was willing to sleep on the floor, and that his horse being tired and completely worn out, he could go no farther. My father then told him that if he could suit himself to circumstances he would be glad to have him remain. The stranger, a fine-looking man, thanked him and went in. When he was conducted into supper he took a seat at the table opposite Mr. Ney, who was occupying his usual seat on the left hand of my father. They glanced at each other, and though not a word was spoken, it was evident to all present that it was a glance of recognition. My mother said a sign passed between them. Immediately after tea Mr. Ney and the stranger, taking their hats, left the house together, and were not seen by the family any more that night. An old negro man (Frederick) reported that he saw them near midnight sitting behind a straw stack in the field, in close conversation, and, although unobserved by them, could hear them distinctly, but could not understand a word they said. The stranger ordered his horse very early the next morning, and left. He gave no information about himself, except in a general way. After the man had gone Mr. Ney went to his room and remained in it all that day, reading and writing. He never made any allusion to the matter, and we had too much respect for him to question him about it. The stranger had black hair, black eyes, and a dark complexion. This incident happened, I think, in 1834 or 1835. Mr.

Ney said he had been recognized as Marshal Ney in South Carolina, and that he came to North Carolina to escape further recognition. He went to Mocksville, perhaps in 1822, for I first saw him in 1823 or 1824. He avoided strangers. His fear of an assassin never left him, though he was as brave and intrepid as any one possibly could be. He said he must protect his friends in France who had aided in his escape. He sometimes, not often, drank to excess. When he was in trouble on account of any bad news which he had received, he would drink more freely than at other times. When intoxicated he would tell any one that he was Marshal Ney, but at other times he would not talk on the subject of his identity with Marshal Ney, except to his intimate friends, and not often to them. He would not permit them to introduce the subject, or to question him too freely. He was greatly attached to his friends. He would do anything for them. In the home circle he was as tender and thoughtful as a woman. He gave us no trouble or inconvenience of any kind, even when under the influence of liquor. Sometimes he would not get drunk for an entire session. He did a great deal of good in the neighborhood; gave many poor children their tuition free, and encouraged them to persevere in their studies after they had left school. So sincere, so sympathizing, so straightforward in all that he did, he was greatly beloved, not only by his pupils (who venerated him), but by all persons who came within the circle of his influence. I have heard him speak of his wife and children; said his wife was a beautiful woman, and had dark eyes and long black hair*—so long that she could sit on it; said he had four children; used to tell the girls about his boys—never heard him say that he had any daughters; gave the names of his boys, but I don't recollect them. One day father asked him why he did not bring his wife to America. He said he had several reasons: one was

* Madame Ney had dark eyes, and it is probable she had dark hair.
"The softness and benevolence of Madame Ney's smile, together with the intelligent expression of her large *dark eyes*, rendered her a very beautiful woman, and her lively manners and accomplishments enhanced her personal graces. I was not a little delighted to meet this charming person at Boulogne."—"Memoirs of Napoleon."—DUCHESS D'ABRANTES.

it would be found out where he was, and it would be dangerous for his wife to come over here. Besides he lived in constant expectation of going back to France. After the death of Napoleon's son, however, he seldom spoke of going back, and in 1836 he seemed to have lost all hope of ever returning to his native country. This is shown by a piece of poetry which he wrote in my album, dated May 26th, 1836.* He told me that he helped to bring Napoleon back from Elba; was in the plot before Napoleon left Elba. He did not regret it. The people wanted Napoleon, and the people ought to rule. Father had a fearful time with him for a week when Louis Philippe was placed on the throne of France; sat up with him; was sick and delirious a great part of the time; drew plans of battles; showed father the scars on his person received in battle. Some of the scars he said were made by his own cavalry. When he fell they ran over him. Have heard him speak of the fine horse he rode on the night of his escape. I think he said he rode eighty miles before sunrise the next morning. Did not like Lafayette; said he was a base ingrate, a traitor to Napoleon and France. Spoke often of Josephine and Hortense. His wife and Queen Hortense were great friends. Blamed Napoleon for divorcing Josephine—the beginning of all his troubles. Said the Austrian woman (Marie Louise) ruined Napoleon, and that she was, for political reasons, accessory to young Napoleon's death. Didn't tell me how he knew this. Told my mother, in 1830, that he saw his son in Virginia in 1828 or 1829. Taught school in Mecklenburg County, Va., in 1828-29. The newspapers stated that one of Ney's sons was in this part of the country in 1828.† In 1830 or 1831 Mr. Ney said, ' My sight

---

* The verses are given in the documentary evidence.

Some one had written in Mrs. Dalton's album a piece of poetry on the transitoriness of all earthly things. In the sixth stanza occurs the following line, "Gone, with their glories gone." Mr. Ney took this line as a kind of text. At the end of it he drew a hand with the index-finger pointing to the opposite page upon which he wrote his verses.

† This is true. See New York *Evening Post* of November 15th, 1828. In April, 1828, General Lafayette wrote to a friend in New England that Count Eugene Ney, son of the unfortunate Marshal Ney, would soon visit

DAVID N. CARVALHO,

Expert Examiner of Questioned Hand-Writing, Inks and Paper,

OFFICE AND LABORATORY: 265 BROADWAY.

New York City, April 5th, 1895.

THOMAS WHITTAKER, ESQ.,
    No. 2 Bible House.

Dear Sir:—I have made a careful analysis of the alleged handwritings of Marshal Ney and P. S. Ney contained in the eight pages of original writings which you submitted to me. As the result of said examination I am of the opinion that the writer of the specimens on the four pages purporting to be those of Marshal Ney and the writer of the specimens on the four pages purporting to be those of P. S. Ney, are one and the same person; the variations of hand being largely due to style of pen used, the quill, gold and steel being all represented, which produces the different quality of line without hiding away the idiosyncracies of the writer.

        Very respectfully,

                DAVID N. CARVALHO.

NO. 1. FACSIMILE SIGNATURES OF P. S. NEY.

NO. 2. FACSIMILE SIGNATURES OF MARSHAL NEY.

never failed me until I was sixty years old.' He was then wearing glasses. I have his first pair. He said no letters from abroad were sent directly to him, but were sent through a man in this country. I don't think he mentioned his name. Blamed Grouchy severely for not coming to Waterloo. Mr. Ney had a strong, guttural voice. He pronounced Grouchy's name in a very peculiar manner—Ge-*roo*-shy. He borrowed Scott's life of Napoleon from a lady in the neighborhood (Mrs. Young), and when he returned it, it was full of marginal notes. Mrs. Young said, ' Why, the man has ruined my book.' I read some of the notes, and I remember that expressions like these frequently occurred : ' That is not true ; ' ' This is a vile slander,' etc. The book, I believe, is now owned by William Young, of Georgia.* Mr. Ney told father he was sorry he burnt his papers when young Napoleon died ; was at a loss for dates in re-writing his history. Blamed Napoleon for his Russian expedition. His description of the horrors of the retreat was awful. Had money in the United States Bank. I once saw a letter which he wrote to Nicholas Biddle. He asked father what he should do with his money when the bank failed. I think he had $10,000 in the bank. Said he had no use for it—intended to send it back to France. He would reprove his pupils sharply for wasting bread, fruit, etc. He said, ' You may come to want, and it is wrong in principle. In the army I was oftentimes thankful for a crust of bread.' I well remember the incident to which my brother refers (the intoxication of Ney by the roadside, etc.). It made a deep impression on my mind. Mr. Ney combed his hair so as to hide the scar on the left side of his head. He was careful to keep it covered. His head was very large and roundish—oval ; did not run up to a point. He said he was five feet eleven inches high when he was a young man, but that old age had settled him down half an inch. He never slept more than five hours out of the twenty-four. Burned out a

the United States. The original letter is now owned by Mr. Warren C. Crane, of New York City.

* I am very sorry to say this book can nowhere be found. It is probably lost.

candle every night. Some persons said Mr. Ney was an infidel, but he was not. He detested hypocrisy in all its forms, but no man ever had a higher respect for the Christian religion and the pure worship of Almighty God."

Colonel Junius B. Wheeler, U. S. Army (1884) : " I knew Peter S. Ney. He was thick set, and had a massive head. His speech was guttural. He had a large scar on the left side of his head. He drank whiskey, and was a great tobacco-chewer. He told me once that he was Marshal Ney, and how he escaped. He said the officer in charge of the troops had served under him in the Napoleonic wars—I think he said he was his aide-de-camp. This officer told him that he would not be hurt ; that he must fall and simulate death. He did so, was disguised, and finally escaped to America. I did not believe that he was Marshal Ney ; but if the officer of the day was really one of his old staff officers, the story is probably true. He was a man of decided ability, and everybody respected him."

Captain F. M. Rogers, Florence, S. C. (1887) : " I was a pupil of Peter S. Ney when he taught at my father's house in Darlington County in 1844 or 1845. I was quite small, but I have a very clear recollection of him. He was then quite an old man, and stooped considerably ; but his eye was still bright, his faculties unimpaired, and he appeared to be unusually strong and vigorous for one of his age. My father * had a very high opinion of Mr. Ney, and was probably acquainted with his history.† When asked about the matter, he would invariably give an indirect answer, and would change the subject as quickly as possible. He corresponded regularly with

* Colonel Robert Rogers.
† See testimony of Dr. A. H. Graham.
A Darlington (S. C.) newspaper says : " In 1842 or 1843 an old Frenchman was engaged as teacher in the family of Mr. Robert Rogers, of Darlington, in this State. Several circumstances conclusively prove that this old man was Napoleon's favorite marshal . . . and . . . Rogers, when he . . . us something ab . . . man." The name and date of the newspaper and a portion of the extract (indicated by the blank spaces) have been torn off. Mr. Robert Rogers was " probably acquainted with P. S. Ney's history."

Mr. Ney until the time of his death in 1846. Some time after Mr. Ney's death a man named Pliny Miles wrote to my father, making certain inquiries about Mr. Ney in the interest of some historical society in New York. My father sent Mr. Ney's letters to Mr. Miles, and they were never returned. One day when my father was absent my mother said she intended to find out who Mr. Ney was. So at the dinner-table she asked Mr. Ney one or two questions, with this object in view. Mr. Ney smiled and said, 'Mrs. Rogers, your dinner is good, very good;' but he did not answer her questions satisfactorily. My father owned a little negro boy, very sprightly and active, who was named Arthur. Mr. Ney taught the boy to call himself Arthur Wellesley, Duke of Wellington, and seemed to take much pleasure in making him repeat this name in the presence of others. He always relished the joke.* Mr. Ney called Mrs. John A. Rogers, *Lady* Frances, because, as he said, of her queenly appearance. At times, in conversation, she looked at him in a way that seemed to revive unpleasant recollections, for Mr. Ney would say, kindly though firmly, 'Don't look at me in that way, Lady Frances —Madame de Staël—Madame de Staël.'† I have always heard that Mr. Ney landed at Charleston in the early part of 1816, and that he afterward went to Georgetown, where, in the early fall of 1819, he was recognized as Marshal Ney by a party of French refugees. These refugees (according to the statement of Chapman Levy, a prominent lawyer of Camden) asserted in the most positive terms that this man was Marshal Ney, as they had frequently seen the marshal in Paris and other places in France. When Mr. Ney heard of these declarations he left Georgetown and went to Cheraw, where my grandfather, Colonel Benjamin Rogers, saw him in the fall of

---

* No doubt there was much sly enjoyment in it.

† Marshal Ney, in all probability, had often seen and conversed with Madame de Staël, and it is equally certain that he did not like her. She was dictatorial, intriguing, meddlesome, visionary. She hated Napoleon and his army, and they hated her. At one time, however (before Napoleon was made emperor), Madame de Staël was very fond of the republican officers. She frequently entertained them at her own home. In 1815 she openly blamed Ney for his "treachery to the king."

1819, and employed him to teach school. He taught about three years, and then went to North Carolina. He named the residence of Colonel John A. Rogers *sans souci*, and his school-house *dans souci*. Mr. Ney liked Monongahela whiskey, and sometimes drank a little too much of it. Notwithstanding, he was a good man and a very great man.''

Wallace M. Reinhardt, Lincolnton, N. C. (1890) : " I went to school to Peter S. Ney in 1838. He taught at Houstonville, Iredell County. All of his pupils, from the greatest to the least, were afraid of him, and yet there wasn't one who wouldn't have shed his blood for him. He was very strict with his scholars. Two things he especially required—absolute obedience and good lessons. Woe to the boy who dared to disobey him, or who came to him with a bad lesson ! He didn't have many rules and regulations. He said he wanted the boys to govern themselves. He liked to put them on their honor. If a boy told an untruth, or imposed upon a smaller boy, or did any kind of dishonest or unmanly thing, Mr. Ney would be certain to punish him for it ; and sometimes, if it were a bad case, the punishment would be quite severe. His school was of a military cast. Even his very small boys were required to take a military posture. A lounging, stooping boy would be straightened up quickly. The sharp, commanding voice of our teacher brought all shoulders square to the front. He required neatness in person and dress, and perfect order at all recitations. When he got excited, his eyes would go clear through you. I couldn't look at him. He was a perfect Bengal tiger. He admired Washington, but said he ought to have pardoned Major André. He ought to have shown his greatness by riding over public clamor and the crazy desire for retaliation. He had no use for General Lafayette. One of his pupils was named after Lafayette. One day Mr. Ney said to him, ' Lafayette, I am sorry for you ; you ought to have another name. Lafayette was not a true man. He treated Napoleon shamefully.' In walking, he used a very long stick or staff, holding it about five or six inches from the end. In the school-room he sometimes walked about with his hands crossed behind him. He seemed to be fond of me, and often asked me to cut his hair, though there was not a great deal to cut. He had a long scar on the left side of his head, and he told me one day, while I was cutting his hair, how he received it. He said that during the battle of Waterloo he happened to come in contact with an English officer named Ponsonby—I think he said General Ponsonby—and that in the *mêlée* Ponsonby gave him this wound; but that he cut Ponsonby down, and broke his sword in doing so. This is my recollection of the matter, and I do not see how I can be mistaken. Mr. Ney had other wounds. One was in his thigh, caused, he said, by a bayonet; another in his foot or ankle. On one occasion, when we were fencing with cornstalks, my stalk broke and a piece of it flew off and hit Mr. Ney on the scar on his head. It brought the blood, but Mr. Ney did not get angry. He asked me afterward if I knew whose head I had wounded. I said I did not. He then told me that I had wounded an old marshal of France. Mr. Ney sometimes attended the militia drills. They amused him in a quiet way. He said he had a Damascus blade which he could bend double; that a sword was worthless unless you could bend it double. One day he broke an officer's sword in trying to bend it. He told the officer he would get him another of better temper; but the officer got mad and wanted to fight. 'Very well,' said Mr. Ney, 'you may take a sword, and I will take a stick.' But the officer backed out, and wouldn't fight after all. Mr. Ney would sometimes drink too much whiskey, and then he would tell a great deal about himself; but you couldn't get him in the presence of ladies when he was drunk. He either talked to the men or shut himself up in his room. He often said to me, 'Young man, don't drink liquor; let it alone. I have troubles that you know nothing of. My old body is greatly relieved by stimulants.' He didn't desire a large school; said people sent him too many scholars. The fact is, they didn't wish any other teacher. Mr. Ney often spoke of his mother, and always with the utmost affection. Never heard him speak of his father. On horseback Mr. Ney had an easy and commanding appearance. Even the horse seemed to feel that he had a master. He would at once prick up his ears and move off quickly. Mr. Ney was in many ways a public benefactor. His influence for good is felt to this day. His old pupils have moulded public opinion in the counties where they lived. They have almost uniformly been sober, honest, industrious, and useful citizens. There is scarcely an exception to this rule."

Witherspoon Ervin, Morganton, N. C. (1890) : * "Some years before my day Peter S. Ney taught school in the Brownsville neighborhood of Marlborough County, S. C. My older brothers attended this school. One day his mail was brought in and delivered to him. He read one of the papers and fell to the floor as if struck by a thunderbolt. He was greatly depressed, and attempted to commit suicide by cutting his throat ; but a surgeon was promptly summoned, sewed up the gaping wound, and Ney recovered from the injury. It was during this period of convalescence that he employed himself in painting in water-colors, from memory alone, a life-size, half-length portrait of Napoleon that for many years occupied a prominent place in our parlor at home. Comparing it with fine steel engravings of Napoleon, I know that it was a wonderfully correct likeness. It could only have been produced by an artist of uncommon skill. It was lifelike, and full of character and expression. The man who painted it must have been born with all the natural gifts that are essential to the artist, and must have had them developed and trained by careful cultivation. The portrait had a fascination for me as if it were a living thing. I remember, when a mere child, lying alone upon the floor in the parlor for hours looking up into that wonderful face. I have often heard the inquiry made of my father as to whether P. S. Ney was indeed the French marshal. His opinion was very promptly given that he was not ; and I think his mere opinion, as a leading lawyer of the State, is entitled to great weight. When the inquiry was made of him, he stated that Ney never claimed to be the marshal except when under the hallucination produced by drinking, and was seriously offended, when sober, if any one pre-

* From the *Statesville* (N. C.) *Landmark*.

sumed to address him by that title. Another reason assigned for his opinion was that Peter S. Ney was a scholar of fine literary attainments, while Michael Ney was a rude and uncultivated soldier, only knowing how to set 'legions in the field.' Another objection was that Peter S. Ney was a somewhat younger man than the marshal was supposed to be. His opinion, founded on what reason I do not know, was that Peter Ney was a nephew of the marshal. My father, Colonel James R. Ervin, died in 1836. I then lived with my elder brother, Samuel. In 1839, I think, while sitting at a window in the parlor, preparing my lesson for the afternoon session at the academy, I saw my brother coming up to dinner accompanied by a tall, soldierly-looking man, of full habit, white locks, looking, in spite of his white hair, like a man of unabated strength and vigor. I at once leaped to the conclusion, from his physiognomy and bearing, that he was a Scotch merchant from Charleston. In five or six minutes several young men came in to dinner. Every one at the table treated the stranger with great deference and respect, and addressed him as *marshal*, which I presumed to be his name. He was a man of notable presence, whom one passing on the street would turn to look at again. As soon as dinner was over I asked my brother who his guest, Mr. Marshall, was. 'Why, that was Marshal Ney! Why did you not come in and speak to him?' With the eagerness of a boy to see something of a noted character of whom he had heard so much, I ran to overtake the party who had just left, when my brother informed me that Mr. Ney had probably left for a distant point in a neighboring county. The young men who had gathered around Ney were his former pupils, whom he had taught some years previously. About this time I spent a day with Colonel B. W. Williamson, a former pupil of Ney, at his pleasant home near Darlington. The conversation turned upon Ney, and when I mentioned the fact of his being addressed as marshal, Colonel Williamson remarked that I must certainly be mistaken in that particular, for it was exceedingly offensive to Ney to have that title applied to him except when under the influence of drink. The reply to this objection was obvious. It probably was true that Ney was under the influence of drink at the time referred to, and that I failed to discover it. The inference to be drawn from Colonel Williamson's statement is that the anger which Ney felt arose from obtruding upon him, when sober, the folly he had committed in his moments of intoxication in setting up a claim to be other than he was. Upon the death of my father his library passed into the hands of my brother. In it were many books with marginal notes in the characteristic handwriting of P. S. Ney, which, in my estimation, added much to their value. Sometimes these annotations were in shorthand, but occasionally in French or in English, and signed by his name or initials. In a volume of Scott's poems is a poem entitled ' To Napoleon Bonaparte at Waterloo.' At the word Waterloo is an asterisk, which refers the reader to a manuscript poem at the conclusion, occupying a page and a half left blank in the old edition. It was in the handwriting of Peter S. Ney, and at the close signed with his name. I read it over once and hurriedly, not dreaming then that it contained evidence as to a fact that might come up for discussion. There were probably thirty or forty lines, but only the first two remained fixed in my memory :

" ' Where broken bones and fractured skull
Had all but ruined this poor hull.'

Then followed several other lines of considerable beauty."

Hon. H. G. Bunn, Camden, Ark. (September 15th, 1892) : "A year ago I was travelling on the cars and made the passing acquaintance of a foreigner of reading and intelligence. His name has escaped me. He had been in this country ten or fifteen years. I think he was a Polish gentleman, but had lived in Paris much of his time before coming to this country. In some way (as such things will happen) we were led to talk of the story of Peter S. Ney. It seemed that he had made himself acquainted with the prominent parts of the story. It will interest you only to repeat here in substance what he said he had heard in Paris or from Paris since he left the city.

"As I understood him, he said in substance this : In 1853 or 1854, after Louis Napoleon had become firmly seated on the imperial throne of France, a question arose as to the integrity of the account of the execution of Marshal Ney. This question somehow affected, or was supposed to affect, the honor of the Napoleonic or that of the Bourbon house; I could not exactly understand from the narrator how this was. Anyway, the story goes that Louis Napoleon became so interested in the matter as to appoint a commission to open the grave of the long-buried marshal. The story goes on to say that no remains were in the decayed coffin, and the evidence was that it had never contained anything."

Vardry A. McBee, Lincolnton, N. C. (1890): "I was a pupil of Peter S. Ney in 1834. There was no man in the country who could compare with him as a teacher. He was *facile princeps*. He easily gained the love and confidence of his pupils, although he exacted implicit obedience to his command, and was in every respect a very strict disciplinarian. He was quite a large man, tall, erect, of soldierly bearing, and imposing presence. He seemed born to command. All persons regarded him as a man of superior parts, and he exerted a controlling influence wherever he went. No pupil, however large, would for a moment think of disobeying his slightest commands. He had a quick temper, and sometimes he would get quite vexed with dull and lazy scholars. On such occasions he would use the rod with considerable freedom. He had a big, round chin, a firm, well-chiselled mouth, large nose, ample forehead, and square, heavy jaws that indicated the greatest determination. His eyes were of a grayish color, sparkling, and unfathomably deep. He looked like a lion. His countenance, his walk, his movements, his bearing, his general expression and make-up had a decidedly leonine cast. Though he would occasionally drink too much, yet this habit never injured him in the estimation of those who knew him, or, I may say, of the people generally. The great influence which he exerted over the community in which he lived was of a pure, wholesome, and elevating character. He left behind him a name of which any one might well feel proud."

Dr. J. R. B. Adams, Statesville, N. C. (1886): "I have been entirely satisfied in my own mind since 1842 that P. S.

Ney, who taught school within a few hundred yards of my residence for two years or more, and is now buried in Third Creek Churchyard, was the veritable Marshal Ney. I met him often, and I observed him closely. I never saw a more level-headed man, or one with greater force of character. He took a plain, practical, common-sense view of everything. There was no circumlocution about him. He came directly to the point, and expressed his views (which were rarely wrong on any subject) with exceeding clearness and power. He despised shams of all kinds, and denounced them in pretty severe terms. There was not the shadow of hypocrisy about the man. Everybody felt this, or, with all his strength of mind, he could not have exercised the power over the people which he did. This was simply marvellous. He was a fine specimen of physical manhood, tall, large, and well proportioned, with a manly and majestic bearing. He had a large, broad forehead, bulging out considerably about the eyes. The perceptive faculties were very large. Very heavy, shaggy eyebrows, which gave him a stern and severe-looking countenance, especially as his eyes were uncommonly brilliant and piercing. They seemed to look clear through you. He was a splendid judge of human nature. It didn't take him long to read a person's true character. He avoided crowds, sought only the best company, and was very quiet and reserved in his general demeanor. He did much for the poor, especially poor children. They remember him with deep thankfulness to this day. He had no vices except drinking. He scorned everything that was dishonest or little, though he was pretty abrupt in his manners. One evening Mrs. Adams's uncle, the Rev. Mr. Hall, held a prayer-meeting at the house at which Mr. Ney boarded. Mr. Hall had a good pair of lungs, and his prayers were long and *loud*. After the meeting was over, Mr. Ney had occasion to walk across the room; and as he passed Mr. Hall he said to him in a gruff voice, 'Is your Maker deaf?' The next morning Mr. Ney apologized to Mr. Hall for the language which he had used. He was not only just, but he was merciful. Mr. Lewis Williams, a member of Congress for many years, offered Mr. Ney a good government position in Washington City, but Mr. Ney unhesitatingly declined it. About the year 1842 I met in Alabama a foreigner who called himself Colonel Lámanouski (the name may be incorrectly spelled). He was making a tour of the Southern States, lecturing on Napoleon's campaigns. He told me that he was perfectly convinced, from what he had seen and heard in France and in this country, that Marshal Ney was not executed. He said that he belonged (I think) to the Polish Corps in Napoleon's army, and was well acquainted with Marshal Ney. He said that if the North Carolina school-teacher were Marshal Ney, he could recognize him at a glance. I do not think he ever met him. About the year 1840 Rev. J. M. Wilson, Professor Hugh R. Hall, and Colonel Thomas A. Allison were appointed by the trustees of Davidson College a committee to draw up a device for the college seal. At their request Mr. Ney assisted them. In a few minutes he prepared both the device and the legend. These were very acceptable to the college authorities, and were at once adopted.* Those who knew him longest and best were firmly convinced that he was Marshal Ney."

Thomas Scott Wood, Cleveland, N. C. (1884) : " I knew Peter S. Ney ; was a pupil of his for several months. In my younger days I was very robust and strong, fond of hunting, fishing, boxing, wrestling, etc. Mr. Ney had been in the habit of whipping his big bad boys ; and as I knew my father expected to send me to school to him, I said publicly that Mr. Ney should never whip me. I was about nineteen years old. The first day I went to school I took my seat at a desk near the door, and put my hat on the desk before me. Mr. Ney came to me and said very pleasantly, ' Every boy has a peg for his hat ; now there is your peg '—pointing to one not far from me. ' Always put your hat on that.' I got up, and, dragging my feet behind me, put my hat on the peg. Mr. Ney was watching me. The next morning I walked into the school-room, took my seat, and placed my hat on the desk before me as I had done the day before. Quick as lightning

---

* See testimony of Rev. Dr. Rockwell.

Mr. Ney sprang from his seat and came to me. 'Sir,' said he, in a deep, stentorian voice which I can never forget, 'take that hat and put it on top of the house!' I looked up and caught his eye—*that* eye. It was flaming, sparkling like diamonds. I began to tremble from head to foot. I had no strength left in me. Mr. Ney, seeing that he had conquered me, changed his tone and manner, and said very kindly, 'Well, if you don't want to put it on top of the house, put it on the door then.' I looked up at the open door, and saw there was a chance to get out of the difficulty. I sprang to my feet, and put my hat on the door. It is needless to say that Mr. Ney had no further trouble with me. From that moment I began to like him, and when I left school he had no more devoted friend in the whole country than myself. I do not hesitate to say that he was the greatest man I ever knew. One of my neighbors, who had long known Mr. Ney, said to me one day, 'Well, if he was not Marshal Ney, he ought to have been.' He was a large, handsome man; broad and full-chested, well made, strong, capable of enduring any amount of privation or fatigue. He had two wounds that I especially remember—a long scar on his head, evidently made by a sabre, and a deep wound on his arm (I forget which one), between the shoulder and elbow. He had a kind of double chin, large, round, protruding, and slightly turned up. His whole countenance was stamped with an air of unconquerable energy and determination. He ate the simplest food; was very fond of soup;* would often eat nothing else for dinner. The school-room was not very far from his boarding-house, and his landlady would generally send him for dinner a bowl of rich soup, some light bread, and two or three large pods of red pepper. He would cut up the red pepper into his soup and eat it with great relish. He said the country people always threw away the best part of what they called a boiled dinner—the *pot liquor*. Mr. Ney died in 1846 at the residence of Osborne G. Foard, in this county. There was a large attendance at his funeral. The sermon was

---

* Soup was the principal dish of the French soldiers.

preached by the Rev. James Adams, a Presbyterian clergyman. His death produced a profound sensation in the entire community. There were many tears shed over his grave. Every one felt that our greatest man, and in God's eyes one of the best of men, had been taken from us."

Editor *Times*, Danville, Va. (1888) : "Anything relating to Peter Ney, whose body was dug up recently in Rowan County, N. C., to see if he was the great Marshal Ney, is interesting. We have a sister who went to school to the said Peter in the year 1829. She was then nine years old, and boarded at Major Thomas Nelson's, in Mecklenburg County, Va. Mr. Ney, she says, taught school at Abbeyville in an old house which had been used as a store—a two-story house. He had a number of scholars, male and female, and was considered a first-rate teacher. He kept a reed stuck in a hole by the mantelpiece, which, when occasion required, he would pull out and use vigorously on the bad boys. One day the little school-girl aforesaid, in company with some of her companions, ran up into the garret, where the old fellow did his painting, and was surprised to see a portrait he had painted of Bonaparte. He painted flowers also, and beautifully, and made poetry. Saturdays he frequently got drunk, and when in that condition he talked about Bonaparte, and said he himself was Marshal Ney. The same little school-girl, now an old lady, distinctly remembers his bald head and a long, deep cut on the left side. She says, as she stood up by him to say her lesson, many a time she felt like putting her finger on the scar. Whether Peter Ney was Marshal Ney or not, there is something very mysterious about his history."

General W. W. Harllee, Florence, S. C. (1888) : "About the year 1840—I forget the exact date—the Governor of South Carolina attended a military review of the State troops. A great many persons were present, and it was an occasion of much interest. The governor invited Peter S. Ney to act as an honorary aide-de-camp. Mr. Ney accepted the invitation, and appeared with the governor on the review mounted on a magnificent charger, which had been procured for him. I think he was without doubt the finest-looking man I ever saw. He was well dressed, and his bearing was superb. He was every inch the soldier. His military form and carriage, his easy, graceful horsemanship, his commanding presence attracted every one's attention. Numerous inquiries were made about him, and he really attracted more attention than the governor himself." *

Hon. J. G. Hall, Hickory, N. C. : " I have often heard of Peter S. Ney. I lived in the county (Iredell) where he taught school for several years. People generally looked upon Mr. Ney with a sort of awe, and thought that he was privileged to drink a little too much. It was a kind of dispensation which even the strictest Presbyterians allowed him—a concession to the man's superiority and greatness."

Dr. Robert H. Dalton, Los Angeles, Cal. (1870) : " I began to practise medicine on the 1st day of May, 1827, in Guilford County, N. C., at a place now called Hillsdale. Some time in 1827 or 1828 a gentleman put up at the hotel where I boarded, and remained several days. He purported to be on his way to Raleigh to confer with the governor of the State in relation to writing the history of North Carolina, and we understood that he had been engaged to do the work. He soon seemed to take to my little office, and was much interested in my small new library, composed of a fair selection of standard medical books and a few choice historical, literary, and poetical works. I shall ever remember a remark he made more than once while standing and looking at my books, so nicely arranged in the little case : ' A few books well read are worth thousands kept to ornament the shelves. Know all in these books, young man, and you will be great.'

* This incident proves that P. S. Ney was highly esteemed by the best men in the country. In antebellum days it was a great honor to be an aide-de-camp of the Governor of South Carolina.

When P. S. Ney first came to the United States his motto was, " Fuge magna"—be modest, be humble, avoid publicity. In the present instance the temptation was probably too strong to be resisted. On all other occasions he seems to have avoided the public eye. In 1846—the year in which he died—he was invited by a friend to attend the Commencement exercises of the State University. His reply was : " No, no, I can't go ; obscurity is my splendor." In his private register he wrote, " Who can be always watching ?"

"We soon understood that he was a Frenchman, and that his name was Ney, though his language betrayed no brogue, but was clear, chaste, and exceedingly fluent. When talking with me he spoke feelingly of Baron Larrey, Napoleon's great surgeon, and seemed delighted to dwell on his character and exploits, relating many incidents and anecdotes which I have never seen in print, proving his great intimacy with that great man.* On evenings at tea and until bedtime we drew him out on subjects involving the history of the French Revolution, and it was very evident that no one but an actual participant in that wonderful drama could have delineated the facts and incidents with such positive clearness and precision; and I am sure that the bitterest enemy of Napoleon and his cause could not have arisen from these discussions with opinions adverse to his honor and his merit. He denied that Napoleon was a tyrant, but represented him as a providential agent of reformation, designed to ameliorate the condition of his people by inaugurating free institutions for France, which could not be done on account of the selfish interest and jealousy of all the crowned heads of Europe, whose very existence depended on the maintenance of absolute government for all the nationalities; that in defence of these just and holy principles he was perpetually assailed by these despotic powers; and for the preservation of his people and their righteous cause he was forced to centralize the powers of the nation to repel invasion; and that for these reasons there never was a time when he could possibly have carried out his views. Hence the empire, with all its semblance of military government. . . . He was, I think, fully six feet high, neither corpulent nor lean, with a florid complexion and auburn hair. His head was large, and

---

* Larrey and Ney had much in common. Both were honest, gentle, merciful, rough, blunt, candid, self-denying, patriotic, brave, plain, practical, strong-minded, persevering, and devoted to *duty*. They must have been great friends. This is evident from Larrey's "Memoirs." "Come here," said Larrey to the soldiers who were slightly wounded, "or I will cut off your ears." One day he said to Napoleon, with great bluntness and boldness, "Let every man attend to his own business." Napoleon said at St. Helena that Larrey was the "most virtuous man that he had ever known."

high behind. He wore no beard ; and his face, though handsome, showed what are called weather-beaten marks. He was a man of the noblest physique and most commanding appearance I ever saw. I remember well the scar on his head, but I had not the temerity to ask about its cause. In discussing the dynasties of Europe in connection with Napoleon, he seemed to enter into the very essence of their constitutions, and his criticisms made a lasting impression on my mind. Taking him altogether, I am sure he was the finest specimen of humanity, physically and mentally, I ever knew. If he lived till 1854 he must have been very old. I ventured once, by way of ascertaining whether he was Marshal Ney or not, to ask him if he was related to the family of that name. I can never forget his startled look. He gave me an evasive answer, which I took as a rebuke for my impertinence. I have seen and conversed with many great men, but with none greater than Peter Stuart Ney."

Mrs. Sarah Anna (Locke) Campbell, Jerseyville, Ill. (1887) : " My maiden name was Sarah Anna Locke. I knew Mr. Ney very well. He often visited my father's house. He was a large man, with a dark red face badly pitted from the smallpox. His nose was very large—not a peaked one. He was a swift runner and a fine horseman. When at the house of my father (Major John Locke) he would often pull down my long back hair and say, sometimes with tears, ' It is just like my wife's.' He often talked about his wife and children. According to my recollection, he said he had three sons, and that his wife was living. He was very kind-hearted—too much so, indeed, for his own good. When he had more trouble than he could bear he would take to drinking sprees. He had no use, however, for any but the best people, and was highly respected."

Mrs. B. G. Worth, Wilmington, N. C. (1887) : " My grandfather, Judge Archibald D. Murphey, believed that Peter S. Ney was Marshal Ney. He taught school in Judge Murphey's family, and my mother was greatly attached to him. She thought him one of the kindest and best men that ever lived. Judge Murphey had the highest opinion of his ability and character. He and Mr. Ney were great friends. Mr. Ney would sometimes stroke my sister's hair and say, 'You look just like my wife, with your dark eyes and your long black hair.'"

Hon. David L. Swain, President of the University of North Carolina (1868) : "I have been familiar with the name and handwriting of P. S. Ney (so called) for about forty years. General James Cook, a lawyer, who died in Mocksville, N. C., some years since, whom I knew very familiarly, went to school to Ney forty years ago and was a firm believer in his marshalship, and entertained lofty ideas of his abilities and attainments. More than thirty years ago Judge Murphey employed Ney to copy historical manuscripts and tracts. He was a neat and ready copyist. Pliny Miles had some manuscripts which once belonged to P. S. Ney. I frankly told him that, in my opinion, his hero was not Marshal Ney. Mr. Miles seemed to be firmly convinced that he was."

Giles E. Mumford, Mocksville, N. C. (1877) : "I was a pupil of Peter S. Ney when he taught one mile north of Mocksville in 1832. He always had a full school. At that time fifteen or twenty grown young men were going to him. I lived in Mocksville, and Mr. Ney got me to bring his mail to him. Thomas McNeely (I think) was postmaster. One Monday morning I came rather late to school. I found my copy-books all ready for writing, and the larger scholars were all out studying their lessons. Mr. Ney always allowed the larger scholars to do so. He took several newspapers. One was the *Watchman*, printed by H. C. Jones, Salisbury. Mr. Ney always read the *Watchman* first, for he wrote a good deal for that paper. If you will see Mr. Bruner, the present editor, you may find several pieces from his pen. His signature was 'O.' When I handed Mr. Ney his mail that morning he stopped writing and opened the *Watchman* and commenced reading. He always read the poetry and deaths and marriages first. As soon as he opened the paper he became deathly pale, rose from his desk, walked to the middle of the room, threw the paper on the floor, jumped on it with both feet, and stamped it to pieces before saying a word. After trampling it to atoms, he said with a perfect tremor, ' Now, damn you, lie there ! ' * He then turned to the scholars in the room and said, ' School is dismissed.' The scholars, not knowing what was the matter, for they were all small, commenced gathering hat and bonnets, which made so much noise that the larger scholars came in and asked Mr. Ney what was the matter. ' Young Napoleon,' said he, ' is dead, and my hopes are all blasted. I can't go back to France.' Mr. Ney commanded the greatest respect from his scholars. We all loved him, I think, as a father. When the news got to Mocksville, the most influential men of the place came up to the schoolhouse and tried to get Mr. Ney to continue the school, but he taught no more for some weeks."

James McCulloh, Mocksville, N. C. (1888) : "I knew P. S. Ney. He came to my father's house one day about the year 1834 or 1835. His eyes quickly fell on a picture of young Napoleon Bonaparte, which was hanging upon the wall. He immediately went to it and stood looking at it intently for some time. When he turned away his eyes were full of tears. ' If that boy had lived,' said he, ' I should not be here.' I have the picture now. Young Napoleon appears to be about twenty years old, and is quite fine-looking. He is dressed in a uniform, with a sword in his hand. Size of picture, about 14 × 12 inches. Underneath are the words, ' Young Napoleon Bonaparte.' "

Rev. E. F. Rockwell, D.D., Iredell County, N. C. (1886) : " When Peter S. Ney was living in this part of the country —say from 1830–42—there was a general belief among all classes, especially those who knew him, that he was the celebrated marshal of the First Empire. Indeed, if he was not Marshal Ney, it is very difficult to tell who he was, for Peter S. Ney bore a striking resemblance to Marshal Ney. It is

---

* P. S. Ney was exceedingly careful not to use profane language in the presence of his pupils. His usual by-words were, ''By Jove !" "By the powers !" "Dash your hide !" etc. In the present instance his grief was simply overpowering. Mr. Burgess Gaither, who was present when Mr. Ney read the announcement of young Napoleon's death, does not think he used the profane language attributed to him by Mr. Mumford.

thought by many persons that the Hon. George Bancroft is in Ney's secret. The writer of this a few years ago, through a friend in New York, addressed a note to him, which was taken to him at his office; but he did not reply. More recently a lawyer in New York, Hiram B. Crosby, wrote to him, and received the following reply :

"'NEWPORT, R. I., October 2, 1877.

"' DEAR SIR : On the subject to which you refer in your letter of September 6th, I have no information beyond that which is open to all the world. I return the document which you enclosed to me, and if you yourself take an interest in the investigation, I am very sorry to be wholly unable to further your inquiries.

"' I remain, dear sir,
"' Very respectfully yours,
"' GEORGE BANCROFT.'

"The 'document' referred to is the copy of a letter to Mr. Crosby relative to the Ney mystery. Mr. Crosby says that Mr. Bancroft's letter is a 'singular one,' and that he is at a loss to understand his position unless he is under a pledge of secrecy to reveal nothing. He expressed an intention to go and see Mr. Bancroft in person.* Mr. Ney kept very close

---

* Mr. Bancroft's letter is indeed a "singular one." Why did he not say plainly that he knew nothing about the subject to which Mr. Crosby and Dr. Rockwell referred ? Of course the "information" of which he speaks was "open to all the world." No one could deny that. Very diplomatic. "I am very sorry to be wholly unable to further your inquiries"—morally unable. Sir Walter Scott said on one occasion, "Upon my honor, I am not the author of 'Waverley.'" And yet he was. Mr. Bancroft is more modest and conscientious than Sir Walter. In 1885 Dr. Draper, of the Wisconsin Historical Society, addressed a letter to Mr. Bancroft, in which he asked him particularly if he was acquainted with the history of Peter S. Ney. Mr. Bancroft replied : "I regret that I can add nothing to your present stock of knowledge on the points to which you direct my attention." This letter is more "singular" than the first. Fortunately I have some information which may throw a good deal of light upon Mr. Bancroft's letters. Dr. Bingham, of Mocksville, N. C., says : "My father, Lemuel Bingham, who was intimately acquainted with Peter S. Ney, told me that he once read a letter which Mr. Bancroft had written to Peter S.

here when teaching; corresponded with the *National Intelligencer* at Washington; had a large sum of money to his credit in the old United States Bank; but he never went to any of the large cities. He could not bear Murat or Grouchy; blamed Napoleon for the Russian campaign and for repudiating Josephine. She and her daughter Hortense were great friends of his wife. His wife, he said, had dark eyes and hair, and was very beautiful. He was athletic, with great power of command, great fascination and discernment of character. When Louis Philippe in 1830 mounted the throne of France, he came near cutting his throat. His friends had great difficulty in quieting him. They had a worse time of it still when young Bonaparte died in 1832. He was greatly attached to Mr. Houston, who had more influence over him than any one else. The manuscripts which P. S. Ney said contained 'something which would astonish the world' were carried off by Pliny Miles, of New York, under the plea of taking them to Europe to be translated, and were never returned. The stenography was Ney's own system, and his pupils here alone understood it. No doubt Miles was employed by some one to suppress these documents. Mr. Crosby searched and found where he had lived, but he died, and left nothing—no property or manuscripts.* Some time after Mr. Ney came to this country he was at Darlington, S. C., at a hotel, on a cold day, seated by the fire, partly intoxicated. A stranger was present who had travelled extensively, and told the company some things he had seen. He had been at the grave of Marshal Ney. Our Mr. Ney roused up and said, 'You may have been there, but Ney was not there.' On another occasion P. S. Ney said that Ney's bones could not be found on the soil of France. I have heard that P. S. Ney broke his sword when young Napoleon died, but I forget the name of my informant. It was also reported that some of his letters came to him through the French consul at

Ney, in which he spoke gratefully of some kindness which had been shown him either by P. S. Ney himself or by his family in France."

* Pliny Miles died on the island of Malta in 1865. He left no papers bearing upon the Ney controversy. No one knows what became of the Ney manuscript. Dr. Rockwell's surmises may be correct.

NO. 3. EXAMPLES OF P. S. NEY'S HANDWRITING.

NO. 4. EXAMPLES OF MARSHAL NEY'S HANDWRITING.

Norfolk or some other influential personage at Norfolk. This is a mere rumor, so far as I know. Mr. Ney is the author of the device on the seal of Davidson College: a man's right hand grasping a dagger, with the point downward, piercing a coiled serpent not far from the head. The hilt of the weapon has rising from it a star or flame that casts rays through the surrounding space. This is encircled by two rings, between which is the legend in Latin, 'Alenda lux ubi orta est libertas' (Light must be sustained where liberty arose), alluding, we suppose, to the Mecklenburg declaration of May 20th, 1775. But there seems to be an incongruity between the radiation of light and the handle of a dagger. It seems to have been customary to set valuable jewels in the hilt of such weapons. The largest diamond known is called Kohinoor, or Mountains of Light, is rose cut, and belongs to Queen Victoria. The second or third in size is called the Pitt diamond. It decorated the hilt of the sword of state of the first Napoleon, was taken by the Prussians at Waterloo, and now belongs to the King of Prussia.* We infer, then, that Mr. Ney, having been familiar with the sight of this most brilliant gem in the hilt of Napoleon's sword, had it before his mind when he drew the device for the seal of Davidson College. I would like to have the opinion of some military men about the idea of originating and sustaining light from the hilt of a sword."

Rev. J. L. Gay, Fayette, Mo. (1888): "In 1827 Peter S. Ney taught school in Iredell County, about twenty miles from Salisbury. I was one of his pupils, and I remember him well. He had some hair at the back and on each side of his head, which was of a reddish or sandy color, though it was then

---

* It is now owned by Sir William Fraser, of London. It has "jewels set in the upper part."

After Eylau, Napoleon attended a special service at Nôtre Dame to give thanks for his victory, etc. Pasquier ("Memoirs") says: "A sword glittering with precious stones was at his side, and the famous diamond called the Regent formed its pommel."

There are two or three statues of Napoleon in Paris where he is represented as grasping with his right hand the hilt of a dagger or short (Roman) sword. The weapon is held in a perpendicular position, the point being downward.

turning gray. His lower face was striking: the heavy jaws, the firmly set mouth, the prominent double chin gave him an air of the most determined resolution. He did not look like a Frenchman; had a Saxon or Scottish-Saxon look. Spoke English well, though you could detect a foreign accent. Was fond of music; had concerts in his school. He wore a long bluish-gray broadcloth surtout cut in the old-fashioned transition style that was common in the first quarter of this century. On the outside of this coat were capacious pockets shielded with large flaps. His shoes were broad of sole, buckled, and always neatly polished. There were no lapels to his coat, and the skirts of it nearly touched his feet. His fame as a pedagogue had preceded him. He had taught school at two or three places in North Carolina before he came to my neighborhood. Everywhere we heard that he was a great teacher. Although I had earlier teachers—two or three for short terms —yet P. S. Ney was the first who really taught me anything worth knowing, or who started me out on the road leading to learning. As we had very inferior and imperfect maps, and no globes for teaching geography, I remember that Mr. Ney directed me to bring him a medium-sized and well-rounded pumpkin, and with this he constructed a geographical globe. He marked out upon the ribs of it the lines of longitude and transversely those of latitude and other lines—the equatorial and the Arctic and Antarctic lines. In the use of the pen and the qualities and powers of numerals he was equally painstaking. He was a dull scholar indeed, or a perverse one, who did not learn to write well and did not obtain a fair insight into the wonderful powers of numeral figures. And I gratefully remember, too, his sympathetic interest in our plays and athletic sports; how agile he was at an age (approaching sixty) when other men are usually oppressed with inertia. He was always as ready to help his pupils in their hours of play as in those of their study. How kind and gentle he was! I delight to recall him as he then appeared at our school and in the walks and playgrounds around it—tall, erect, but slightly bending under the weight of years, broad-shouldered, large-chested, with a kindly beaming eye, yet blazing up instantly when anything unusual awoke him from his repose. His whole countenance would at once show the most evident marks of his emotion. In this connection I recall his appearance as we were marching on the morning of our school exhibition to the place—the wide piazza in front of Mr. Gracey's house—where we were to speak our little pieces and perform our allotted parts. An improvised country band was gotten together, and were playing such airs as they were equal to. Simple and primitive as the music was, it had an almost electric effect upon our old teacher, for he straightened himself up and instantly caught the old military fire and manner of his army life. Everybody noticed it, but Mr. Ney said nothing about it. At that performance I experienced much needed encouragement from the dear old man, for, like most boys, it was with me the critical moment of my life. With glad hearts we were released from school, saddened only with the thought that we would have to part with our dear old master, and probably never see him again. One day at school one of the older scholars asked him if he were related to Marshal Ney, as he had the same name. 'Yes,' he replied, with some show of annoyance at the question or the questioner—'yes, some connection'—a nephew I think he said—and turned away, and so abruptly closed the subject. This, with the admission that he had been in the Napoleonic wars and had been wounded in some battle or other, was all that we could get out of him. It began indeed to be surmised that he was none other than Marshal Ney himself; but it was only an idle surmise, that, like thousands of others, was dropped, and so passed out of our minds."

Rev. R. H. Morrison, D.D., formerly President of Davidson College, North Carolina, Lowesville, N. C. (1885): "I knew Peter S. Ney. As far as I could learn, his conduct was upright and marked by propriety except when drinking to intemperance, and even then he seemed to avoid collision with others. There were some points in his behavior so different from the ordinary pursuits of men as rendered it difficult to account for them. He avoided towns and cities and sought schools in the country, and seemed to care for only a bare support, when he might, from his talents and attainments, have obtained much more profitable positions. He also avoided efforts to gain the honors and distinctions in society which learning and integrity often prompt men to seek. He evidently had strong motives to avoid notoriety. He taught school in my neighborhood, and one of my sons went to school to him. He was a fine scholar and a good teacher. He sometimes attended my preaching, and gave the most respectful attention to the services of the sanctuary, as a courteous gentleman always does."

Hon. Victor C. Barringer, N. C. (1887): "When I saw him [P. S. Ney] he was always duly sober, and nobody could be more silently polite, less pretentious, or less likely to excite remark or notice. Pliny Miles told me he had found a treasure in the manuscript shorthand of Ney, which he admitted he could not read; but he was sure it was a golden egg."

P. H. Cain, Felix, Davie County, N. C. (1886): "I was a pupil of P. S. Ney in 1831. He was the grandest of men. Saw him in the latter part of 1832. He said, 'By Jove! old boy, I came near killing myself since I saw you. The d——d rascals have poisoned young Napoleon, and my hopes of returning to France are forever blasted.' He then spoke of his wife and children; said he once knew what happiness was, but that he should never see his family again; spoke of his wife with a good deal of emotion; had soldiers shot for insulting or outraging ladies; gave me and another student lessons in loading and shooting—shot some himself at our target practice; said he and Napoleon's brother-in-law were equally matched in fencing—frequently up till ten o'clock at night; that Napoleon made them quit, saying something serious might result from it; said to me and another student at our target practice that if we should ever go into the artillery service to keep well behind our guns when firing. He believed in early marriages; said young people as a rule ought to get married when they are twenty-one years old, but not before. In 1832 Mr. Ney appeared to be sixty-five or seventy years old."

Colonel C. C. Graham, Memphis, Tenn. (1885): "I saw

P. S. Ney sometimes at county musters. When slightly intoxicated he could handle a company or battalion with great skill, showing a fine knowledge of military tactics."

J. H. Ennis, editor *North Carolina Farmer*, Raleigh, N. C. (October, 1887): "I knew P. S. Ney in Salisbury, N. C. I have often talked with him. He was a man of rare intelligence; could talk well on almost any subject. A man of fine common sense. Took a practical view of things. Would drink too much sometimes, but was never quarrelsome, though very talkative. Appeared to have some great trouble on his mind and trying to get rid of it or to avoid thinking of it. He appeared to be of Scotch-Irish descent. Eyes rather large and extraordinarily searching. Chin very prominent, square and curved or stuck up at the end. Nose a little hooked at the end; wings of his nose very broad and full. Lips compressed, not sensual-looking. Rather duck-legged, though his legs were well suited to his body. He was at all times polite and gentlemanly; there was no letting down in his demeanor. He was highly respected by everybody."

Dr. John A. Allison, Statesville, N. C. (1887): "I was well acquainted with Peter S. Ney. He taught school near the residence of my father, Colonel Thomas A. Allison, some three or four years, and I was his pupil the greater part of the time. He boarded at my father's house, or, rather, he was an honored guest, for my father and mother thought so much of him that they would never look upon him as a boarder. Mr. Ney was about five feet eleven inches in height. He was broad and full all the way from the hips up, yet exceedingly well proportioned. He had a fine head, large and roundish, rather long from forehead to back. Forehead large and full, especially near the eyes. Perceptive faculties unusually well developed. He had a magnetic eye. He could just make you love him and fear him and obey him too. Nose large, particularly at the base, and slightly turned up at the end. Lips medium—my impression is they were rather thin. Considerable distance between his nose and upper lip. Was very neat in his person and dress. A fine horseback-rider, though he seldom rode a horse. We had a fiery, vicious horse that no one seemed to be able to ride. Mr. Ney mounted him one day and rode him with the utmost ease. Everybody was astonished at his horsemanship. A splendid marksman. He sometimes went out hunting with me. I never saw him miss a squirrel. He would hit him every time. Every pupil who studied hard was a favorite of Mr. Ney, but the bad, idle boys were pretty severely dealt with. Still, they all loved their teacher. The best fencer, perhaps, in the whole country. His skill was perfectly marvellous. I have seen splendid swordsmen stand in front of him and try to hit him, but they couldn't touch him. He would play with them as if they were little babies. When he became tired of the fun he would tap them on the side of the head and say it was time to stop. One day near the barn he picked up two large corn-stalks, and handing one to me, said, ' Now we'll fence a little.' We went at it, but it so happened that his corn-stalk broke all to pieces ; then I managed to hit him a pretty good lick, but I was badly frightened. I thought he would get mad, but he didn't. He patted me on the head and said it was all right. One day, in the winter of 1840 or 1841, Mr. Ney went to Statesville and stayed away three or four days. He seldom went to town, and we were uneasy about him. He finally came back intoxicated, and told my mother that he had been with his son in Statesville. Upon inquiry we found that a young man, evidently a foreigner, well dressed and of good appearance, had been in Statesville for some days past, and that he and Mr. Ney had been constant companions. The young man was very quiet and reserved, and did not tell any one who he was or what was his business. Mr. Ney kept perfectly sober while the man was with him, but as soon as he left he got drunk. He went home, burned up some papers, and was greatly depressed for several days. Mr. Ney had an old hair trunk, in which he kept his papers written in shorthand, paintings, drawings, etc. I used to get a glance at them sometimes, though he always kept his trunk locked. He had another trunk which contained his clothing, etc. He was not so particular about this one. My father thought Ney had a sword in his hair trunk. I heard Milus Bailey say that Mr.

Ney told him some time in the thirties that he was Marshal Ney. Bailey had somewhere procured a picture of Ney's execution. He showed it to Mr. Ney. Mr. Ney said, 'That is not correct. The positions are wrong, etc.* Some day I'll draw it for you. Ney was not shot. I felt safe as soon as I knew that the old soldiers composed the firing party.' I knew Barr, the German, who recognized Mr. Ney as Marshal Ney at a public gathering not far from Statesville.† Barr was an old soldier, covered with wounds, and would fight in a minute if any one doubted his word. He was a thoroughly reliable man, a real stanch, honest old fellow. Mr. Ney walked rather quickly, but with firm military tread; he infused into his pupils a military spirit; said it would not hurt them, and might be of great benefit to them in after life. He had his bywords, such as 'By Jove!' 'Dash your skin of you!' sometimes 'God dash your skin of you!' He did very little square cursing, only when he got mad. He was very particular with his boys in this respect. In combing his hair he always turned it up over his ears and the top of his head. He had a wound on the left side of his head, made, I suppose, by a sabre stroke; also one in his foot. He said to me one day, 'I was in a tight place when I got that wound in my foot.' He made a great point of promptness and punctuality at home and in the school-room. Never late at breakfast; a very early riser, though he sat up late at night reading and writing. His mind was as clear as a sunbeam. He could explain a subject better than any man I ever knew. He was very useful in the neighborhood. He wrote deeds, wills, and other documents for the neighbors, told them how to doctor their horses, how to build bridges, dykes, embankments, flood-gates, etc. Without doubt he was one of the greatest men that have ever lived in this part of the country. My father was firmly convinced that he was Marshal Ney, and so were the most intelligent people of this section."

William M. Haynes, St. Louis, Mo. (1887): "I went to

* This is no doubt true. The common representations of Ney's execution (see Abbott's "Napoleon") are notoriously inaccurate.
† See testimony of Mr. William Sidney Stevenson.

school to P. S. Ney when he taught at Colonel Allison's, not far from Statesville. I was but a boy at the time, but he made a lasting impression on my mind. When under the influence of strong drink he was perfectly harmless and very liberal. He would thrust his hand in his large vest-pocket and take out a handful of small silver coin and scatter it broadcast before the boys. It greatly amused him to see them scramble after it. I never heard him use profane or indecent language. When sober he would not refer to his past life (except in some of his poetry), but would occasionally speak about it when partially intoxicated. When not especially engaged in school duties he seemed to be engrossed in deep thought."

W. H. Trott, Newton, N. C. (1890): "I went to school to P. S. Ney. He walked quickly, and took tolerably short steps. High, full forehead, especially near the eyes. Eyebrows beetling, so heavy and projecting as partly to hide his eyes when he looked at you. Eyes keen beyond description. Very strict as a teacher, but good-natured and obliging. Conducted his school in a sort of military style. Everybody had to toe the mark. Sometimes called the boys pet names—called Fred Leinster Duke or Dunk.* He looked somewhat like Judge Armfield,† though Armfield would run quicker than Ney. Armfield is a brave man and wouldn't run, but he would run quicker than Ney. Ney was a perfect bull-dog—never let go his hold. Ruled everybody. I never saw any one like him."

Mrs. Hall, Newton, N. C. (December, 1891): "I was acquainted with Peter S. Ney. He was a very large man, weighing, I suppose, about two hundred pounds. His eyes were keen and sparkling. His nose was broad at the base and slightly turned up, or appeared to be so. He was very kind-hearted. He once gave me a pair of fine gloves, and

---

* See testimony of Frederick Leinster.
† Hon. R. F. Armfield, a judge of the Superior Court, Statesville, N. C. Judge Armfield is a large man, of fine presence, great force of character, and one of the ablest lawyers in the United States. Mrs. Dalton thinks P. S. Ney looked a little like Judge Armfield. So does Mr. William Sidney Stevenson.

would have given me a more costly present if I had consented to accept it. One day he went with a party of girls to hunt strawberries. He would pick a handful with great care, and then go and put them in the basket. He was very fond of children, and they all loved him. I once heard Mr. Ney say that some of Napoleon's officers who were condemned to be shot escaped by putting on their wives' dresses,* but that he could not escape in that way, because his wife was a small woman† and he was a large man. He possessed great force of character, and no man stood higher in the community in which he lived."

Wilfred Turner, Turnersburg, Iredell County, N. C. (1883) : " I was a pupil of P. S. Ney in 1825 and 1826, and saw him afterward from time to time until his death in 1846. In 1825 his hair was getting gray, though you could easily see that it was originally of an auburn or reddish-sandy color. His head was bald on top, and his face appeared to be marked from the small-pox. No pupil, however dull, could fail to learn something from him—more, doubtless, than he could have learned from any other teacher. He applied the hickory freely to bad boys, especially to the big bad boys, but he was very indulgent to the smaller children, and to all, indeed, who were obedient and showed a disposition to study. He had a quick temper, but never did any one an intentional wrong. He was too noble for that. If he found out that he had wounded any person's feelings, he would seek him out and apologize. He did much good in our community."

Frederick Leinster, Statesville, N. C. (1884) : " I went to school to Peter S. Ney in 1846. He used to call me *duke*, because my name was Leinster ; said he knew the Duke of Leinster, and didn't like him ; once had a difficulty with him. It seems to me he said the Duke of Leinster gave him that cut on the head. I know he said he didn't like him, and that there had been some trouble between them. He used to pet me at times. We boarded at the same house. One of his

---

* Notably Lavalette. He probably meant him.
† "Madame Ney was tall and slight."—"Memoirs of Madame de Rémusat.

scholars had been to school to Bishop Ives, at Valle Crucis, and was very much stuck up—thought he knew about as much as Mr. Ney. One day, in reciting his Latin lesson, Mr. Ney stopped him and said, 'That translation is not correct.' 'Well,' said the boy impatiently, 'that is the way they taught me at Valle Crucis.' 'Did they?' said Mr. Ney; 'we want no dog Latin here.' He then gave the boy a few good raps with his hickory switch. We heard no more of Valle Crucis.''

Joseph Barber, Cleveland, N. C. (1887) : '' I was a pupil of P. S. Ney. He carried on his school in military style. Made his pupils, when spelling, stand with their feet together, toes turned out, hands down, perfectly erect. On one occasion I was a little perverse—I stood with my feet a considerable distance apart. Mr. Ney came along and put his big foot on mine and mashed it pretty hard. I did not forget the lesson. His scholars thought he was the greatest man on earth. My sister fairly worshipped him.''

Joseph McKnight, Hickory, N. C. (1886) : '' I have often seen Peter S. Ney. He looked like a soldier, and seemed born to command. He had a deep, powerful voice, which carried much force with it. Large ears, stood off somewhat from his head. His head was tremendous, but it just suited his body. Rather fat underneath the chin, which was very large. He kept the strictest order in his school. Sometimes the parents of his pupils would visit him, but if they began to talk or whisper in ever so low a tone he would check them, it mattered not who they were. Discipline, he said, had to be maintained.''

Mr. James Andrews, Houstonville, Iredell County, N. C. (1883) : '' I knew P. S. Ney for many years. I owned a mill not far from the place where he boarded when he taught school in this part of the country, and he used often to come to the mill as well as to my house and have pleasant and familiar talks with me. One day, in my mill, he took up a handful of wheat out of a hogshead which contained two or three bushels of the grain, and turning to me, said, 'Joemes, if a man had had this much wheat in the Russian campaign, it would have been worth a fortune to him. Men were starving on every hand, and those that were able would mortgage whole estates and give everything they had for a loaf of bread.' He has told me a great deal about his army life, but I cannot remember all that he said. He spoke of the great sufferings which his men endured, and that seemed to hurt him more than anything else. He said that in crossing a certain river— I forget the name *—so many men were killed or wounded or drowned that they almost formed a bridge over which the others could walk. He blamed Napoleon for dividing his army, when the retreat began, into so many separate columns, with two or three days' march between them. He said that it was perfectly ruinous; that the whole army ought to have retreated in one compact body, and to have fought its way directly through. He said that in doing so the army would have encountered many difficulties, but that there were many more difficulties in the other plan of marching in separate columns. He said that he put the stragglers and disbanded men between his main body and the Russians, so that the Russians might fall on them first.† It was a desperate measure, he said, but he had to do it, sometimes at the point of the bayonet. A Russian woman and her daughter came to him one day and swore that one of his officers had committed rape upon the daughter the night before. The officer was tried and sentenced to be shot. He afterward found out that the accusation was false; that it was gotten up by a man who wanted the officer's place, and he had him court-martialed and shot. Discipline, he said, had to be preserved. In speaking

---

* The Beresina, I suppose—hardly the Dnieper.

† "The enemy opened upon them with the whole of his artillery. The disarmed stragglers, of whom there were still between three and four thousand, took the alarm. This disorderly multitude wandered to and fro, running about in utter uncertainty, and attempted to throw themselves into the ranks of the soldiers, who drove them back. Ney contrived to keep them *between him and the Russians*, whose fire was principally absorbed by these useless beings. While the marshal was making a *rampart* of these poor wretches to cover his right flank, he regained the banks of the Dnieper, and by that means was enabled to cover his left flank."— Ségur, "Napoleon's Expedition to Russia."

of the scarcity of food, he told me one day that even before the retreat began many of the soldiers had nothing to eat but a little parched wheat. He told me more than once, when he had not tasted a drop of strong drink, that he was Marshal Ney, and how he escaped; how the soldiers fired as he gave the command; how the balls passed over him; how he was taken up and secretly conveyed to some point on the coast, where he took passage for America. I well remember the sabre cut on his head. He told me, I think, that he received it at the battle of Waterloo, in the last charge of the Old Guard. The man who wounded him was cut down by one of his aids. He saw Lord Wellington and his staff with his spyglass. He was so badly hurt that he was left behind—couldn't keep up with the army in its retreat.* It always gave him pain to speak of Napoleon's defeat at Waterloo. It was like drawing a rasp over a saw. He had wounds, it seemed to me, all over his body. There were prints of horses' hoofs on his legs and breast. He had a wound in the fleshy part of his arm above the elbow. He told me that the surgeon, Larrey, put salt in it. He said that he asked him if that was all he was going to do to the wound. 'Yes,' replied the surgeon, 'I treated the emperor so.'† Mr. Ney was a great teacher. His pupils were devoted to him, though he was strict with them, and they advanced rapidly in all their studies. He taught them to be obedient to their parents, and honest and true and merciful in their dealings with their fellow-men. He made an impression upon them which remained throughout life. He was a man of feeling heart. He did a great deal for the poor, especially the poor children of the neighborhood. He taught many of them from year to year without charging a cent for their tuition. His salary was small. He

* See Ney's letter to Fouché, Duke of Otranto.
† "I asked Napoleon if he had not been frequently slightly wounded. He replied, 'Several times. . . . At Marengo a cannon shot took away a piece of the boot of my left leg and a little of the skin,' said he, showing the mark to me, 'but I used no other application to it than a piece of linen dipped in salt and water.'"—O'Meara's "Napoleon in Exile."
"In treating General Cammas, I applied over the whole wound linen dipped in salt water."—Larrey.

taught for $200 a year and his board. He had a good deal of fun and humor about him, loved a joke, and would sometimes take out of his pocket a handful of small change and scatter it over the grass to see the boys scramble for it. It appeared to amuse him very much. He told me that he could speak the English language when he came to this country; that his mother was a Scotchwoman, and taught it to him in his youth. I think he said, though I am not certain, that his father went to Scotland to escape persecution, and there married a Scotchwoman who was related to a Presbyterian clergyman. Her maiden name was Stuart, or she was related to some family of that name. He dearly loved his wife and children, though I do not think he gave me their names. He spoke of them often, and said it was sweet to think that some day he should see them again and die among his own people. After the death of Napoleon's son he gave up all hope of going back to France. I felt very sorry for him, for I never saw any one grieve so much. I do not think he ever got over it. He told me that if it were known in France that he was living in the United States, his friends in France, who aided in his escape, would suffer severely, and that his own life would be in danger, for his enemies would not hesitate to hire some one to come over and assassinate him. In teaching, he would not allow his pupils to undertake more than they could do. He said it was better to know a little well than to have a smattering of a great deal. I remember two of his bywords: 'By Jove!' and 'By the powers!' He taught school in several places in this part of the country. I don't think he wished to remain permanently in any one place. He was braver than Julius Cæsar or anybody else, in my opinion; but I think he had good reasons for changing about as he did. Mr. Ney was not a religious man, though he was a firm believer in the Bible. Not long before he died he said to me, 'Jeemes, hold on to your religion. It is a good thing to have. Don't let it go.' I loved Mr. Ney. Indeed, I feel that it is the greatest privilege and honor of my life to have known such a man."

Matthew Brandon, Elmwood, N. C. (1887): "I was well acquainted with Peter S. Ney. Saw him often at the mineral springs, in Lincoln County, N. C., in 1842. I was with him almost every day for two or three months, and I can truly say that I never knew a man with a sounder, stronger mind, or a kinder heart. He seemed to take a liking to me, and we often had long talks in his room. He read a great deal ; had several books in his room. He had one book, a good-sized volume, on Napoleon and his wars, which he generally kept locked up in his trunk. I forget the name of this book, but it was full of criticisms or notes in his own handwriting. He allowed me to look through the book on several occasions, but would not let me carry it out of his room. The book contained an account of the execution of Marshal Ney. Just opposite this account, on the margin of the book, was written, ' Ney was not shot.' There was no other comment. He was reticent about his history, and I did not feel at liberty to ask him any questions. He didn't court company ; stayed much in his room, though he was polite and affable to all who approached him. He was wrinkled, and looked sunburned and weatherbeaten. In his notes on Waterloo he called Grouchy a ' traitor.' He couldn't get over his failure to come to Waterloo. He corrected some mistakes of history, and explained certain points which the writer did not seem to understand or failed to make clear. ' If Grouchy had come up,' he said one day, ' Wellington would have been swept away.' Often alluded to Grouchy ; had no fancy for him ; he didn't obey orders. It always excited him to talk about the battle of Waterloo. I never saw him under the influence of strong drink. It was said that he would sometimes get drunk, but I certainly never saw him in that condition, though, as I have said, I was with him almost every day for two or three months. His head was always clear when I saw him. My wife was very fond of him, and showed him much attention. He was very grateful for her kindness. He was quite a lion at the springs. Much consideration was shown him by every one."

General John A. Young, Charlotte, N. C. (1885) : " I was well acquainted with Peter S. Ney ; was his pupil when he taught in Iredell County, near the residence of Colonel Placebo Houston. He was a man of marvellous strength and vigor, both of body and mind. He never seemed to need any recreation or rest, was little affected either by heat or cold, slept little (only about four or five hours during the night), and was always ready and in good condition for work. His eyes were different from any that I ever saw. When he was in a good humor they were very soft and gentle, but when he became angry or excited they would change almost with the rapidity of lightning—and indeed they looked like lightning. At such times few men could look at him with composure. You felt that he was entire master of the situation. His lips were not thin, though they came firmly together ; nose and head large ; his hair was turning gray when I first saw him. It must have been originally sandy or auburn. He had a florid complexion, and his face was marked with the small-pox. As a teacher I do not hesitate to say that I have never seen his equal. He would explain any question in such a way that no pupil, not even the dullest, could fail to understand it. Those who were disposed to be idle were properly punished. He made them study. He especially insisted upon three things—punctuality, good lessons, and obedience. If a pupil were punctual, and recited good lessons and obeyed him, he would grant him almost any favor. He would allow no pupil to impose upon or in any way to be unkind to another. I remember an incident which will illustrate my meaning. One of the larger boys was deeply in love with a beautiful young lady in the neighborhood. The lady in question was not disposed to favor his suit, and the young man was greatly dejected. The boys laughed at him a good deal, and Mr. Ney himself one day teased him a little about it ; but seeing that the young fellow was hurt by his bantering, quickly desisted. In a little while the boys went out into the grove to play. They formed a circle about the disconsolate lover, and began to jeer him worse than ever. Mr. Ney saw us, and came out quickly to the playground. I can see him now, erect, dignified, his hands crossed behind him under his long blue broadcloth coat, his eyes sparkling, with a grave and determined face, as fine a specimen of genuine manhood as any one ever beheld. ' Boys,' said he, ' you must stop this. It isn't just ; it isn't manly ; it isn't kind to tease your playfellow in this way. You must stop it instantly and forever.' It is needless to add that he was obeyed. Although he drank intoxicating liquors, and sometimes to excess, it never seemed to have any bad effect upon his boys, or, I may say, upon the people generally. He was so good and noble in every other respect that they were willing to pardon this infirmity. He taught hundreds of boys during his stay in North Carolina; and I will venture to say (for I do not speak without some knowledge of the subject) that you will find few, very few among them who became drunkards, or who ever in any way dishonored their teacher. He left an indelible impression for good upon the minds and hearts of all his pupils. He was a man of most capacious intellect. He seemed to be familiar with almost every branch of learning. He was a fine linguist, but he was especially expert in mathematics. It took him but a few moments to see through and make plain to others the most intricate problems presented to him. He always looked at everything in a practical, matter-of-fact light. He said that if a man did not have common sense, no mere knowledge of books would amount to anything. He could handle the sword with incredible skill. In the opinion of the best professional fencers, no one in this country could begin to equal him. Mr. Ney had an exceedingly kind heart. Indeed, he was so sympathetic that he would sometimes be imposed upon, and his charities would be imprudently bestowed. But he didn't care. He said it was better to do too much in that direction than to do too little. I must say that, in my opinion, a truer, gentler heart never beat in the breast of man."

David Gaither, Newton, N. C. (1886): "I was a pupil of P. S. Ney, I think in the year 1830. No one who knew him can possibly forget him. Quick-tempered, cross at times, but generally good-natured; always just. His head was full of thought. A great Whig—didn't like the Democrats. Sometimes attended Whig club meetings and made short speeches; but he wasn't much of a success as a public speaker.* Still,

* "I am no speech-maker."—Marshal Ney on his trial.

what he did say was to the point, and had great weight with those who heard him."

Major James H. Foote, Dellaplane, N. C. (1886) : "In the years 1837 and 1838 P. S. Ney was teaching on the farm of Captain Placebo Houston, and it was then I was one of his students. He was in the employment of that noble circle of citizens, Captain P. Houston, Captain John Young, Samuel Young, and Colonel Francis Young (who all lived on adjoining plantations), and was patronized by the leading men of the county. North Carolina at that time afforded no better, no more patriotic, high-toned gentlemen in her borders ; and among them, honored and loved by all, was our teacher, Peter Stuart Ney. Who he was and whence he came we knew only from himself. As a teacher none excelled him. Many of his older pupils regarded it a degradation to join any other school after leaving him. In hearing the recitations, he seldom held a book in his hand. He would criticise the military tactics of Julius Cæsar while the class recited from that author, pointing out his mistakes and blunders. His features were well marked, and readily gave expression to the passion dominant in his mind. His head was very bald, with a broad, elevated forehead, and an eye—ah ! what an eye ! He looked as if he penetrated the depths of your soul and knew your very thoughts. An air of great determination and firmness was marked by a prominent chin and resolute countenance. He always dressed well, but not fastidiously. He taught his students the art of stenography, and could himself take down a discourse *verbatim et literatim*, while the speaker was delivering it. He wrote a beautiful but plain hand, and always with a quill pen. I never heard him use profane language. He had his bywords, such as ' Dash your skin of you ! ' ' I give the lie to that ! ' etc. He had a brogue more like the Scotch, I think, than French, and still he was in every sense a thorough Frenchman. He claimed, on his mother's side, relationship with the Scotch, and always wrote his name Peter Stuart, or the initials P. S., which makes me think his mother was Scotch and not Irish, as Mr. (Burgess) Gaither thinks.*

* He could have been related both to the Scotch and the Irish, and this

Although he followed teaching as 'a visible means' of support, he was in no want of funds, for it was known that he had credit in the United States Bank at Washington City. His price for teaching was only $200 per session of ten months, including his board. He spent his money freely, but not foolishly; for no man was more charitable than he. If he saw any one, man, woman, or child, in want or distress, he would readily divide with them of what means he had in hand. He would take the poor boys in his school and charge their tuition to himself and have it deducted from his salary. His whole deportment was that of the true gentleman. He had one fault that many great men have—that of drinking at times to intoxication; and when drinking was very communicative; when sober he was rather reticent. In 1837 P. S. Ney appeared to be about seventy years old. I think he sometimes wrote his name P. S. M. Ney. These initials, I suppose, stood for Peter Stuart Michael. He often spoke of his wife and children; seemed to have the greatest affection for them. He was a great expert with the sword. When he was teaching at Mocksville (I believe), a French fencing-master came and proposed to Mr. Ney's pupils to teach them the art of fencing. They told him if he would take a tilt with their teacher and hit him they would get him up a big class. This was agreed to, and Mr. Ney was introduced to him. The fencing-master opened his trunk and invited Mr. Ney to select his sword. They repaired to the playground, and after parrying thrusts for awhile, Ney clave the Frenchman's hat in two, just brushing his ear. The professor immediately threw down his weapon and said, 'Boys, you have a master; you have no use for me.' I have heard General James Cook, who was an eye-witness, relate this incident. He never went about large cities; remained far in the interior of the country, and lived in obscurity for some purpose. I do not think he could have been a refugee for crime, one so noble in his bearing, so capable of filling any station in life. Royalty sat upon his brow, and Genius claimed him for her own. I have no

is probable. Michael is an Irish name; and certain features of Ney's face, and his temper, rather indicate that he had Irish blood in his veins.

doubt he was here for some political offence. I was a mere lad the first day I went to his school, and was afraid of him. He called me to his desk and inquired my name. Taking up his pen, and while I stood by his side, he wrote a beautiful acrostic on my name, a part of which is as follows :

> " ' Jehovah made thee what thou art,
> A youth of warm and feeling heart ;
> Make, then, thy genius and thy time
> Employ themselves in things sublime.
> Sweet are the musings of the just ;
> Heaven always holds their lives in trust.'

From that moment he won my heart."

John A. Butler, County Line, N. C. (1888) : " My father, L. Q. C. Butler, was well acquainted with Peter S. Ney. He was his pupil for a long time, and thoroughly understood his system of stenography. Mr. Ney said to him one day, pointing to a desk which contained his private papers, ' In that desk is a document written in shorthand. After my death I wish you to get it and translate it. There is something in it that will astonish the world.' I have heard my father speak of the conversation often. Mr. Ney died in November, 1846, and my father did not hear of his death until several months afterward. He went at once to the residence of Mr. O. G. Foard, where Mr. Ney died ; but Mr. Pliny Miles, of the New York Historical Society, had already obtained the manuscript from Mr. Foard, with the distinct promise that he would get it translated and would then return it with the translation to Mr. Foard. That promise he failed to fulfil. My father always deeply regretted that the manuscript was carried off in that way. I have often heard my father speak of Mr. Ney's fine personal appearance. . . . He said his lips were rather thick, but came evenly together. His hands were fat, tender, and freckled. Mr. Ney was a man of great nobility of character. There was a man in our neighborhood, said my father, that nobody liked. He was selfish and mean. Some one asked Mr. Ney to give his opinion of him. ' No,' he replied, ' I shall not do it. I have been that man's guest. I can't put my feet under a man's table and then go off and talk about him.' It is needless to say that my father worshipped the man."

Dr. Peter C. Jurney, Olin, N. C. (1885): "I was a pupil of P. S. Ney for several months. He had a very quick and excitable temperament. When aroused on any subject, his eyes would flash, he would talk rapidly, and his whole countenance would quiver with the emotion which he felt. One day at school, during the noon recess, a young man named Naylor came to the schoolhouse and said to some of the boys that he would like to fence with Mr. Ney. One of the boys, watching his chance (for Mr. Ney was very approachable at times), told him what the young man had said. Mr. Ney, who had been walking up and down the schoolhouse, apparently in deep thought, answered pleasantly that he would be glad to fence with Mr. Naylor. When they took their positions Mr. Ney noticed that the young man was left-handed. He didn't like it. 'Dash it!' or 'Dash your hide!' said Mr. Ney, 'you are left-handed. I never saw but one man that I dreaded, and he was left-handed. He gave me this scar or lick on my head,' or words to that effect. But they went at it, and the young man proved to be but a baby in Mr. Ney's hands. He could not touch Mr. Ney, while Mr. Ney could hit him at any time he pleased."

Rev. William A. Wood, D.D., Statesville, N. C. (1887): "I knew Peter S. Ney. I was a pupil of his for a considerable time. I was quite young, but I have a very clear and distinct recollection of him. Indeed, it would be almost impossible to forget such a man. I may safely say that I never knew one with a warmer, truer heart, a stronger mind, or more commanding presence. As a teacher it would be difficult for any one to equal him, much less surpass him. He was painstaking, conscientious, and thorough. He could not tolerate superficial work of any kind. He ruled the older pupils—some of them very wild and reckless at home—as easily as he ruled the little boy but eight years old. To the younger pupils he was exceedingly kind. My health was delicate, and I sometimes rode to school on horseback, especially when the weather was inclement. On such occasions Mr.

NO. 5. EXAMPLES OF P. S. NEY'S HANDWRITING.

NO. 6. EXAMPLES OF MARSHAL NEY'S HANDWRITING.

Ney would come out of his log academy and help me off my horse with a tenderness and a delicacy which to me was most embarrassing. In the evening he helped me on the horse in the same gentle way, and was so thoughtful and considerate of my comfort that I was glad to get away to hide my blushes and perhaps my tears of joy and gratitude. During recess he would often take crumbs of bread and throw them to the mice which came out timidly from their hiding-places to look for something to eat. He would not permit the smallest act of injustice or cruelty. When cases of this kind among his pupils were reported to him, he would fire up instantly. His eyes, so calm and gentle in repose, would flame with passion, and the offender would certainly be punished, and sometimes with severity. He taught his boys to be truthful, honest, manly, generous, merciful. He paid as much attention perhaps to the moral as to the mental development of his pupils. In this way he accomplished a vast deal of good. Few teachers, I venture to say, have left so deep, so lasting an impress upon the minds and hearts of their pupils as Peter Stuart Ney. He had but one vice—that of occasionally drinking to excess; but his general conduct was so pure, so honorable, so upright, so noble, that every one, from the highest to the lowest, had the sincerest respect for him, the fullest confidence in him. His oath would have been received in any court of justice as quickly and as readily as that of Judge Pearson or Governor Morehead. His influence for good in the community where he lived can hardly be overestimated. It is felt to this day, and will continue to be felt by succeeding generations. One day, when I was at Davidson College—probably in the year 1847—I saw in the library a book entitled, I think, 'Napoleon and his Marshals.' In that book was a fine engraving of Marshal Ney. On the page opposite was a pencil sketch or drawing of Marshal Ney which closely resembled the engraving in the book, and was also a good likeness of Peter S. Ney. Underneath this pencil sketch, in P. S. Ney's handwriting, were the words, 'By Ney himself.' I often looked for the book afterward, searching diligently through the library, with the aid of the librarians, but I could not find it. I can hardly doubt that this great man—for I must call him great—was Napoleon's most famous marshal."

John L. Jetton, Davidson College, N. C. (May 1st, 1893): "I went to school to P. S. Ney in 1846. I remember him well. There were some persons in the neighborhood who were very anxious to find out who Mr. Ney was. Among them was Colonel John H. Wheeler, author of a 'History of North Carolina.' Colonel Wheeler had a high opinion of Mr. Ney, and often invited him to his house. But Mr. Ney seldom accepted his invitations. He said one day, 'Mr. Wheeler tries to *pick* me in a gentlemanly way. He asks too many questions. I cannot answer them, and sometimes I am embarrassed in his presence.' One day during recess, while we were playing shinny, one of the boys was struck on the head by the ball and rather seriously hurt. Mr. Ney came out and, taking hold of my stick, said, 'I will show you how to strike the ball so that it will go near the ground. As he drew back his stick to strike, one of the boys on the opposing side, seeing his opportunity, took the ball away from Mr. Ney and carried it on to the goal. Mr. Ney was delighted. 'That's right,' said he—'that's right.' It is 'one of my old tricks. Once, while one of my brother officers was getting ready to attack the enemy, I charged the enemy with my troops and drove him back before the officer could get his troops in motion.' I remember the book of which the Rev. Dr. Wood speaks. I first saw it, I think, in 1848. It remained in the library until about 1851, and then disappeared. I saw it a dozen times or more. I am quite sure the book was 'Napoleon and his Marshals,' by J. T. Headley.* The drawing was very distinct and

---

* Headley's "Napoleon and his Marshals" was published in 1846. The *Southern Literary Messenger*, in its June number (1846), acknowledges the receipt from Baker & Scribner, New York, of a "copy of 'Napoleon and his Marshals,' by the Rev. J. T. Headley." The work therefore must have made its appearance about May 20th. P. S. Ney's school was but a short distance from Davidson College. He probably visited the college during his summer vacation, and spent much of his time in the large and well-equipped libraries of that famous seat of learning. At this time, doubtless, P. S. Ney drew the pencil picture to which the Rev. Dr. Wood and Mr. Jetton refer. He died in the following November.

well executed. It looked like the portrait of Ney in the book, allowing for age, etc., and was an exact likeness of P. S. Ney. It was often shown to visitors. Underneath the sketch, as Dr. Wood says, P. S. Ney had written the words, '*By Ney himself.*' I never knew a more honorable man. His word was his bond. He would have been believed, either in court or out of court, as quickly as any man in North Carolina. Mr. Ney couldn't bear an informer or spy. One day some of the boys robbed a watermelon patch. The owner was angry, and asked Mr. Ney to punish the boys. 'I will do so,' said he, 'if I can find out who they are.' 'One of the scholars,' said the man (giving his name), 'knows who they are, but he won't tell me.' Mr. Ney asked the boy if he knew who the raiders were. 'Yes,' he answered, 'but I can't tell.' 'Why?' 'Because the boys told me they were going to take the melons, and I can't betray them. I can't violate their confidence.' Mr. Ney's face instantly changed. 'You are right,' said he, 'perfectly right. I hope all the boys will imitate your example.'"

Mrs. G. N. Beale, Washington, D. C. : "I knew Peter S. Ney; have often played chess with him near Beattie's Ford, N. C. He was very courteous and gentlemanlike, though rather brusque in his manners. One day, when slightly under the influence of wine, he said to Miss Martha Graham, a niece of Governor Graham, 'You look like the Duchess of Argyle.' The Grahams were descended from the Argyle family. Some years ago I attended an entertainment given in this city by a Professor Stoddard. It consisted of a series of movable pictures, representing the principal events, etc., in the life of Napoleon Bonaparte. When the portrait of Marshal Ney appeared upon the canvas I instantly turned toward my husband and said, 'There is Peter Ney, the man I used to play chess with.' 'Why,' said my husband laughing, 'you must be very ancient. You must have been born before the flood.' A few moments after this conversation occurred Professor Stoddard said that the picture which he was then exhibiting was that of Marshal Ney, the 'bravest of the brave.' It was a perfect likeness of Peter S. Ney. Colonel

John H. Wheeler observed Mr. Ney closely, and he was satisfied that he was an officer of high rank in Napoleon's army, though he did not think he was Marshal Ney. The only reason he gave for this opinion was that Marshal Ney was an illiterate man, while Peter S. Ney was an accomplished scholar."

Alexander F. Brevard, Machpelah, Lincoln County, N. C. (October 28th, 1892): "I went to school to Peter S. Ney in 1841, when he taught near Catawba Springs. He walked very briskly, especially for a man of his age. Beetling brows, very shaggy; tuft of hair at each inside end, nearest the nose. When talking his lips came firmly together. Nose very broad at base—spread out in folds or curves. He told me he was the 'best fencer in the French army with one exception'—presumably Murat. One day, when slightly in liquor, he said, 'Some people say I was educated for a Roman Catholic priest. It is a lie. I am the poor old marshal.' Once, when hearing a recitation in history, he described by way of illustration the battle of Waterloo. It was a magnificent description. The old man's eye lighted up, and he appeared truly grand. He gave many incidents connected with the battle which were deeply interesting to the class. At last, when he came to Blücher's arrival, his voice faltered and his eyes moistened. 'Blücher,' said he, putting his hands to his eyes to conceal his emotion—'Blücher ruined everything.' Mr. Ney permitted the older pupils to study in the grove during school hours, but they had to know their lessons. There could be no better teacher, and everybody had the sincerest esteem for him, whether he was drunk or sober."

Colonel George N. Folk, Blackstone, N. C., Judge John Gray Bynum, Morganton, N. C., A. W. Haywood, Raleigh, N. C., T. H. Cobb, Asheville, N. C. (1889): "We have often heard Chief Justice Pearson speak of Peter S. Ney. He had a very high opinion of his character and his abilities, and was firmly convinced that he was Marshal Ney."

H. H. Helper, Mocksville, N. C.: "I knew Peter S. Ney. He talked at all times with a German brogue. Had glittering blue-gray eyes, sunk deeply into his head. Face, if I may so express myself, both long and round. Was fond of music. In speaking of the female sex generally he never used the world *lady*—always said *woman*. He refused to ride a horse one day because it was named Wellington. Said he prepared himself for teaching English after he came to this country. He often said to his pupils : ' Any boy of good common sense is capable of mastering any and all branches.' "

Dr. Bingham, Mocksville, N. C. (1889) :* ". . . I have often seen a copy of Labaume's ' Russian Campaign ' which contained a great many marginal annotations by P. S. Ney. These were very interesting. He would often correct Labaume as to matters of fact connected with the retreat, and would give fuller information as to other points which he considered important, but which were briefly noticed by Labaume. The book, I think, was owned by P. S. Ney, and was given by him to my father. It was certainly left at my father's house, but I do not know who has it now. P. S. Ney also wrote in this book a piece of poetry on the Moscow fire. My father had a very high opinion of Mr. Ney's ability and general character. He said Mr. Ney looked like a Scotch bishop —that he was too highly educated for Marshal Ney. In other respects he thought he bore a striking resemblance to the great French soldier."

Rev. Basil G. Jones, M.D., Kingstree, S. C. (1887) : " When I came from Alabama to Davie County, N. C., in 1829, there was a mysterious person teaching school near Mocksville, calling himself Peter Stuart Ney. He was regarded by the *literati* and everybody else as a finished gentleman and scholar. He seemed to be perfectly at home in any branch of learning known in that day. He seemed to understand well the Scotch, French, Italian, English, Latin, Greek, Hebrew, Russian, and Polish languages. He said he could read and converse in all of them. He was frequently put to test in at least some of them, as Latin, Greek, French, Scotch,

---

* A part of Dr. Bingham's testimony has already been given. See testimony of the Rev. Dr. Rockwell.

and Hebrew. He was acknowledged by those who professed to understand the Hebrew to be a superior Hebraist.

"Mr. Ney taught at other places. At Mr. Placebo Houston's, in Iredell, the Houstons, Youngs, and others, the most wealthy and respectable citizens of Iredell County, were his pupils; a part of them are still living. Mr. Ney was a man about five feet ten inches high, heavily set, and compactly built; he weighed about one hundred and seventy or one hundred and eighty pounds, and was of extraordinary muscular development. He had every appearance of a large, rough Scottish Highlander, of symmetrical proportions, well adapted to energy and endurance, qualities which Mr. Ney possessed in a high degree. He was more adapted to herculean strength than to agility. His back was straight, shoulders broad and a little stooped, head well balanced, the top bald, the back and sides of the head covered with hair once auburn, but then a little silvered; his nose was straight and very large, with a massive end; his mouth large and broad; lips firm, the under apparently a little thicker than the upper; complexion florid; face full and pitted with small-pox; countenance a little down but stern, thoughtful, and intelligent; his eyes not large, but rather brilliant, indicating a strong, perceptive, and penetrating intellect. One day Mr. Ney received bad news from France. He said his hopes were destroyed. He could never go back. He wept like a child, and large tears found their way rapidly down his pale cheek. While in that condition he could not be trusted alone. He was sick, frantic, and almost ungovernable. During this time the writer and a few others spent a night with him. I never can forget that night. He raved of France, Napoleon, his wife and family, Waterloo, Moscow, etc.; *called for Phesinac*,* *issued his commands*, sketched his past history, gave

---

* The italics are mine. P. S. Ney doubtless said *Fezensac*, and the witness understood him to say *Phesinac*. The Duke of Fezensac was for a long time Ney's loved and honored aide-de-camp, and in the Russian retreat he was Ney's right arm. Ney trusted him as he trusted no other officer, and it is but just to say that not even the "bravest of the brave" could have accomplished what he did accomplish without the loyal and

an account of his birth, connection with the family of the Stuarts, and his relation to the Bonapartes ; how he came to be made a marshal of the Empire ; how the battle of Waterloo was planned by Napoleon and his Cabinet, etc. Mr. Ney then showed us the wounds or rather scars which he received at Waterloo and elsewhere—wounds of precisely the kind described in history. I was a pupil of Mr. Ney in 1831 or 1832. Moral courage, firmness of principle, fixedness of purpose, strength of nerve, indomitable perseverance, honesty and truth, are traits of character which he held in the highest admiration. He used to impress these upon us boys as essential elements of a man. He told me once how he escaped. He said the French people thought Marshal Ney was dead, but he was not. He fell by preconcerted arrangement, as if he were dead ; was taken up, disguised, and finally escaped to the United States, the Ancient Fraternity* aiding in his escape from the first. I never heard Mr. Ney say what

hearty co-operation of the Duke of Fezensac. Ney and Fezensac were the only men with " thoroughly tempered souls," and it is perfectly clear that next to Ney, Fezensac is the hero of the Russian retreat. The " Memoirs" of the Duke of Fezensac prove that he almost worshipped Ney, and that Ney loved him as a son, and had the very highest opinion of his character as a man and his genius as a soldier.

A short time after the Russian retreat, Ney wrote the following letter to the Minister of War :

"MONSIEUR LE DUC : I seize the present moment to inform you how highly I appreciate the services which Monsieur de Fezensac has rendered the army. This young man has been placed in the most critical circumstances, and in every instance he rose superior to them. I present him to you as a veritable French chevalier, and you may henceforth regard him as an old colonel."

Fezensac says : " I have the original letter. Every one must understand how great a price I attach to such a document."

In his delirious ravings it was but natural for P. S. Ney (if he were the marshal) to fight over his old battles, to " issue his commands," to " call for" Fezensac, for so long a time his chief aide-de-camp, and who in the Russian retreat, as colonel of the Fourth Regiment, so nobly held up the hands of his chief as the savior of the army, of Napoleon, of the Empire. Fezensac is a singular name, and it is extremely probable that the witness, then but a youth, had never heard of the Duke of Fezensac.

* The Masons, I presume.

became of Phesinac. It seems to me he said Phesinac kept him from being slain at Waterloo, or protected him in some way. His wife, he said, sent him packages—he didn't say how. One day when he was staying at my home a tremendous thunderstorm came up. It was about sunset, and the storm was the most terrific I ever saw. My father and every member of the family were badly frightened. Mr. Ney alone appeared calm and undismayed. Presently he rose from his seat, and began to walk rather briskly about the room. Then we thought *he* was frightened, but he was not. In a few minutes he opened the door, and taking in his hand a stout cane, he walked out under the large trees and quietly surveyed the storm. Now and then he would raise his stick and wave it, as if in the act of fencing. When the storm subsided Mr. Ney came back into the house, and said, 'By Jove, colonel, I never saw such sublimity, except at Waterloo!'"

George A. Miller, Davie County, N. C. (1870): "I was well acquainted with P. S. Ney. From 1833 until his death in 1846 our intercourse was as familiar as could be between persons of different ages and pursuits. The venerable and dignified deportment of Mr. Ney, his imperial air, his great learning and unexampled scholarship, his perfect acquaintance with the Greek and Latin classics, the modern languages, and especially the history of the French Revolution and every particular in relation to the personal, civil, and military career of the great Napoleon—these qualities of mind and person, united to an impenetrable mystery which clung around his own history—a mystery which nothing could surprise or remove—attracted every one like the secret properties of the magnet. There was a something about the man which once seen seemed to say, 'I dare you to forget me.' It stamped itself on the brain in letters never to be blotted out, 'I am not *booked on the common roll of men.*' He appeared to others what we often heard him say in regard to Napoleon, 'that he was the only mortal he could never look full in the eye.' We have seen Mr. Ney under all circumstances. We have seen his courage tested, and his face never blanched and his nerves never trembled. We have seen him when the saying of Horace, '*In vino veritas*,' could be best verified. We have seen him at midnight, courting and recording the inspiration of the muses. We have seen him kiss the portrait of Josephine while the tears of affection and . . . (lines obscured). With the permission of Mr. Foard we examined the papers of Mr. Ney soon after his death. We found any quantity of poetry and prose on all subjects, but nothing to throw light on the object of our search—his own life. The longest and most labored production of his mind was a history of the French Revolution written in ciphers (of his own invention), which we could not understand, but in part was explained to us by Dr. Matthew Locke, one of his former pupils. Mr. Foard told us that a night or two before he died he destroyed all of his more private correspondence, and among them some ship letters lately received from France, which contained valuables."

Mr. A. H. Graham, Bagdad, Tex. (1879) : "Peter S. Ney, as he styled himself, came to my father's in Lincoln County, N. C., in 1842, to teach school. He was employed by my father and others for about four years in teaching. He had a sabre wound on his head and numerous gunshot wounds on his body and limbs, and one particularly near the knee-joint, from a musket-ball, part of which he still retained, and at times, in his long walks to and from school, gave him much pain. In 1845 he appeared to be seventy-five or eighty years old. He was well preserved, as he had taken good care of himself. His habits, diet, exercise, cleanliness of person were all conducive to good health. He used Florida water and cologne constantly. Shaved every day. I was his almost daily companion for three years ; slept near him, helped him to undress when in his cups. Complexion florid, pale only when sick. Hairs on his arms and legs even of an auburn color. A small eater—rarely ate more than two meals a day. Spent most of his time in reading, writing, etc. The portrait of Lord Elgin, Governor-General of Canada, is a fair likeness of Ney. He dressed very much as Elgin, although he wore no jewelry. Had a large English silver watch. No side whiskers, and always dressed the side hair of his head over the top and back of his head, and not straight down, as in the Elgin engraving. He wore a white neck-tie like our Episcopal ministers—a black one at times. Had cat or hazel eyes, sprinkled with grains of powder; said he received powder burns on his face at Borodino. Often spoke of Lord Nelson and battle of Trafalgar; didn't say he was in the battle; said Lord Nelson was a brave and great Englishman. He had a German brogue. He frequently made use of such words as mŏn for man, and ye for you, as the Germans use them. In pronouncing algebra, he made the last a sound like r. Spoke much of the excellence of the German language; said it was a great language; seemed to be very fond of it. Spoke it perfectly, as he also did the French and dead languages. I have sat for hours and listened to him tell of his battles and campaigns, especially of the dreadful march from Moscow, and the great battle of Borodino. Also spoke often of Hohenlinden. Said the victory at Borodino was due to him, as Napoleon was too unwell to command in person, but sat astride a cannon the greater part of the day, being afflicted with strangury. Said Lord Wellington saved his life. He feared to make himself known on this account and for his family's sake, as well as for other reasons. As a rule he would not talk about himself except when in wine; but he was rarely intoxicated. He knew what he was talking about. I once saw a letter which he wrote to Wellington. He seemed to be agitated when he wrote it. Said, according to my recollection, that the French Government owed him 60,000 francs. I do not think he sent the letter. Talked about Wellington in a very excited manner. Said he or some of his friends appealed to him in person. Wellington, with his hat drawn down over his eyes, stamped upon the ground, and said with much emphasis, 'I cannot and will not interfere with the laws of the French Government.' Said his friend Rogers in South Carolina was fully acquainted with his history. In 1844 said his wife was still living. Spoke of her with much affection. Said she was a small woman, and very beautiful. For a man of his age he was an excellent and graceful horseman, although he seldom rode a horse. I once saw him ride at full gallop a

NO. 7. EXAMPLES OF P. S. NEY'S HANDWRITING.

NO. 8. EXAMPLES OF MARSHAL NEY'S HANDWRITING.

large, fiery horse, which showed him off to much advantage, and surprised us all very much. This proved to us that he had long been accustomed to the saddle. He used to punish his pupils by pinching their ears. Said that was Napoleon's habit with his officers. My sisters occasionally played 'Bonaparte's Retreat.' Mr. Ney didn't like to hear it—sometimes shed tears. I don't think he ever voted or was naturalized. Was a great fencer. Said Murat only was a better swordsman. He often spoke of an adopted child that he rescued during the march from Moscow. He called him Phesnac or Fesnac.* He appeared to have a greater affection for him than any one of whom I heard him speak—not even excepting his wife and children. Always spoke of Phesnac or Fesnac as a youth; called him 'my son.' I think he said Murat cut down the soldier who gave him the sabre wound. Did not say in what battle he received it. I have often seen the manuscript containing an account of his life. He kept it securely in his trunk. In writing it he often consulted Thiers's 'History of the Consulate and Empire.'"

* I have no doubt P. S. Ney said *Fezensac.* Headley says: "As they left the gates of Smolensko, a French mother, finding she had not room in her sledge for her infant child, cast it from her into the snow in spite of its piercing cries and pleading tones. Ney, touched by the spectacle, lifted up the infant himself, and replaced it on the mother's breast, bidding her cherish and protect it. Again did she cast it away, and again did he carry it in his own brave arms back to her; and though the mother was finally left to die on the frozen ground, that tender infant survived all the horrors of the retreat, and lived to see France."—"Napoleon and his Marshals."

"At the gates of the city" (Smolensko) "a mother abandoned her little son, only five years old; in spite of his cries and tears, she drove him away from her sledge, which was too heavily laden. . . . Twice did Ney himself replace the child in the arms of its mother, and twice did she cast him from her on the frozen snow. . . . The infant was entrusted to another mother; this little orphan was then in their ranks; he was afterward seen at the Berezina, then at Wilna, again at Kowno, and finally escaped all the horrors of the retreat."—Ségur's "Expedition to Russia."

At Smolensko (p. 59) Fezensac was almost as heroic, almost as great as Ney himself. It is very probable that Ney adopted this orphan boy, and named him Fezensac in honor of his lion-hearted lieutenant. See testimony of the Rev. Dr. Jones.

Mrs. Elizabeth P. Sloan, Brenham, Tex. (1886) : "I was well acquainted with Peter S. Ney. I was his pupil for a considerable time. My brother" (Dr. A. H. Graham) " wrote on a piece of cardboard ' Academy of P. S. Ney,' and tacked it on a tree near the road. Mr. Ney was enraged, and ordered my brother to take it down, saying he did not wish his whereabouts to be known. I have frequently heard him speak of his wife. Said she had an elegant necklace* (diamond, I think) which cost several thousand dollars—I forgot how many. One day our class read 'On Linden when the sun was low.' Mr. Ney shed tears, as he did on another occasion when the class read about Waterloo. When on horseback, as old as he was, he was grand—so erect—and rode beautifully."

N. F. Hall, Blackmer, Rowan County, N. C., 1886 : "I saw P. S. Ney several times when he taught near Mocksville. Judge Pearson knew him well. He said to me one day, 'This Peter S. Ney likes whiskey. I believe he is an impostor. I haven't the slightest idea that he is Marshal Ney.' Later Judge Pearson was convinced that he was Marshal Ney. I saw P. S. Ney a short time before he died. He appeared to be very aged. A good fencer. One day a left-handed man was his antagonist. Ney shrank back, and pointing to a heavy sabre scar over the eye, said, ' A left-handed man gave me this scar, or this was made by a left-handed man.' "

Moses Lingle, Third Creek, N. C. (1886) : "I knew P. S. Ney. He was a passionate man, and would sometimes give vent to his temper. Osborne G. Foard told me that Ney when drunk would tell who he was, how he got away, etc., but silent as to these points when he was sober. I bought a few books that once belonged to P. S. Ney. Some of them were scorched or injured by the fire. It is said that once when in great trouble he started to destroy them."

General D. H. Hill, Charlotte, N. C. (1887) : " Many of my acquaintances were pupils of P. S. Ney. In some way they were much impressed with the learning and ability of this man of mystery. They all believed him to be the re-

---

* See portrait of the Princess de la Moskowa.

doubtable marshal ; but the claimants for the marshalship overdid the work. They talked a great deal about the scholarship of P. S. Ney, for which the real marshal was not distinguished. However, the boys in an old field school are apt to imagine that their teacher is a new edition of Solomon. Ney said to Mrs. Hill that he took great interest in her, as her name (Christian) had the same initials* as the name of his mother. He showed considerable skill in versification, but, as I remember, no poetic talent. The Rev. Mr. Frontis, a native Frenchman, said he never believed Ney to be a Frenchman until he heard him pronounce Augereau. The pronunciation was such, said he, as only a native could give. Ney wouldn't talk French with Frontis, and that excited his suspicions."

Mrs. H. M. Irwin, Charlotte, N. C. (May 13th, 1887) :†
" P. S. Ney's mother, according to his assertion to a member of my family, was a Scotchwoman whose name was Isabella Stuart. The way he happened to speak of it was this : he sometimes, at the request of his pupils and other parties, would write acrostics on their names. He would dash off these productions with no apparent effort, give the origin of the name, and state to what language it belonged. In writing an acrostic for a young lady whose name was Isabella,‡ he said, ' I take much pleasure in putting this into verse, as it was the name of my mother,' adding that she was a native of Scotland."

Mrs. D. H. Hill, Charlotte, N. C. (1894) : " I have often seen Peter S. Ney. He wrote a beautiful acrostic on my name. He said his mother was connected with a family of Stuarts who lived (as I understood him) in Scotland, not far from the residence of Sir James Graham. I once dined with Mr. Ney at the home of my uncle, Mr. J. D. Graham. Mrs. Graham was dead, and his young daughter, Miss Martha, acted as hostess. She asked me to assist her. Mr. Ney was

* General Hill married Miss Isabella Sophia Morrison, a sister of Mrs. Stonewall Jackson.
† From the *Charlotte* (N. C.) *Chronicle*.
‡ Mrs. D. H. Hill.

amused at our inexperienced efforts at entertaining, and serving the table. He remarked : ' I hope, young ladies, you will excuse personal remarks, but I cannot help criticising occasionally.' My cousin said, ' I expect my teacher to criticise me.' He made no reply, but after we went into the parlor he took a seat near us and remarked, ' Composure of feature and steadiness of person are the highest evidences of good breeding.' I was so struck with these words that I immediately wrote them in my diary."

Mrs. Sally Nelson Hughes, Halifax Court House, Va. (1889) : "Peter S. Ney taught school near the residence of my father (Mr. William Nelson), Mecklenburg County, Va., in 1828-29. I was his pupil a great part of the time. He kept a large life-size portrait of Napoleon hanging up in the school-room. He also had a picture of Napoleon's grave at St. Helena. We all thought he was a wonderful man. My father asked him to write an acrostic on the names of the different members of his family. He did so. The acrostic is exceedingly beautiful and in excellent taste. My youngest sister was named after Mr. Ney's mother—Catharine Isabella. Mr. Ney himself asked my mother to let him name her infant child after his mother. She readily granted the request. He was very proud of the honor. It gratified him very much, as he seemed to have great affection for his mother. In the acrostic the different names are connected together in a single piece of composition. That part of it which refers to my youngest sister is as follows :

" ' Conduct us to the climes above.
Assume, O Muse, a deeper tone,
To animate, inspire, inform :
Harmonious numbers well may claim
A child that bears my mother's name ;
Right forward be her path ; may time
Inspire her heart with truth Divine ;
No vices stain, no passions wild
Entice away this lovely child.

" ' In charity and peace, oh may
She ever think of Stuart Ney !
Around her head may Virtue throw,
Beaming and bright, her robe of snow :

Emblem of innocence and worth,
Look up to them who gave thee birth ;
Look up to Him who's higher still,
And act obedient to His will.'

"The first line is connected with the preceding name, thus :

"' Wisdom and faith and pious love,
Conduct us to the climes above.'

"He also wrote the acrostic in shorthand, and said to my oldest sister, 'Copy it, and time will repay you.' He was fond of music, and often played on a flute. He gave my father a large spy-glass. When extended, I think it would measure three feet, and it commands a distance of several miles. It is now owned by my nephew in Spartanburg, S. C. The only thing on the glass is, 'Carpenter, London. Improved day and night.'"

J. W. Sanders, Iredell County, N. C. (1886): "About the year 1840 Peter S. Ney was recognized as Marshal Ney by John Snyder, of Iredell County. Snyder was a Bohemian German born and raised near Prague. He said he was conscripted by order of Napoleon on the very day he was twenty-one years old. He was assigned to Murat's command, and charged in the snow-storm with that renowned marshal on the bloody field of Eylau (as called by Snyder, 'Ilau'). He was afterward under Davout, then under various other marshals, including Marshal Ney. Said he had seen Bonaparte (to use his own words) 'hundred times.' Had been in sixteen regular battles, besides several smaller engagements. Napoleon, seeing defection in his German troops, sent them away, I think to the West Indies. Synder said that after enduring great hardships and suffering he deserted and came to the United States, landing at Charleston, S. C. He afterward settled in Iredell County. Snyder saw P. S. Ney in Statesville about 1840, and immediately recognized him as Marshal Ney. He said he was frightened. He raised his hands and exclaimed : 'Lordy God, Marshal Ney !' P. S. Ney gave him a sign not to talk, and he afterward conversed with P. S. Ney. He said he knew Ney perfectly. Belonged at one time to Ney's command, and was personally acquainted with him. He told me the following incident among many others: On one occasion in a severe battle (I forget the name) Marshal Ney had several horses killed under him. He then walked on foot along the line, animating his desponding troops, with his sword in one hand and a broken standard in the other. Snyder saw that the men were being killed all around him, and he began to dodge at the whistle of the bullets. Ney saw him and tapped him on the shoulder, and said, in German, 'Snyder, the bullets you hear won't kill you.' Snyder said that Ney knew a great many of the private soldiers, and would often go among them and talk to them in his blunt but kind-hearted way. He said Ney's soldiers loved him, and almost worshipped the ground he walked on. He said that the marshal would look out for them as nobody else would. He would see that they had plenty of food and clothing, and that the sick and wounded were properly cared for. He would take the part of any soldier that was abused or imposed upon, and would see that justice was done him. Frederick Barr, one of Napoleon's old soldiers, also recognized P. S. Ney as Marshal Ney. Snyder and Barr were from the same country, and generally spoke the German tongue. They were men of high character, and enjoyed the confidence and esteem of the community in which they lived."

Daniel Snyder, Statesville, N. C. (1889): "I have often heard my father (John Snyder) say that he knew Marshal Ney in Europe; that he had served in Ney's command as a private soldier. When my father saw Peter S. Ney in Statesville about the year 1840, he knew him at once, but he was 'astonished,' he said, 'almost out of his senses.' He had no idea of seeing him. There was a political meeting in Statesville on the day that my father saw Peter Ney. He said when he recognized him as Marshal Ney, Mr. Ney intimated to him to say nothing more, and that after the meeting was over he and Ney had a private talk. I have heard my father say dozens of times that Peter S. Ney was Marshal Ney; that he knew Marshal Ney by sight as well as he knew his own father. Germany was my father's native country, and his people were in good circumstances. He said he knew

Marshal Ney personally, as Marshal Ney was in the habit of going among his soldiers and making the acquaintance of the humblest in the ranks. My father solemnly asserted to his dying day that Peter S. Ney was Marshal Ney."

William Sidney Stevenson, Statesville, N. C. (1887) : "I knew Peter S. Ney. He taught school not far from my home for a considerable time, and I have a most distinct recollection of him. He was a man whom, having once seen, you could never forget. His large, well-formed head, his broad, full massive face, with piercing magnetic eyes and very prominent chin, showed great strength of mind and great force of character. He was a man, too, of great personal dignity, of marked simplicity and kindliness of manner, free from hypocrisy or any sort of affectation whatever. In the year 1840 I attended a political meeting in Rowe's Township, about nine miles from Statesville. It was during the gubernatorial campaign. Judge Saunders, of Raleigh, and Governor Morehead, of Greensborough, were to address the people on that occasion. A little while before the speaking began I was talking to two of my friends, not far from the speaker's stand. They were John Young, county surveyor and member of the Legislature, and Dr. James B. McClellan, both men of the highest character. During this conversation Dr. McClellan left us and walked over to a small gathering of men about sixty yards distant, who were discussing the ordinary topics of the day. In a little while Dr. McClellan came back, walking quickly, and manifesting considerable excitement. He made substantially the following statement : 'Just now, while I was talking to Daniel Hoke, Frederick Barr, and others, Barr suddenly raised his hands in great excitement and said something in German which the rest of us except Daniel Hoke did not understand. We all asked Daniel Hoke what was the matter with Barr—what it was he had said ? "Why," answered Hoke, pointing to Peter S. Ney, who, with Colonel Thomas Allison, was then walking past us on the opposite side of the road, "he says, ' Yonder is Marshal Ney. They told me he was shot ; but he was not. Yonder he is. I know him, for I fought under him off and on for five or six years, in Napoleon's wars.'" This information greatly staggered Mr. Young and myself. We had occasionally heard the reports that some persons believed Peter S. Ney was Marshal Ney, but we had attached little importance to them. We had no faith in them; but we could no longer doubt the truth of these reports. Both of us knew Barr, and had known him for years, and we believed him to be an honest, reliable, truthful man. He certainly bore that reputation in the community in which he lived. Barr was a German, and talked English very brokenly indeed. He had several wounds which he said (long before he saw P. S. Ney in 1840) he had received in the Napoleonic wars. He was a very brave man, and would permit no one to doubt his word or cast the slightest imputation upon his honor. He drank too much beer at times. That was his chief infirmity. Daniel Hoke (upon whose farm Barr lived) was a cousin of the Hon. Michael Hoke, a distinguished lawyer, and was a man of intelligence, wealth, and influence. He was thoroughly acquainted with the German language, and he and Barr frequently talked with each other in that language. Hoke had the highest opinion of Barr as an honest, industrious, truthful, and generally sober tenant. After Barr's declaration about Peter S. Ney, Hoke said he was compelled to believe that P. S. Ney was Marshal Ney. A short time after Barr's statement at the political meeting in reference to P. S. Ney, he suddenly left the county, and went, I think, to Indiana—certainly somewhere out West. No one knew why he left. His sudden departure puzzled his neighbors. Hoke valued him highly as a tenant; he was prosperous and contented, every one respected him, he was in no trouble of any kind, and his neighbors could not imagine why he should suddenly leave the county and remove to a distant part of the country. It was reported that Daniel Hoke helped him to get off—furnished him with money, etc. Possibly P. S. Ney's friends had something to do with his removal.* I never heard from Barr afterward.

"Peter S. Ney, as I remember him, looked somewhat like

---

* It is very probable.

Judge Armfield. Armfield's forehead is not as high and full as Ney's, especially the upper part of his forehead. His eyes, too, are different. Still, there is some resemblance. P. S. Ney also bore some resemblance to the Rev. Henry Nelson Pharr, Presbyterian clergyman (with whom Mr. Ney was quite intimate), and to Sidney E. Morse, the first editor of the New York *Observer*."

Rev. R. W. Barber, Wilkesborough, N. C. (1888) : " In the year 1846, not long before Christmas, in company with the Rev. Mr. Gries, I was at the house of Major E. P. Miller, in Caldwell County. We were there several days, and while there, Mr. Gates (Gétz), a well-known teacher of Caldwell County, came in and spent the most of one afternoon. As he was a native German, and Mr. Gries, as he termed himself, a 'Pennsylvania Dutchman,' they seemed to enjoy a great deal of conversation, of which the rest of us were, perhaps blissfully, ignorant. There were intervals, however, when they conversed in English. Mr. Gries had heard of P. S. Ney, and seemed to be impressed with the claim of his being Marshal Ney. Up to that time I did not share the impression. In the course of conversation he mentioned the matter, and asked Gates what he thought of it. To which Gates replied, ' Poh ! old hypocrite,' repeating the epithet very contemptuously three times. He then went on to state his reasons. I will endeavor for the sake of brevity to use his own language, and will write in the first person. He went on to say : ' Some years ago I was in search of a situation as a schoolteacher, and was advised to go to the house of Mr. Graham, in Lincoln County. Soon after my arrival I presented my letters of recommendation from various persons, whose patronage I had before enjoyed. Mr. Graham replied that some weeks before they wanted a teacher, as I had been informed, but had been so fortunate as to secure one with whom they were well pleased. He went on to state his name and claim sometimes made. He then asked me if I had ever seen Marshal Ney. To this I replied, " *Once* and only *once.*" " Do you have any distinct recollection of his appearance, so as to be able to detect the same in one now claiming to be the marshal?" I replied that the impression made on my mind by the looks and bearing of Marshal Ney was indelible. He was a German by birth, and having then, when I saw him, attained very eminent distinction, I eyed him closely. Mr. Graham proposed that I should have a personal and private interview with Mr. Ney. To this I assented, and he sent a servant to ask Mr. Ney to come into the sitting-room, as a gentleman from the old country wished to see him. Ney very soon made his appearance, and, as he stepped into the room, the marks of identity were so strong that I said to myself, "It is no farce, this must be the identical Marshal Ney." We had a prolonged conversation. I drew him out in conversation about parts of Germany with which I knew, if he was Marshal Ney, he must be familiar. I found him not only familiar with the topography of the sections, but with families whose names had not found a place in history or in fame. The conviction was overpowering. I drew my chair close to him, and in a low tone of voice said, "Are you not Marshal Ney?" Upon my saying this, or asking this question, the old hypocrite, as I now felt that he was, sealed his lips, arose from his chair, and placing his hands behind him under his surtout coat, walked off to his room, not making his appearance any more during my stay.'* This is Gates's statement as accurately as I can remember and relate it.

"I never saw P. S. Ney. Whatever impressions I have were derived from intelligent persons who were well acquainted with him. By conversations with them I have been convinced that those entertaining the notion of P. S. Ney's identity with Marshal Ney cannot be justly deemed mere victims of a pleasing illusion, or liable to the charge of credulity. It is not true that he alluded to his identity with Marshal Ney only when in his cups. These were generally

---

* I care little for Mr. Gates's *opinion*. His testimony is valuable, for those who knew him well say that his character for truth was unimpeachable. Mr. Gates fully believed that P. S. Ney was Marshal Ney until his *pride* was touched, and then he called him an old hypocrite. Had P. S. Ney been an impostor, it is clear that he would have acted differently

his occasions for asserting it ; but he asserted it to several individuals when cool sober. My brother, Colonel William Barber, was his pupil, and a favorite one. Under him he read Cæsar's Commentaries. He told me at the time, and many years afterward, that Cæsar was the old man's favorite classic ; that during recitations he would discuss Cæsar's strategic movements with a freedom and apparent ability which no one but a military man could or would have done ; that he was in the habit of comparing or contrasting them with those of Napoleon on various occasions, and, incidentally, and with apparent unconsciousness, would state his own part in the drama. My brother may be said to have been one of those who cherished the *pleasing illusion*. It may have been attributed to childish credulity, for he was then only thirteen years of age. But after going through college, studying law, and entering the practice of it, he said to the last that time and reflection had not effaced in the least his impressions."

Dr. J. G. Ramsay, Cleveland, N. C., 1887 : "I knew P. S. Ney. It seems to me to be more difficult to say who he was than to believe he was Marshal Ney. I once asked Dr. Locke how he came to let Ney die. Locke replied, ' He wouldn't take the medicines I prescribed for him ; took only such as pleased him ;* said it was no use, etc. I was acquainted with Snyder, who recognized him as Marshal Ney in Statesville. Snyder was an honest, truthful man. The Hon. Burton Craige, M.C., of Salisbury, told me once that he believed P. S. Ney was an Irishman, and educated for a Roman Catholic priest. I do not remember that he stated why he thought so."

Dr. Daniel Burton Wood, Elmwood, N. C. (1888) : " I knew P. S. Ney. His physique was almost perfect. A phrenologist would have gloried in his head—large, finely shaped, full of brains, and well developed. His whole expression and bearing were simply magnificent. He was a born leader of men. I once saw in the Eumenean Society,

* Napoleon at St. Helena would not take O'Meara's medicines ; said, " It's no use. One's days are numbered," etc.

Davidson College, a book on the French Revolution (I forget the title) which contained quite a number of marginal notes by P. S. Ney. In these notes Mr. Ney corrected several historical errors, and explained other points which needed elucidation. The Rev. Barnabas Scott Krider, who was educated at Davidson College, said P. S. Ney borrowed the book and returned it with the annotations. The day after Mr. Ney's death I rode over to Mr. Osborne Foard's, and went into the room where Mr. Ney was laid out for burial. I placed my hand upon his ample, noble forehead, and said to myself, 'Can it be possible that I have my hand upon the forehead of the "Bravest of the brave"?' I was deeply affected by the thought. He looked grand even in death."

Dr. James M. Spainhour, Lenoir, N. C. (1888): "My father, Noah Spainhour, who died in Caldwell County in 1881, was acquainted with Peter S. Ney. He met him in Rowan County in 1846, a short time before P. S. Ney's death. He said in substance: 'In the summer of 1846 I went to Salisbury, N. C., for the purpose of employing Miss Emma J. Baker to teach school in Lenoir. She had previously taught in Lenoir, and was then staying with her brother Alfred, who lived in Salisbury. In passing through Rowan County I lost my way, and asked the first man I met to show me the road to Salisbury. He asked me who I was, and where I lived. I said, "My name is Spainhour, and I live in Caldwell County." "*Spainhour, Spainhour*," said he, repeating the name slowly and reflectively. "Why, I had some soldiers of that name in my command in Switzerland." "Very probable," I said, "for my family came from Switzerland, and we have several relatives in that country." He then asked me to go home with him; said it was nearly dark, and Mr. Foard, the gentleman with whom he boarded, would be glad to entertain me. I accepted his invitation. After supper he asked me to walk out with him into the grove, not far from the house. I did so, and we had quite a long talk. He said he thought he had three soldiers named Spainhour belonging to his command in Switzerland; that he had a distinct recollection of the name. He then told me that Marshal

Ney had command of Bonaparte's troops in Switzerland, and that he was not executed, as history states that he was. He said the arrangement was that the soldiers detailed to execute him were not to fire until they heard the word of command from the marshal himself; that he was to fall while giving the command *fire*, so that the balls might pass over him. This arrangement was carried out. He was quickly taken up and carried to a neighboring hospital. He then disguised himself, made his way to the coast, and sailed to the United States. He said that when he walked to the place appointed for his execution he had in his left bosom a bag of red fluid resembling blood, and that when he struck his hand upon his heart or breast in giving the command *fire*, the bag bursted, and the fluid spurted over his person, etc. I think he also told me that he went on board the boat which carried him to America disguised as a servant, carrying a valise. His clothes did not fit him, and it made him mad. They were too small for him. During the voyage he said he was recognized by an old soldier who had been in the Napoleonic wars, and that when they reached Charleston he remained on board the vessel until the old soldier had gotten off and disappeared. He saw him leave from the cabin window.

"I have heard my father make this statement more than once, and I cannot be mistaken as to its substantial accuracy. My father further stated that P. S. Ney told him that Marshal Ney was then living, but he would not say positively that he was Marshal Ney."

Valentine Stirewalt, Davidson College, N. C. (1894): "I went to school to P. S. Ney in 1842. He boarded at my father's, and I saw him often—sometimes had long talks with him in his room. He was fond of his toddy, and my father gave him a dram every morning for breakfast. He didn't drink much at a time, and he rarely went beyond proper bounds. I appeared to be one of his favorites, and he would occasionally talk to me about his past life. He once told me he was Marshal Ney, and how he escaped. He said that when he marched out for execution he had in his bosom a sack of red fluid, and that when he gave the command to fire he struck the sack with his right hand, and the liquid spurted out on his face and clothing. He fell, and appeared to be dead. He was taken up and carried off, and finally escaped to the United States."

R. A. Henderson, attorney-at-law, Topeka, Kan. : "I was born in England ; was educated at the Royal Military College, and served three years in the regular army. My grandfather (Robert Laird) was an English soldier in the Peninsular War and at Waterloo. In the Peninsular War he was a member of the Eighty-eighth Regiment, known as the Connaught Rangers, and at Waterloo he was a sergeant in the celebrated Sixth Inniskillen Dragoons, who were almost annihilated in their charge against the cuirassiers. After the battle of Waterloo he went to France, and remained there with the army of occupation. He was one of the persons representing the English army, appointed to witness the execution of Ney. I have heard him say often that Ney was not executed—that he saw the muskets discharged, saw Ney fall, viewed the body, saw it taken up and carried away, saw it in the hospital, but that Ney was not hurt ; that the so-called execution was a farce. He always affirmed this in the most positive manner. Said Ney's fall was not natural, and that the supposed bullet marks upon his person were artificial. I think he also stated that some Prussians were present at the scene. My impression is that he said the guns contained blank cartridges. The report made by the commission, of which he was a member, to the military authorities was this : 'Marshal Ney was not shot.' I may be mistaken as to some minor matters, but the essential facts are as I have given them. My grandfather was a man of approved courage. He had a great many medals which were given to him for gallantry in the Peninsular War and at Waterloo. He was born in Fermanagh, six miles from Inniskillen, Ireland, and was very old when he died. While in the army he kept a private diary, which he bequeathed to me. I have it among my books in Canada. In that diary will be found a confirmation of what I have said and other details of the alleged execution.

"My grandfather further said that at the time of the so-called execution it was the common talk in the army and elsewhere that Ney was not shot."

Correspondent of the St. Louis *Republic*, Rocheport, Mo. (1891) : " Major Thomas W. Sampson, of Rocheport, gives some very interesting facts in regard to the mysterious Ney which seem to establish the fact conclusively that he was not shot on that dismal and foggy morning when so many brave men fell victims to the merciless decree of the French Council of Peers. Major Sampson states that the late George H. C. Melody, of St. Louis, spent several weeks in Paris, France, in 1845, during the reign of Louis Philippe, King of the French. His Majesty extended to the American commoner many tokens of friendship in recognition of courtesies extended to the king by Mr. Melody in St. Louis during the king's exile years before.

"In the course of a confidential conversation during this visit, Mr. Melody asked Louis Philippe the question : ' Is the statement in history that Marshal Ney was shot true ? '

" The king replied : ' Mr. Melody, I know the fact that you are one of the highest Masons in America. I am known as one of the most exalted Masons in Europe. Marshal Ney held a position among Masons equal to either of us. The prisons were full of men condemned to be shot. These men were daily being marched out to meet their fate. Some other man may have filled the grave intended for Marshal Ney.' Mr. Melody replied very quietly : ' May it please your Majesty, Ney was not shot.' " *

Mrs. E. D. Austin, Mocksville, N. C. (1888) : " When Peter S. Ney taught school near Mocksville, N. C., about the year 1834 or 1835, he lived very near my house, and I frequently saw him. My husband, Colonel E. D. Austin, had a carpenter shop not far from the house, and was often called upon to furnish coffins for persons who had died in the town

---

* The Rev. Dr. Basil G. Jones states that P. S. Ney told him that the '*ancient fraternity* aided in his escape from the first." Hon. John S. Henderson, Salisbury, N. C., says : " I have heard my father say that Peter S. Ney was a Mason." Wellington was a Mason. Comment is unnecessary.

or the surrounding country. Mr. Ney would sometimes go into the shop and sit down and talk with Colonel Austin and his workmen. One night, between nine and ten o'clock, while they were engaged in making a coffin for a person who had recently died near the town, Mr. Ney walked into the shop to see what was going on. He had been drinking a little, but he was by no means intoxicated. One of the workmen, who was much attached to Mr. Ney, said to him, 'Mr. Ney, we are making a coffin for a man just about as large as you are. This coffin will exactly fit you.' 'Ah,' said Mr. Ney, quickly looking up, 'they thought they had me in a coffin once, but they didn't.' My husband, Colonel Austin, heard this conversation, and related it to me."

Thomas D. Graham, Davidson College, N. C. (1888) : " I was well acquainted with Peter S. Ney. I helped to nurse him in his last illness. He was sick several days, and I sat up with him every other night. I saw him die, shaved him, and helped to dress him and bury him. He had wounds all over his body—I don't remember how many. He had a scar on the left side of his head, one on his breast, one on his thigh, one on his arm, and one in the calf of his leg. He would ask those who waited on him to rub his leg for the cramp, but to be careful, for there was a ball in the calf of his leg which sometimes gave him pain. He had many other scars, but I have forgotten where they were located or how many there were. Mr. Ney boarded at Mr. Osborne G. Foard's. I often saw him there, and sometimes had long talks with him. He described to me one day the battle of Waterloo—drew a plan of it on the sand, marked off the position of the army, also that of the English army ; showed me how the battle was conducted, etc. I think he told me that he received the sabre cut on his head at the battle of Waterloo ; that he cut down the man who gave him the blow, but broke his own sword in doing so. I have his old hair trunk and shaving-box, brush and strap. During his last illness I heard him say four or five times that he was Marshal Ney. He died on the 15th day of November, 1846, about five or six o'clock in the evening. About ten o'clock in the morning Dr. Matthew

Locke, his physician, and one of his old pupils, came into the room and said to him, 'Mr. Ney, it pains me deeply to tell you that you have not long to live.' Mr. Ney looked at Dr. Locke and said calmly, 'I know it, Matthew, I know it.' About three o'clock in the afternoon Dr. Locke returned. He was much affected. 'Mr. Ney,' said he, 'you have but a short time to live, and we would like to know from your own lips who you are before you die.' Mr. Ney, perfectly calm and rational, raised himself up on his elbow, and looking Dr. Locke full in the face, said, 'I am Marshal Ney of France.' Two or three hours later he died.

"Archie Foard, a colored man, was present when Mr. Ney told Dr. Locke he was Marshal Ney. Mr. Foard, I think, was also present."

Mrs. George F. Shepherd, Elmwood, N. C. (1890) : " When Peter S. Ney died I was living at my old home, not far from the residence of Osborne G. Foard. A few hours after Mr. Ney's death my father (Joseph Irwin) came home, and said that Mr. Ney had made some revelations which cleared up the mystery of his life ; that just before he died he told his friends who he was, etc. I was quite young, but I distinctly remember that my father said this."

Archie Foard (colored), Cleveland, Rowan County, N. C. (1890) : " I belonged to Mr. Osborne Foard. Mr. Peter Ney died there, and I nursed him while he was sick. He was sick, I think, about two weeks. He had rheumatism and pains in his back, with a good deal of inflammation at times. He was very thankful for what I did for him, or for what anybody did for him. He said to me, ' You are very good to me. I will reward you when I get well.' Sometimes he would hug his pillow and say, ' Oh, my wife ! my wife !' I felt so sorry for him, for he was just as good to me and the other colored people as any man could be. One day he said, ' Oh, I can't stand it any longer ! If I get well I must go back and see my wife and children.' Often when he was in pain he would say, ' Oh, my God ! ' * not ' Oh, *my* God ! ' like most

---

* M. Batardy said that when he told Marshal Ney that Napoleon had

people, but, 'Oh, my (me) God!' I heard him say two or three times that he was Marshal Ney. I didn't know who Marshal Ney was, but that is what he said. He had wounds all over him. I don't know how many he had. He was awfully marked up. I used to rub his back. He said it did him a great deal of good, and he would thank me over and over again for it. He wasn't out of his head at any time except a little while before he died. He said not long before he died that he was Marshal Ney. When Mr. Ney was well he would often go out into the garden before breakfast and get an onion and eat it with a biscuit; sometimes he would eat red pepper with his biscuit. Everybody, white folks as well as colored, looked up to Mr. Ney as the biggest man in that country. We were all sorter 'jubus' of him; stood off from him because he was so fur ahead of us. I never seed such a man."

John M. Steele, Statesville, N. C. (1887): "I went to school to P. S. Ney in 1826 and again in 1829. He had originally auburn or reddish hair, but in 1826 it was turning gray. He had splendid teeth, but they were considerably worn, because the upper and lower ones came evenly together, one square upon the other. He was without doubt the greatest man that ever lived in North Carolina. One day Mr. Ney borrowed a horse of Mr. Gay, of Iredell, to ride to Statesville, a distance of twelve miles. When he returned he said to Mr. Gay in his deep bass voice, 'This is a good horse, but not so good as the one I once rode eighty miles, from dark to daylight.' At the close of the school in 1826 Mr. Ney said to his pupils, 'Stick to your books; read and study at home; you have better advantages than I had when I was a boy.' Mr. Ney died near Third Creek, Rowan County, in 1846. It was the common talk of the neighborhood immediately after his death that he had told Dr. Locke and others that he was Marshal Ney. I heard the report often."

Mrs. Osborne G. Foard, Newton, N. C. (1887): "I knew P. S. Ney when he taught school near Third Creek in Rowan

landed from Elba, Marshal Ney answered, "O my God, what a misfortune!"

County. I remember him well. He walked rather briskly at all times, even in going about the house. Had small marks or spots on his face, produced, I suppose, by the small-pox. Skin a little rough, though of a healthy hue. Loved fun and jokes when he had nothing to do. A hearty laugher when anything amused him. A great fencer. His sword or stick would fly like lightning. Hawk-looking eyes, with a good deal of white in them. One day when he was sick, he said, 'O France! France! why can't I— No, I must not!' Talked rapidly when excited. Had a wound on his arm between shoulder and elbow so deep that the flesh appeared to adhere to the bone. He had an Irish brogue, a deep, rolling voice. I have his writing-desk, comb, and knife. He had a fine sword, with the point broken off; but I do not know what became of it. I have seen it often. It was highly polished, as bright as new silver, with a richly ornamented hilt. About one fourth of the sword was broken off. Mr. Ney noticed everything. Mr. Foard used to say, 'What Mr. Ney couldn't see was not worth seeing.' Mr. Foard was very sorry that he allowed Pliny Miles to carry off Mr. Ney's shorthand manuscript. Mr. Foard wrote to Mr. Miles about the document, and he replied that he would return it after awhile. Some months afterward Mr. Foard wrote again to Pliny Miles, but he received no answer to his second letter. The manuscript was never returned. Mr. Foard had the monument put to Mr. Ney's grave, and my impression is that he and Colonel Austin composed the inscription. I have frequently heard Mr. Foard speak of Mr. Ney's last illness, and of his dying declaration that he was Marshal Ney. He said in substance that not long before Mr. Ney died, Dr. Locke approached his bedside and said, 'Mr. Ney, I have done everything for you that I could do, and it grieves me to tell you that I do not think you can possibly get well. We would like to know who you are before you die.' Mr. Ney answered, 'I might as well tell you. I am Marshal Ney of France.'"

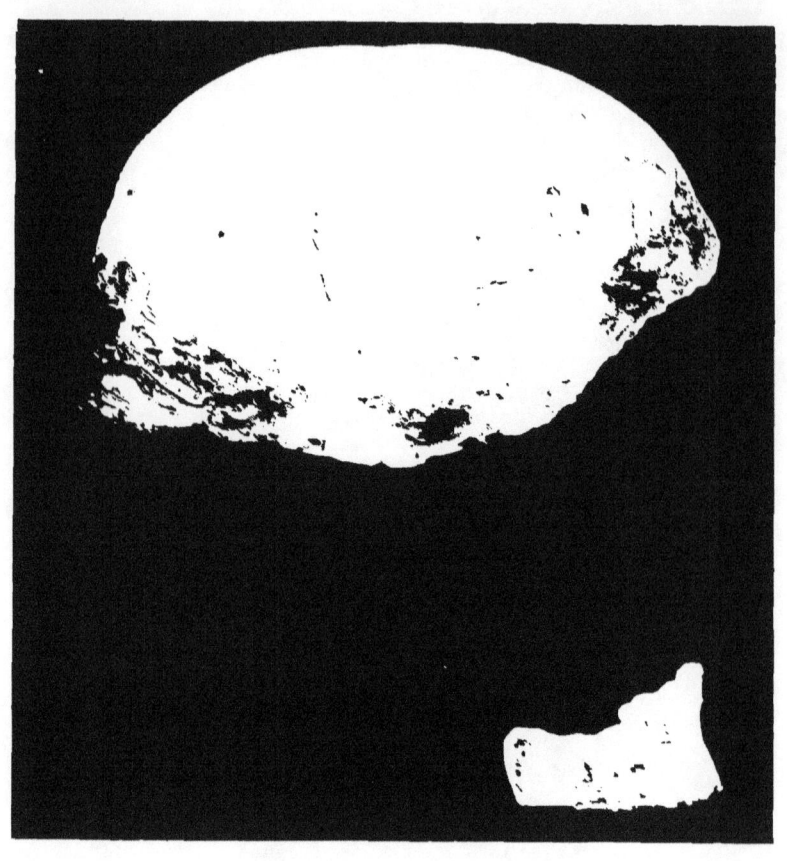

NOTE.

The body of P. S. Ney was exhumed on the 3d day of May, 1887. The physicians present say :

" The undersigned physicians wish to state that, according to a previous notice, we did to-day cause to be exhumed the remains of P. S. Ney in the presence of a great number of witnesses, some of them from Washington City, Raleigh, and other parts of the country. We found some of the bones only, and these in a state of such decay that we cannot state positively whether the skull had ever been trepanned or not. We made diligent search for bullets said to have lodged in the body, but found none. We succeeded so far, however, as to ascertain that the skeleton was about five feet ten inches long, and the skull around about the eyes about twenty-four inches in circumference.

" (Signed) J. G. RAMSAY, M.D.,
D. B. WOOD, M.D.,
S. W. STEVENSON, M.D.,
JAMES McGUIRE, M.D.,
C. M. POOL, M.D.,
S. W. EATON, M.D.,
THOMAS E. ANDERSON, M.D.,
J. H. WOLFF, M.D.,
J. B. GAITHER, M.D.

" THIRD CREEK CHURCH, N. C., May 3, 1887."

The inscription on P. S. Ney's tombstone is as follows :

IN MEMORY OF

PETER STUART NEY,

A NATIVE OF FRANCE AND SOLDIER OF THE FRENCH REVOLUTION

UNDER NAPOLEON BONAPARTE,

WHO DEPARTED THIS LIFE

NOVEMBER 15TH, 1846,

AGED 77 YEARS.

[OVER.]

Brief Description of Lower Maxillary by Dr. J. H. Wolff.

"THE body or anterior part of the inferior maxillary bone (lower jaw-bone) was found in a better state of preservation than the other bones of the skull. That part of the bone on the right side, posterior to the location of the second molar (jaw tooth), and on the left side posterior to the first molar (jaw tooth), was missing. The dimensions, shape, etc., indicated a lower jaw developed somewhat above the average of the human race—the chin being prominent, bordering on protrusion. The sockets (receptacles for the teeth) were well marked, showing that the full complement of teeth were present in this jaw when the subject died, except the second inferior molar on the right side, which had, no doubt, been removed, as the soft bone which encases the teeth had been absorbed and a smooth surface left on the bone proper. The left inferior *lateral incisor cuspid*, first and second *bicuspids* were the teeth found intact, the others having been dislodged evidently in removing the skull from the grave.

"The teeth were in a better state of preservation than other parts found, showing that, notwithstanding they had done duty as grinders for seventy-seven years, and had lain in the ground forty years, they yet served as signboards to point out certain characteristics and to tell of the malformation of their owner. To be plainer, the teeth being evenly abraded or worn down half the length of the crowns indicate the closing of the teeth of the upper jaw directly upon those below instead of the anterior teeth closing over, *scissors fashion*, which is normal.

"The abnormal articulation of the teeth accounts for the slight protrusion of the lower jaw heretofore referred to."

DOCUMENTARY EVIDENCE
AS TO NEY'S IDENTITY.

MR. ROBERT MACFARLAN, attorney-at-law, Florence, S. C., has in his library a valuable book which once belonged to Peter S. Ney. This book was written by Dr. Barry E. O'Meara, and is entitled "Napoleon in Exile; or, a Voice from St. Helena." It is in two volumes, and was published by Carey & Lea, Philadelphia, in 1822. Each volume contains several marginal annotations in P. S. Ney's handwriting. P. S. Ney wrote his name once in Vol. I. and twice in Vol. II.

The notes by P. S. Ney are copied literally from the book, exactly as they were written, and are here printed in italics.

Enough of the text is given to make the notes intelligible.

NOTES IN "NAPOLEON IN EXILE," VOL. I.

" ' I never knew anything about that document until it was read to the troops. It is true that I sent him orders to obey me. What could he do? His troops abandoned him.' "[1]—Page 16.

P. S. NEY'S NOTE.—[1] *The Return was meditated prior to N. Bonaparte's quitting fontainbleau for Elba, and when Napoleon re-landed, Ney used all his influence to induce his Division to join the Emperor . . . ! ! ! which they hesit . . .* *

"Nor since I knew him had he ever taken more than a very small cup of coffee after each repast, and at no other time. I have also been informed by those who have been in

---

* Unfortunately the book was rebound, and some of the most important notes were cut off.

his service for fifteen years, that he had never exceeded that quantity since they first knew him.'"—Page 17.

P. S. NEY'S NOTE.—[1] *This is a mistake.**

"He smiled and said, '*Sarebbe difficile a credere.*' "[1]—Page 115.

[1] P. S. NEY'S NOTE.—(Shorthand).

"'At Moscow the fire advanced, seized the Chinese and India warehouses; . . . most terrific sight the world ever beheld!!'[1] *Allons docteur.*' "—Page 127.

P. S. NEY'S NOTE.—[1] *Grand.*

"'There was a Major Douglas[1] who behaved very gallantly at Acre.'"—Page 135.

P. S. NEY'S NOTE.—[1] *Sir John Douglas.*

"'If the government I established had remained—best thing that ever happened for Spain.'"[1]—Page 136.

P. S. NEY'S NOTE.—[1] *True.*

"'But Soult did not betray Louis, as has been supposed, nor was he privy to my return and landing in France. . . . Were I on his jury[1]. . . Ney stated I told him so—that Soult was privy to my return. As to the proclamation which Ney said that I had sent him, it is not true.[2] I sent him nothing but orders. I would have stopped the proclamation had it been in my power, as it was unworthy of me.'"—Page 249.

P. S. NEY'S NOTES.—[1] *Soult is alive!!! therefore the policy of Napoleon* . . .
[2] *I do not know exactly who framed the proclamation. But it assuredly augmented Bonaparte's army from 3400 to 50,000 in* . . .†

* P. S. Ney is right. See "Memoirs of Duchess d'Abrantes." When Napoleon lost Egypt he "ordered three cups of coffee in one hour." On board the Northumberland, "coffee was frequently served up to him on deck." The *Monthly Magazine* states that he was "extremely fond of coffee."

† The Duke de Rovigo states that an officer told him that he saw General Bourmont "drawing up the proclamation in Marshal Ney's quarters."

"'He [Ney] could not prevent the troops from joining me, nor indeed the peasants; but he went too far.¹ There was no plot, no understanding with any of the generals in France.² Not one of these men knew my intentions. Mouton Duvernet and others, because my having effected.'"—Page 250.

P. S. NEY'S NOTES.—¹ *An error !!! Too much vanity or disguise. Ney had as much influence over the troops* AS ANY MAN, *and acted according to preconcerted measures. Ney was ordered by the Bourbons to march against Napoleon without coming to Paris, but he did come to Paris to inform the Bonapartists of his design of . . . and to preconcert measures; then . . . intention, paid his devoirs to Lewis, and promised to bring Bonaparte to Paris in an iron cage. No man could use . . . to induce both m . . .*
² *The scheme of the plot was formed before Bonaparte quitted Fountainbleau ! ! ! and communications between B. and some of the generals facilitated by Lavalette before Napoleon re-landed from Elba ! ! !**

"'I have always gone with the opinions of great masses and with events. *J'ai marché toujours avec l'opinion de cinq ou six millions d'hommes.*¹ Of what use, then, would crime have been to me? . . . I am not uneasy for the result. Had I succeeded, I should have died with the reputation of the greatest man² that ever existed. As it is, my ambition was great, and caused by the opinions of great bodies.'"—Page 261.

P. S. NEY'S NOTES.—¹*You will not get "de cinque ou six millions de hommes" to agree with you in these assertions and opinions.*
² *All admit you to have been the greatest—but not the best.*

"'If ever policy,' continued he, 'authorized a man to commit a crime¹ . . . not only did I refuse to consent, but I positively prohibited that any attempt of the kind should be made. . . . Perhaps my greatest fault was not having deprived the King of Prussia of his throne, which I might easily

---

Ney, on his trial, said Napoleon sent him the proclamation. It is not at all probable that Ney wrote it. The style is entirely too bombastic and wordy. It sounds like Napoleon. The framework of it, to say the least, is probably due to Napoleon. Capefigue ("Les Cent Jours") says it was "dictated by the Emperor."
* See Appendix A.

have done. After Friedland I ought to have taken Silesia and
. . . from Prussia, and given them to Saxony . . . they would
have been content.' " ²—Page 262.

P. S. NEY'S NOTES.—¹ *Your opinion is ill founded—the Bourbons* . . .
² *This measure was actually in agitation after the battle of Friedland. But
the solemn engagements and importunities of the King.* . . .

" ' Warden has been incorrectly informed that Maret* was
privy to my return to France. He knew nothing about it,
and such a statement may injure his relatives in France.
He has acted also unguardedly in asserting matters upon the
authority of Count and Countess Bertrand, as it may cause
. . . saying that the information came from me.' " ¹—Page
270.

P. S. NEY'S NOTE.—¹*This is the real motive which induces Napoleon to assert at all* . . .

" ' Ney,' said he, ' never made use of haughty language at
Fontainebleau in my presence ; on the contrary, he was always
submissive before me, though in my absence he sometimes
broke out into violence, as he was a man without education.¹
If he had made use of unbecoming language toward me at
Fontainebleau, the troops would have torn him to pieces.²
Lavalette,' ³ added Napoleon, ' knew nothing of my return
from Elba, or of what was hatching there. Madame Lavalette
was of the family of Beauharnais. She was a very fine
woman. Louis, my brother, fell in love with her, and wanted
to have her, to prevent which I caused her to espouse Lavalette, to whom she was much attached.' "—Page 289.

P. S. NEY'S NOTES.—¹ *He had a good, though not classical education* . . .
² *Indeed.*
³ *Lavalette is alive ! ! ! or was at the date of this conversation. It is very
prudent in Napoleon to say this—but Lavalette and Ney knew of and aided
the Return.*

" Napoleon added that he had never told Ney that he had
entered France with the privity and support of England ;

* At Auxerre Napoleon said to Ney, " Write to our friends in Paris.
Write to MARET."

that, on the contrary, he had always disclaimed and reprobated the idea of returning by the aid of foreign bayonets, and had come purposely to overturn a dynasty upheld by them. That all he looked for was the support of the French nation."*—Page 289.

"'Pichon had been consul in America. He was disgraced by me for having embezzled three millions. This Pichon published a libel against me, and was afterward sent by me to London as a spy—at least, he was so far sent by me that I suffered it. This man who, in 1814, had written such a libel against me, went, in 1815, as a spy for the police of the very person whom he had so grossly libelled.'"[1]—Page 295.

P. S. NEY'S NOTE.—[1] *This is greatly to be doubted.*

"'I knew of Bulow's arrival[1] at eleven o'clock; but I did not regard it. I had still eighty chances out of a hundred in my favor.'"—Page 299.

P. S. NEY'S NOTE.—[1] *He could not have known of Bulow's arrival at so early an hour, for the Prussians did not arrive before 3 P.M., and then the greater part of the reserve were ordered to oppose . . .*

"'These were the two principal causes of the loss of the battle of Waterloo:' (1) Tardiness and neglect of Grouchy, and (2) the Reserve engaged without orders and without my knowledge.'"—Page 300.

P. S. NEY'S NOTE.—[1] *Blucher came in about sunset with 10,000 fresh troops which decided the . . . which was the reason that Bonaparte had no reserve to meet the British Cavalry† . . . simultaneous movement . . . nearly dark at this time—perhaps Napoleon did not distinctly observe the commencement of these. . . . The fact is, that on the retreat of the old guards each offr. acted for himself.*

* Marshal Ney on his trial said that Napoleon wrote to him that he had left Elba with the knowledge and consent of England. Napoleon here denies the truth of this assertion. It is probable that Napoleon is right, as P. S. Ney has no observation to make on Napoleon's statement.

† Napoleon himself, it appears, sent off his reserve, or the greater part of it, to oppose the Prussians. Who believes his statement that they "engaged *without orders, and without his knowledge*"?

"'The Doctor in his book makes me say that I never committed a useless crime.¹ I never committed a crime.'"— Page 302.

P. S. NEY'S NOTE.—¹ *few will acquiesce with you in saying that you never committed* A CRIME. *It must be granted that none in your situation could have committed* FEWER CRIMES. *It would be blind adulation to say less. But,* " *Cur non dices veritatem*"?

"'Is this the result of the conduct of a merciless, unfeeling tyrant . . . but I never employed crime or assassination to forward it . . . le mensonge pape, la verité reste¹ . . . like Lord C——² . . . C'est un homme ignoble.'" ³— Page 302.

P. S. NEY'S NOTES.—¹ *Falsehood will die, and truth live.*
² *Castlereagh.*
³ *He is a base man.*

"'. . . To believe that abstaining from flesh and eating fish, which is so much more delicate and delicious, constitutes fasting! *Povero homo.*¹

P. S. NEY'S NOTE.—¹ *Poor men.*

"'If Hoche had arrived, Ireland was lost to you.'" ¹—Page 311.

P. S. NEY'S NOTE.—¹ *The ships were taken by the British.*

"'If the Irish had sent over honest men to me, I would have certainly made an attempt upon Ireland.¹ But I had no confidence. . . .'"—Page 312.

P. S. NEY'S NOTE.—¹ *Naper Tandy was an intelligent, active man, and an Envoy from Ireland to France.*

"'The King's legs are covered with ulcers, which are dressed for him by the Duchess of Angoulême. He gorges . . . When I returned to the Tuileries I found my apartments poisoned with the smell of his legs, and of divers sulphureous baths which he was in the habit of using.'" ¹—Page 314.

P. S. NEY'S NOTE.—¹ *These observations are beneath the dignity of Napoleon, though correct in point of fact.*

AS TO NEY'S IDENTITY.

" ' . . . with the body of a beautiful dancer, but *per Dio* [1]
. . . To the Emperor and to the Prince de Neufchâtel.' " [2]
—Page 316.

P. S. NEY'S NOTES.—[1] *By God.*
[2] *Marshal Berthier.*

" I took the liberty to observe that it might naturally be supposed . . . 'Yes,' replied Napoleon, 'I would strictly have complied with that treaty.¹ I would not have made it myself, but finding it made [Treaty of Paris], I would have adhered to it.' "—Page 317.

P. S. NEY'S NOTE.—[1] *In fact the Return of Napoleon was preconcerted at fontainbleau before the signature.* . . .

" I then asked who in his opinion now was the first.'
. . . ' Suchet, Clausel, Gerard are in my opinion the first of the French generals.' [2] . . . He also mentioned Soult in terms of praise.' " [3]—Page 318.

P. S. NEY'S NOTES.—*N. B. Kleber, Dessaix, Ney, Duroc, Hoche, etc., are now dead.* . . .
[2] *Now.*
[3] *He merited them.*

" ' Before I went to Elba, Lord Castlereagh said to Caulaincourt, ' Why does Napoleon think of going to Elba? Let him come to England . . . he will be received with the greatest joy, and be much better than at Elba. This,' added he, ' had much influence with me afterward.' " [1]—Page 321.

P. S. NEY'S NOTE.—[1] *And would have been accepted then—only for the secret design formed in concert with his officers at fontainbleau to Return to France.* . . .

" ' . . . I should have extinguished her like that ' (raising one of his feet, and stamping as if he were putting out the snuff of a candle). ' I could,' continued he, ' have dethroned the King of Prussia or the Emperor of Austria upon the slightest pretext as easily as I do this ' (stretching out one of his legs). ' I was then too powerful for any man except myself to injure me.' " [1]—Page 322.

P. S. NEY'S NOTE.—[1] *This is the true spirit of the man.*

". . . Following tenor relative to Metternich : 'One or two lies are sometimes necessary, but Metternich is all lies—nothing but lies, lies, lies from him.' Napoleon laughed and said : '*C'est vrai.*' " ¹—Page 323.

P. S. NEY'S NOTE.—¹ *It is true.*

" ' . . . You say that it has been stipulated that only prisoners, and not slaves, are in future to be made. . . . I fear much that if any difference be made . . . I think that your ministers ordered Lord Exmouth *not* to endeavor to abolish piracy altogether, but merely to give it a check, to punish the Algerines in a certain degree.' " ¹—Page 325.

P. S. NEY'S NOTE.—¹ *Solid Remarks.*

" ' You say that you lost a thousand men in killed and disabled, and got five or six ships knocked to pieces. Now the lives and limbs of a thousand brave English seamen are of more value and consequence than the *whole of the piratical States.*' Blockading the port with a seventy-four and two or three frigates under Captains Usher or Maitland would have gained you just as good terms as you have got without the loss of a man. . . .' "—Page 326.

P. S. NEY'S NOTE.—¹ *. . . Come with an ill grace from a man who was never remarkable for preventing Bloodshed.*

" . . . Lord Cornwallis, to which his Excellency [Lowe] replied that Lord Cornwallis' was too honest a man to deal with him ! ! ! . . . This man never could have been brought up in good company, and has *l'air*² *d'un sons lieutenant de l'ancien régime.*"—Page 328.

P. S. NEY'S NOTES.—¹ *Lowe confesses his own . . .*
² *the manner of . . . old Government.*

officer retired, and the Russian batteries opened a fire of grape-shot, at the distance of only two hundred and fifty yards, while at the concussion the mist arose, and showed the devoted column of French, with a ravine in front manned by their enemies, subjected on every side to a fire of artillery, while the hills were black with the Russian troops placed to support their guns. Far from losing heart in so perilous a situation, the French Guards, with rare intrepidity, forced their way through the ravine of the Losmina, and rushed with the utmost fury on the Russian batteries. They were, however, charged in their turn with the bayonet, and such as had crossed the stream suffered dreadfully. In spite of this failure, Ney persevered in the attempt to cut his passage by main force through this superior body of Russians, who lay opposed to him in front. Again the French advanced upon the cannon, losing whole ranks, which were supplied by their comrades as fast as they fell. The assault was once more unsuccessful, and Ney, seeing that the general fate of his column was no longer doubtful, endeavoured at least to save a part from the wreck. Having selected about four thousand of the best men, he separated himself from the rest, and set forth under shelter of the night, moving to the rear, as if about to return to Smolensk. This, indeed, was the only road open to him, but he did not pursue it long; for as soon as he reached a rivulet, which had the appearance of being one of the feeders of the Dnieper, he adopted it for his guide to the banks of that river, which he reached in safety near the village of Syrokovenia. Here he found a single place in the river frozen over, though the ice was so thin that it bent beneath the steps of the soldiers.

Three hours were permitted, to allow stragglers from the column during the night-march to rally at this place; should their good fortune enable them to find it. These three hours Ney spent in profound sleep, lying on the banks of the river, and wrapped up in his cloak. When the stipulated time had elapsed, the passage to the other side began and continued, although the motion of the ice, and the awful sounds of its splitting into large cracks, prevented more than one from crossing at once. The wagons, some loaded with sick and wounded, last attempted to pass; but the ice broke with them, and the heavy plunge and stifled moaning, apprised their companions of their fate. The Cossacks, as usual, speedily appeared in the rear, gleaned up some hundreds of prisoners, and took possession of the artillery and baggage.

FACSIMILE OF P. S. NEY'S NOTES IN "LIFE OF NAPOLEON BUONAPARTE." PAGE 379.

nation, instead of brutifying them by ignorance and superstition."

"Those English," added he, "who are lovers of liberty will one day lament with tears having gained the battle of Waterloo. It was as fatal to the liberties of

Oui en vérité, vous et moi nous sommes d'accord — Malgré tout le monde.

FACSIMILE OF P. S. NEY'S NOTE IN O'MEARA'S "NAPOLEON IN EXILE," VOL. II., PAGE 243.

NOTES IN "NAPOLEON IN EXILE," VOL. II.

"21st April, 1817,¹ Napoleon has been for some days in very good spirits. On Saturday, the 19th, some captains . . ."
—Page 1.

P. S. NEY'S NOTE.—¹ *Voilà l'homme!*

" . . . The charlatans¹ will kill . . . Molière's doctors." ²—Page 3.

P. S. NEY'S NOTES.—¹ *Quacks.*
² *Women.*

"'When at Elba the Princess of Wales informed me of her intention to visit me. . . . I knew that at the time it could not fail to injure the princess [Queen Caroline], and therefore I put it off. It is astonishing that she desired it, for she had no reason to be attached to me, as her father and brother were killed fighting against me.¹ She went afterward to see Marie Louise at ——,² and I believe that they are great friends.' "—Page 21.

P. S. NEY'S NOTES.—¹ *Her Brother, the Duc de Brunswick, was killed on the 1st day of the Battle of Waterloo at Quatre Bras; subsequent to the period alluded to—He was with Wellington's Right Wing in advance.*
² *Young Napoleon and Billy Austin, Caroline's adopted son, used to play and frequently fight. Billy was stronger, but Nap more active.*

"During the conversation I mentioned that Bernadotte¹ had been strongly suspected of being lukewarm in the cause of the allies, . . . and supposed to be likely to join him if any reverse happened."—Page 27.

P. S. NEY'S NOTE.—¹ *Bernadotte was subsidised by England [with] 1 million per month. He at last advanced with 60,000 men; to him was chiefly owing the victory at Leipsig.*
His previous knowledge of Bonaparte's tactics and Dispositions in Battle give him great ascendency . . . Napoleon . . .

"'Murat's boiling courage carried him into the midst of the enemy, *couvert de pennes jusqu'au clocher*, and glittering with gold, . . . he was a paladin—in fact, a Don

Quixote in the field ; but take him into the Cabinet, he was a poltroon, without judgment or decision. Murat and Ney[1] were the bravest men I ever witnessed.' "—Page 61.

P. S. NEY's NOTE.—[1] *Ney could both act in the field and the Cabinet without his previous arrangements and subsequent . . . observation. Bonaparte . . . O'Meara makes Napoleon say that Ney betrayed him at Fontainbleau! Bah! his having first joined him with 36,000 men when he had it in his power to capture B. refutes that insinuation.*

"' Murat, however, was a much nobler character than Ney. Murat was generous and open. Ney partook of the *canaille*.'"[1] —Page 62.

P. S. NEY's NOTE.—[1] *Bah!*

" Josephine died worth about eighteen millions of francs."[1] —Page 64.

P. S. NEY's NOTE.—[1] 18,000,000 × 10 =

12)180,000,000 *pence*

20)15,000,000

£750,000 *sterling*.

" Josephine was grace personified. She had grace even *en se couchant*.[1] Her toilet was a perfect arsenal."—Page 65.

P. S. NEY's NOTE.—[1] *In bed.*

" Napoleon gazed on the statue of his son with great satisfaction and delight, his face strongly expressive of paternal love. No person who witnessed this scene could deny that Napoleon was animated by the tender affections of a father."[1] —Page 66.

P. S. NEY's NOTE.—[1] *Yet the American Reviewer says that Napoleon had no sympathy! Ecce!*

"' What reason had Murat to complain of the Emperor of Austria, who had behaved generously and offered him an asylum ; . . . as Murat had endeavored to deprive him of Italy.' Murat behaved like a madman ; he engaged without judgment in an expedition without a plan. . . . In his procla-

P. S. NEY's NOTE.—[1] *Moscow.*

mations to the Italians he never mentioned my name, though he knew they adored me.² He terminated his life like a madman.' " ³—Page 67.

P. S. NEY'S NOTES.—² *Oho!**
³ *Murat died like a Gallant Soldier on the Ruins of his throne.* . . .

"'I ought to have died at Waterloo. But the misfortune is, that when a man seeks the most for death he cannot find it. Men were killed around me, before, behind, everywhere, but no bullet for me.'"'—Page 69.

P. S. NEY'S NOTE.—¹ *True.*

"I told him that in Lord ——'s' speech there were three calumnies and ten lies."—Page 70.

P. S. NEY'S NOTE.—¹ *B——'s.*

"'I was called to that of France by the votes of nearly four millions of Frenchmen.'"'—Page 72.

P. S. NEY'S NOTE.—¹ *Polls gave more.*

"The Emperor was so firmly impressed with the idea that an attempt would be made forcibly to intrude on his privacy, that . . . he always kept four or five loaded pistols and some swords in his apartments, with which he was determined to dispatch the first who entered against his will."'—Page 85.

P. S. NEY'S NOTE.—¹ *He might have been disarmed.*

"Napoleon then said that, notwithstanding the occupation of Paris by the allies, he should still have succeeded but for the treachery of Marmont. He was to have entered Paris in the dead of the night.¹ The *canaille* were all ready (I think he also said he would have cut off the allies from their park of artillery)."—Page 100.

P. S. NEY'S NOTE.—¹ *Napoleon, Ney and others did aproach the lines*

* P. S. Ney is right. The Italians did not "adore" Napoleon. They hated him because of his tyranny and his vile treatment of the Pope. See Thiers' "History of the Consulate and the Empire," and Ney's letter to Napoleon after the battle of Dennewitz.

in the middle of the night to reconnoitre,* and found it prudent to retire and abandon the plan of surprise.

"The English cavalry approached to within a hundred or a hundred and fifty toises of the spot where the Emperor was standing with only Soult,¹ Drouot, Bertrand, and himself, . . . exclaiming, '*Il faut mourir ici, il faut mourir sur le champ de bataille.*' "²—Page 103.

P. S. NEY'S NOTES.—¹ *Soult was not in the battle. Certainly.*
² *He shall die by a blow at once. He shall die on the field of Battle.*

" ' . . . or in the hope that I might commit suicide. The fact is, that had it not been for their broils and quarrels among themselves, I should never have thought of dispossessing them '¹ [the Spaniards]. I said that some of the publications against him asserted that he had been the contriver of the whole plot.' "—Page 107.

P. S. NEY'S NOTE.—¹ *Vide Vol. I. The intentions of Napoleon with regard to Spain. These two statements are irreconcilable. Bonaparte certainly . . .*

" ' In some respects Robespierre may be said to have been an honest man.¹ All the crimes committed by Hébert, Chaumette . . . When I commanded the Army of Italy, Barras made the Venetian Ambassador . . . with which I [here he made use of a most significant gesture].² I never paid any attention to such letters.' "—Page 109.

P. S. NEY'S NOTES.—¹ *Yes, if honesty means to be sincere in the most flagitious crimes and . . .*
² *Drawn to the life.*

* We know certainly that Marshal Ney was at Fontainebleau on the night of April 5th. He had a long private interview with Napoleon, and one of the subjects discussed was that of Marmont's defection. Thiers says, "It is difficult to know what passed in this interview. Marshal Ney has left no written record, and Napoleon in his St. Helena memoirs has observed a profound silence on the subject."

It is very probable the "scheme of the plot to return from Elba" was then considered, and that the reconnoissance by "Napoleon, Ney, and others," was made during the night. About this time it was officially reported at the headquarters of the Emperor Alexander that Napoleon

"'Barrère? parceque c'est un homme sans caractère.' Carnot, c'est le plus honnête des hommes.² Madame Campan,' continued Napoleon, 'had a very indifferent opinion of Marie Antoinette. She told me that a person well known . . . but discovered a pair of breeches,³ . . . which were immediately recognized.'"—Page 110.

P. S. Ney's Notes.—¹ *Because he is a man without character.*
² *He is the most honest of the* . . .
³ *Unworthy Repetition.*

"'Fouché,' added he, 'never was my confidant. Never did he approach me without bending to the ground. For *him* I never had esteem. . . . He never was in a situation to demand my confidence, or even to speak to me without being questioned, nor had he the talents requisite for it.¹ Not so Talleyrand.'"—Page 111.

P. S. Ney's Note.—¹ *The ablest Minister of Police that ever lived.*

"The princes and chief mandarins performed the *ko-tou*. The English and Russian ambassadors ought to have done the same. The Emperor of China had a right to require it. If a Chinese ambassador were received in London, he would have no right to perform the *ko-tou*. He ought to follow the same etiquette as that observed by the princes, . . . which would be the English *ko-tou*.¹ The simple principle that in negotiations as well as in etiquette the ambassador does not represent the sovereign, and has only a right to experience the same treatment as the highest grandee of the place, clears up the whole of the question, and removes every difficulty."²—Page 113.

P. S. Ney's Notes.—¹ *Damn such frippery.*
² *Certainly.*

had fled from Fontainebleau with fifty mounted Chasseurs of his guard. Macdonald in his "Memoirs" alludes to this report. He says that he does not know how it originated; that he was never "able to get to the bottom of the story." I have little doubt that it had its origin in the reconnoissance of which P. S. Ney speaks.

"'The time for libels against me is past. A moderate criticism upon my actions . . . than all the furious diatribes in the *Quarterly Review* style.

"'Fouché, if even so inclined, never would have dared to do it. He knew me too well.' The fact is, that Wright killed himself. That Fouché may have threatened him,² with a view of extracting discoveries, is possible.'"—Page 116.

P. S. NEY'S NOTES.—¹ *Midshipman Mansel, who was captured with Capt. Wright and imprisoned in the next room to him, stated on his return to England that he often heard Captain W.'s groans as if in agony and . . . to rack. That one night Capt. W. after giving some directions touching his family affairs, etc., said that he had fallen into the hands of cruel Enemies, and would never more see England as he had but a short time to live. Such was the Report circulated by Mansel. The French Government . . . committed suicide.*
² *And also tortured him!*

"'Sidney Smith knew, from having been so long in the Temple,¹ that it was impossible to have assassinated a prisoner' [Wright]. I give this report as an *on dit.*"²—Page 117.

P. S. NEY'S NOTES.—¹ *Whence he escaped and crossed the British Channel in a small boat.*
² *As reported.*

(Note at bottom.) ". . . And only surpassed by the manifestation of generosity which he [Wellington] displayed in the fate of his old antagonist Ney."¹—Page 118.

P. S. NEY'S NOTE.—¹ *Viz., Wellington had military occupation of Paris when Ney was tried. The Bourbons refused in evidence the 12 Article of the Capitulation of Paris stipulating a general amnesty signed by Blucher, Wellington and the Bonapartists. Ney called upon Wellington to cause the 12 article to be complied with on his trial. Wellington replied that he had no authority to interfere with the acts of the Bourbons!!! Though by virtue of that very Capitulation which he had signed they could . . . Ney was sacrificed by . . .*

" I observed that I had been told by some English officers, who had been present at the battle of Albuera, that if Marshal Soult had advanced after the attack made by the lancers,

lowed the arrest, and the execution the trial, was an outrage upon humanity. On the trial no witnesses were produced, nor did any investigation take place, saving by the interrogation of the prisoner. Whatever points of accusation, therefore, are not established by the admission of the duke himself, must be considered as totally unproved. Yet this unconscientious tribunal not only found their prisoner guilty of having borne arms against the Republic, which he readily admitted, but of having placed himself at the head of a party of French emigrants in the pay of England, and carried on machinations for surprising the city of Strasburg; charges which he himself positively denied, and which were supported by no proof whatsoever.

Buonaparte, well aware of the total irregularity of the proceedings in this extraordinary case, seems, on some occasions, to have wisely renounced any attempt to defend what he must have been convinced was indefensible, and has vindicated his conduct upon general grounds, of a nature well worthy of notice. It seems that, when he spoke of the death of the Duke d'Enghien among his attendants, he always chose to represent it as a case falling under the ordinary forms of law, in which all regularity was observed, and where, though he might be accused of severity, he could not be charged with violation of justice. This was safe language to hearers from whom he was sure to receive neither objection nor contradiction, and is just an instance of an attempt, on the part of a consciously guilty party, to establish, by repeated asseverations, an innocence which was inconsistent with fact. But with strangers, from whom replies and argument might be expected, Napoleon took broader grounds. He alleged the death of the Duke d'Enghien to be an act of self-defence, a measure of state polity, arising out of the natural rights of humanity, by which a man, to save his own life, is entitled to take away that of another. " I was assailed," he said, " on all hands by the enemies whom the Bourbons raised up against me; threatened with air-guns, infernal machines, and deadly stratagems of every kind. I had no tribunal on earth to which I could appeal for protection, therefore I had a right to protect myself; and by putting to death one of those whose followers threatened my life, I was entitled to strike a salutary terror into the others."

We have no doubt that, in this argument, which is in the original much extended, Buonaparte explained his real motives; at least we can only add to them the stings of obstinate resentment, and implacable revenge. But the whole resolves itself into an allegation of that state necessity, which has been justly

FACSIMILE OF P. S. NEY'S NOTES IN SCOTT'S "LIFE OF NAPOLEON." PAGE 18.

he would have cut the English Army to pieces.[1] Napoleon acquiesced in this, and said that he had censured Soult for having neglected to do so. . . . Graham, he observed, was a daring old man, and asked if he were not the same who had commanded in the affair near Cadiz.'"[2]—Page 124.

P. S. NEY'S NOTES.—[1] *The Polish Lancers charged through the British lines and threw them into great disorder; then took a position in their rear. A thick shower of rain concealed the effects of this movement from Soult, and when it cleared up, it was too late to take advantage of it. The lancers, not being supported, had to sustain a furious assault from the Reserve and left wing, and were dreadfully cut up . . . Retreated with the* . . .*
[2] *Yes, beat Victor.*

"I mentioned Toussaint L'Ouverture, and observed that some of his enemies had asserted that he had caused him to be put to death privately in prison. 'It does not deserve an answer,' replied Napoleon. 'Had he died in St. Domingo, then, indeed, something might have been suspected; but after he had safely arrived in France, what object could have been in view?'"[1]—Page 127.

P. S. NEY'S NOTE.—[1] *None. But his imprisonment was a great crime.*

"'Indeed the nation had *la rage* to regain St. Domingo, and I was obliged to comply with it; but had I, previous to the peace, acknowledged the blacks, I could under that plea have refused to make any attempts to retake it; in doing which I acted contrary to my own judgment.'"[1]—Page 128.

P. S. NEY'S NOTE.—[1] *Why?*

"'Nothing ever done by your ministers enraged the French and other nations against them so much as their system of pontons.'"[1]—Page 129.

P. S. NEY'S NOTE.—[1] *He cannot forget the pontons, neither will the Americans forget the British . . .*

* Masséna and Ney had their well-known quarrel a short time before the battle of Albuera was fought. Masséna deprived Ney of his command, and sent him into the interior of Spain to await the Emperor's orders. Ney doubtless went to Soult's headquarters, and was there when the battle took place.

"He then made some remarks upon the *Manuscrit venu de Ste. Hélène*. 'The *Edinburgh Review*,' said he, 'will find out directly that I am not the author of it.'"[1]—Page 131.

P. S. NEY'S NOTE.—[1] *Great compliment to the Edinburgh Reviewers.*

"'It is, however, composed with good intentions toward me. If I had written a work of the kind, it would indeed be different. Every line of it would be a subject of discussion for nations.'"[1]—Page 132.

P. S. NEY'S NOTE.—[1] *Aye, aye.*

"Count Montholon called Captain Blakeney and myself this day to look at the state of his apartments. The walls were damp and cold to the touch. I never saw a human habitation in a more mouldy or humid state."[1]

P. S. NEY'S NOTE.—[1] *O fye.*

"Napoleon said that a man's conscience was not to be amenable to any tribunal; that no person ought to be accountable to any earthly power for his religious opinions."[1]—Page 135.

P. S. NEY'S NOTE.—[1] *This sentiment forms the very Essence of toleration.*

"'Sir Hudson said I might have books in my rooms, to be shown to the French, of a very improper tendency, which they might read in my absence.'"[1]—Page 137.

P. S. NEY'S NOTE.—[1] *This is like the pope's prohibiting the Laity from Reading the holy Scriptures.*

"Napoleon then rallied me upon my supposed attention to Miss ——."[1]—Page 140.

P. S. NEY'S NOTE.—[1] *E. Balcome.*

"'That circumstance of the *déjeuné de trois amis*[1] I never told to any person.'"—Page 144.

P. S. NEY'S NOTE.—[1] *3 young friends.*

AS TO NEY'S IDENTITY.

" ' After the abdication at Fontainebleau, upward of forty millions of francs, my private property, was seized. Of this money, about five-and-twenty millions were divided¹ among T——, M——, H——, and C——.' "—Page 146.

P. S. NEY'S NOTE.—¹ *Talleyrand, Metternich, Hardenburg and Castlereagh.*

" ' Judging from Wellington's actions, from his dispatches, and, above all, from his conduct toward Ney, I should pronounce him to be *un homme de peu d'esprit sans générosité¹ et sans grandeur d'ame.*' "—Page 147.

P. S. NEY'S NOTE.—¹ *A man of little wit, devoid of generosity, and without greatness of soul.*

" ' You ought not to suffer the Americans to send a ship there ;¹ you give up Batavia to the Dutch. . . . After my fall you might have had anything you liked² to ask for.' "—Page 150.

P. S. NEY'S NOTES.—¹ *They would find it difficult to prevent that.*
² *Not from the Americans.*

" ' I disagreed with him [the admiral], and thought him *un homme dur*,¹ still I felt confidence in his character and integrity.
" ' Had I any intention of committing suicide, a pistol would be my resource. *Je n'aime pas la longue guerre.*' " ²
—Page 154.

P. S. NEY'S NOTE.—¹ *A rude man.*
P. S. NEY'S SHORTHAND NOTE.—² *I am not a friend of long wars.*

" ' The French admiral was an imbecile, but yours was just as bad.¹ I assure you that if Cochrane had been supported, he would have taken every one of the ships.' "—Page 186.

P. S. NEY'S NOTE.—¹ *Admiral Gambier.*

" ' The Pope proposed to me to canonize Bounaventura

Bonaparte. "*Saint Père,*" said I, "*pour l'amour de Dieu epargnez moi le ridicule de cela.*" ' " ¹—Page 189.

P. S. NEY'S NOTE.—¹ *O Holy Father, for the love of God, spare me the ridicule of that.*

"Lieutenant-General Sir Hudson Lowe, K.C.B.,¹ etc., was duped."—Page 191.

P. S. NEY'S NOTE.—¹ *Knight Commander of the Bath.*

"I asked him if he believed that ——¹ was privy to the death of ——." ²—Page 215.

P. S. NEY'S NOTES.—¹ *Alexr.*
² *his father.*

"But in truth there was nothing to be feared from France under any sovereign. Until she has an army of five hundred thousand men France is not to be dreaded." ¹—Page 216.

P. S. NEY' NOTE.—¹ *She brought kingdoms to her feet with half of that number.*

"'There was nothing to be feared from me, for if I had attempted new conquests, the opinion which brought me back from Elba would have thrown me to the ground again.'

"'Masséna lost himself in the campaign of Portugal. If he had been what he formerly was he would have followed Wellington so closely as to be able to attack him while entering the lines before Lisbon, before he could have taken up his position properly.'" ²—Page 217.

P. S. NEY'S NOTES.—¹ *Certainly.*
² *The heights of Busaco and Torres Vederas were previously fortified by the British and Portuguese, by a succession of circumvallations . . . the Enemy . . . Ney, D'Erlon and many others were present whose conduct and courage have never been questioned. If Bonaparte himself had been there he would have been . . . months before the place and his convoys and communications cut off.*

"'Twenty-one guns were to have been fired for the birth of a princess, and one hundred and one for a prince. At the discharge of the twenty-second gun the Parisians rent the skies with acclamations and expressions of universal delight.¹ Almost all the powers of Europe sent ambassadors extraordinary.' "—Page 233.

P. S. NEY'S NOTE.—¹ *The same parisians rent the air with vive la Republique! Vive le premier consul!* . . .

"'It has been said,' added Napoleon, 'that the marriage of Marie Louise was one of the secret articles of the Treaty of Vienna, which had taken place some months before. This is entirely false. In fact, the marriage with the Empress Marie Louise was proposed in council, discussed, decided, and signed within twenty-four hours, which can be proved by many members of the council¹ who are now in existence.'"
—Page 235.

P. S. NEY'S NOTE.—¹ *They did so decide on the proposition made by Napoleon himself. But no report ever gained more credit in* . . .

"'Those English,' added he, 'who are lovers of liberty, will one day lament with tears having gained the battle of Waterloo.¹ It was as fatal to the liberties of Europe in its effects as that of Philippi was to those of Rome.'"—Page 243.

P. S. NEY'S NOTE.—¹ *Oui en vérité, vous et moi nous sommes d'accord— malgré tout le monde.*

"'It [the victory at Waterloo] has precipitated Europe into the hands of triumvirs, associated together for the oppression of mankind, the suppression of knowledge, and the restoration of superstition.'" ¹—Page 244.

P. S. NEY'S NOTE.—¹ *Holy Alliance.*

"The Emperor then shook me by the hand and embraced me, saying, '*Adieu,*¹ *O'Meara, nous ne nous reverrons jamais encore. Soyez heureux.*'" ²—Page 264.

P. S. NEY'S NOTES.—¹ *Adieu. L' honneur au revoir O'Meara une homme a recompenzer. C'est une affaire a la perdre avec le Roi sotte d'Angleterre. H. Lowe c'est le plus méchant; il seriot retranche de la . . . malheureux. . . .*
² *God be with you, O'Meara. We shall never meet again. May you be happy.*

"'The instructions which I [Lowe] have received from the British Government direct me to limit the expenditure of General Bonaparte's establishment to £8000 per annum; they give me liberty at the same time to admit of any further expense being incurred, provided he furnishes the funds whereby the surplus charges may be defrayed.'" [1]—Page 284.

P. S. NEY'S NOTE.—[1] *The object was evidently to discover what funds Bonaparte had at his command in Europe.*

"Supplies for General Bonaparte daily:

Meat, beef and mutton included (lbs.)	82
Fowls (no.)	6
Bread (lbs.)	66
Butter (lbs.)	5
Lard (lbs.)	5
Salad oils (pints)	3¼
Sugar candy (lbs.)	4
Coffee (lbs.)	2
Tea, green (lbs.)	½
Tea, black (lbs.)	½
Candles, wax (lbs.)	8
Eggs (no.)	30
Common sugar (lbs.)	5
Cheese (lbs.)	1
Vinegar (qts.)	1
Flour (lbs.)	5
Salt meat (lbs.)	6
Fire wood (cwt.)	3
Porter or ale (bottles)	3
Vegetables (in value)	1*l*.
Fruit (in value)	10*s*.
Confectionery (in value)	8*s*.
Champagne or Vin de grave (bottles)	1
Madeira (bottles)	1
Constantia (bottles)	1
Claret (bottles)	6"[1]

—Page 287.

P. S. NEY'S NOTE.—[1] *Ecce! Sir Hudson is Deputy Butler to the Prince Regent, who acts as chief* . . .

taken a position in the rear of a piece of woods which secured their flanks, they maintained it until night. Ney fixed his head quarters at Quatre Bras, his line being two cannon shot distant from the enemy. He was joined by count Erlon with the corps of reserve. The loss of the English troops was estimated at 9000; that of the French at 3400.

The night of the sixteenth and seventeenth, the third corps of the French army rested on its arms on the field of battle in advance of St. Amand; the fourth corps in advance of Ligny; marshal Grouchy at Sombref, and the sixth corps in reserve behind Ligny. The Prussians retreated in two columns towards Wavres, where the fourth corps under general Bulow arrived from Liege about 11 o'clock at night. The dispersed Prussians covered the country like a swarm of locusts, and committed dreadful ravages. The defeat of the Prussians occasioned great joy to the inhabitants on the left bank of the Rhine.

The duke of Wellington had reached and passed the night at Quatre Bras; where his troops, exhausted and fatigued, continued to arrive. They had been on their march since the night of the fifteenth.

At break of day on the seventeenth, general Pajol, with the 6th corps, and a division of light cavalry was ordered to pursue the Prussians in the direction of Wavres; and marshal Ney received orders to march at day break on Quatre Bras, and attack the rear-guard of the English. Count Lobau was directed to march by the road of Namur, towards the same place, to aid the attack of marshal Ney. Marshal Grouchy with the third and fourth corps

FACSIMILE OF P. S. NEY'S NOTE IN "MEMOIRS OF NAPOLEON." PAGE 316. TRANSLATION OF THE SHORTHAND IS: "COUNT D'ERLON WAS CALLED AWAY (OR OFF) BY NAPOLEON, WHO CRIPPLED MY MOVEMENT."

AS TO NEY'S IDENTITY.

" ' You ask me, sir, *est ce à ce que cés objets ne sont pas arrivés parle canal du ministre?* ' " etc.'—Page 296.

P. S. NEY'S NOTE.—¹ *Is it on account that these things have not arrived through the medium of the Minister?*

" ' You observe, sir,' *Servit ce parceque sur les jettons il y a une couronne,* etc.
" ' *Vous n'avez pas le droit d'en faire.*²
" ' *L'Empereur ne veut de grace,*' " ³ etc.—Page 298.

P. S. NEY'S NOTES.—¹ *Can it be because a crown surmounts the counters?*
² *You have not the right to make* . . .
³ *The Emperor begs no favor.*

" ' . . . not execute my duty as a *consigne*.¹
" ' *Aucune inspection directe ou publique*.²
" ' *L'Empereur me charge de protester contre l'existence de toute restriction*.³
" ' Your most obedient and humble servant,
   " ' H. LOWE, *Lieutenant-General.*' " ⁴
—Page 299.

P. S. NEY'S NOTES.—¹ *An agent.*
² *No personal inspection, immediate or public.*
³ *The Emperor directs me to denounce the existence of all restriction.*
⁴ *Ou il est mechant, ou il est fou.*

" ' Do your duty, come what may [Bertrand].' *Fais ce que tu dois* ;² *advienne que pourra.*' "—Page 304.

P. S. NEY'S NOTES.—¹ *Bravo!*
² *je ne la croyois pas si brave or aussi brave qu'il est—beaucoup plus grand Bertrand.*

"The powers declare that Napoleon Bonaparte is placed out of the pale of civil and social relations ; and that as an enemy and disturber of the world he is delivered up to public vengeance!"

Then follow the signatures:

Austria { Le Prince de Metternich.[1]
Le Baron de Wessemberg.

Spain—P. Gomez Labrador.

France { Le Prince de Talleyrand.[2]
Le Duc d'Alberg.
Latour Dupin.
Le Comte Alexis de Noailles.

Great Britain { Wellington.[3]
Clancarty.
Stewart.

Sweden—Lowenheim.[4]

—Page 306.

P. S. Ney's Notes.—

[1] *Pandemonium* { Beelzebub.
Moloch.
au Diable Roi inferne.
Baal.

[2] (*Talleyrand's portrait is here drawn—a caricature, yet a striking likeness.*)

[3] (*A fair portrait of Wellington is here drawn—it is slightly caricatured. At Wellington's mouth is the word* OUI.)

[4] ... toute merite au ... au pendere.

" ' I came voluntarily on board of the Bellerophon. I am not the prisoner, but the guest of England. I appeal to history.' " [1]—Page 307.

P. S. Ney's Note.—[1] *You have no reason. History speaks regardless of Appeals.*

NOTES IN SCOTT'S "LIFE OF NAPOLEON."

Mr. S. A. Kelley, Charlotte, N. C., owns a copy of Scott's "Life of Napoleon" (published in three volumes by J. P. Ayres, Philadelphia, 1827), which contains some notes of great value written by Peter S. Ney. Of this book Mr. Kelley says: "It originally belonged to my father, who lived in Mocksville, N. C. When Peter S. Ney taught school near Mocksville he was a frequent visitor at my father's house. He borrowed Scott's "Life of Napoleon," and while it was in his possession wrote the notes which the book contains. The first volume contained a steel engraving of Napoleon. P. S. Ney wrote underneath the portrait : 'This is not a correct likeness of Napoleon.' "

On a fly-leaf of the first volume P. S. Ney wrote : "This book should be thrown in the fire. P. S. Ney." (*P. S. Ney* in shorthand.) On a fly-leaf of the second volume P. S. Ney wrote : "This book should be read with great caution, for it contains more falsehoods than facts. P. S. Ney." (*P. S. Ney* in shorthand.)

"It is little more than a historical romance. P. S. N." (*P. S. N.* in shorthand.)

NOTES IN VOLUME II.

"On the trial [of the Duke D'Enghien] no witnesses were produced, nor did any investigation take place, saving by the interrogation of the prisoner. Whatever points of accusation, therefore, are not established by the admission of the duke himself must be considered as totally unproved.[1]

"Yet this unconscientious tribunal not only found their prisoner guilty of having borne arms against the republic, which he readily admitted, but of having placed himself at the head of a party of French emigrants in the pay of England, and carried on machinations for surprising the city of

P. S. NEY'S NOTE.—[1] *Bah!*

Strassburg—charges which he himself positively denied, and which were supported by no proof whatsoever." [1]—Page 48.

P. S. NEY'S NOTE.—[1] *A large bundle of Proclamations, calling on the French to rise in arms against Napoleon, were found in the Duke's bureau when arrested!**

"The prince may be lamented who is exposed, from civil disaffection, to the dagger of the assassin, but his danger gives him no right to turn such a weapon even against the individual person by whom it is pointed at him.[1] "In every point of view the act was a murder;[2] and the stain of the Duke D'Enghien's blood must remain indelibly upon Napoleon Bonaparte." [3]—Page 49.

P. S. NEY'S NOTES.—[1] *Why?*
[2] *No.*
[3] *So say you.*

"General indignation of Europe, in consequence of the murder[1] of the Duke D'Enghien."—Page 52.

P. S. NEY'S NOTE.—[1] *Execution.*

"A single Russian officer appeared, and invited Ney to capitulate. 'A marshal of France never surrenders,' answered that intrepid general. The officer retired.[1] . . . Miloradovitch lay here at the head of a great force."—Page 378.

P. S. NEY'S NOTE.—[1] *The officer was not suffered to retire, for during the parley a volley of grape was fired from Russian cannon, and he was disarmed and detained for this violation of the flag of truce. Miloradovitch wished to prevent any terms offered by Koutousoff then present.* (Shorthand.†)

"The hills were black with the Russian troops. . . . Far from losing heart in so perilous a situation, the French Guards, with rare intrepidity, forced their way through the ravine of the Losmina, and rushed with the utmost fury on

* Colonel Ordener, who arrested the Duke D'Enghien, said: "I found in his house sacks of papers sufficient to compromise the half of France."

† "The world he for this reason caused by fealty to be veered."—Deciphered by one of P. S. Ney's pupils.

the Russian batteries. . . . Ney persevered in the attempt to cut his passage by main force through this superior body of Russians, who lay opposed to him in front. Again the French advanced upon the cannon, losing whole ranks, which were supplied by their comrades as fast as they fell. The assault was once more unsuccessful, and Ney, seeing that the general fate of his column was no longer doubtful, endeavored at least to save a part from the wreck. Having selected about four thousand of the best men he separated himself[1] from the rest. . . . Here he found a single place in the river frozen over, though the ice was so thin that it bent beneath the steps of the soldiers.[2] . . . The wagons, some loaded with sick and wounded, last attempted to pass,* but the ice broke with them, and the heavy plunge and stifled moaning apprised their companions of their fate."—Page 379.

P. S. NEY'S NOTE.—[1] *No. Not before dark, and ordered all to follow.*
P. S. NEY'S SHORTHAND NOTE.—[2] *Blockhead be I see, or say.*

"We return to the Grand Army, or rather to the assemblage of those who had once belonged to it, for of an army it had scarce the semblance left. . . . If Ney and some of the marshals still retained authority, they were only attended to from habit, or because the instinct of discipline revived when the actual battle drew near. . . . The stragglers, which now comprehended almost the whole army, divided into little bands. . . . Those associated into such a fraternity would communicate to none save those of their own party a mouthful of rye dough, and a handful of meal was a sufficient temptation for putting to death the wretch who could not defend his booty."[1]—Page 390.

P. S. NEY'S NOTE.—[1] *Base traducer.*

"He [Napoleon] had no expectation that the mild climate of Fontainebleau would continue to gild the ruins of Moscow

* See Testimony of Burgess Gaither. See also Ségur and Horne. The drowning of the sick and wounded made a lasting impression upon Ney and his entire army.

till the arrival of December ; but he could not forego the
flattering belief that a letter and proposal of pacification must
at last fulfil the anticipations which he so ardently entertained.
It was only the attack upon Murat that finally dispelled this
hope." '—Page 399.

P. S. NEY'S NOTE.—' *The letter was not forwarded by Koutousoff.*

NOTES IN "MEMOIRS OF NAPOLEON BONA-
PARTE."

I have still another book—"Memoirs of Napoleon"—
which contains a few notes of priceless value written by Peter
S. Ney. The book belongs to Mr. A. B. Andrews, Jr.,
Attorney at Law, Raleigh, N. C., who obtained it from his
grandfather, Colonel William Johnston, Charlotte, N. C.
Colonel Johnston writes : " The ' Memoirs of Napoleon,'
containing marginal notes by Peter S. Ney, was in my
father's library* when I was a boy, and was read with much
interest by me. Peter S. Ney taught school in our immediate
neighborhood, and my youngest brother, Rufus M. Johnston,
was one of his pupils. P. S. Ney sometimes went home
with him. He had full access to my father's library, and
read with avidity everything which in any way related to the
life of the Emperor Napoleon. His conversation was intellectual, his manner dignified and impressive, and he would
have attracted attention in any society."

The title-page of the book is as follows : " Memoirs of the
Military and Political Life of Napoleon Bonaparte, . . .
Embracing also an Authentic Narrative of the Conduct of
Napoleon during his Voyage to St. Helena, and while in
Exile, and of Events attending his Confinement, . . . with
Numerous Private Documents, Collected chiefly from the
Writings of Dr. B. E. O'Meara, Surgeon to Napoleon at St.
Helena. Hartford : Published for Chauncey Goodrich,
1822."

* On a fly-leaf of the book is the signature of Robert Johnston, father
of Colonel Johnston.

security, or destroyed; as they compromised the lives of so many persons. But M. Blacas was only intent upon saving his *quattrini;** and gave himself but little concern about the lives of those who had been the means of bringing himself and his master back. He was then minister of the king's household. Every thing was trusted to him by Louis, who is incapable himself, and whose chief qualities are dissimulation and hypocrisy. His legs are covered with ulcers, which are dressed for him by the Duchess of Angouleme. He gorges to that degree every day, that they are obliged to give him God knows what to enable him to disencumber himself of his load. Some morning he will be found dead in his bed. He has some ignorant *imbéciles* of physicians about him. They wanted Corvisart to attend him, but he refused, saying, that if any accident happened, he might be accused of having contributed to his end. When I returned to the Thuilleries, I found my apartments poisoned with the smell of his legs, and of divers sulphureous baths, which he was in the habit of using."

* Money.

FACSIMILE OF P. S. NEY'S NOTE IN O'MEARA'S "NAPOLEON IN EXILE," VOL. I., PAGE 311.

army was expected to be concentrated, and prince Bernard of Saxe, had taken a position between that place and Genappe. The position of the prince of Orange was an important one, being the point at which the different divisions of Wellington's army were concentrating. Had it not been for the delay of marshal Ney, he might have secured this position, and been enabled to attack separately the divisions of the English army on their march. These advantages were lost. But the marshal having received the orders of the emperor, with about half his force com-

FACSIMILE OF P. S. NEY'S NOTE IN "MEMOIRS OF NAPOLEON," PAGE 315. TRANSLATION OF THE SHORTHAND IS: "DELAY! SAY THE EMPEROR TOOK AWAY MY RESERVE."

AS TO NEY'S IDENTITY.   253

" The general sarcastically replied, ' *C'etoit une vraie capucinade* '—' it was a true farce.' " [1]—Page 208.

P. S. NEY'S SHORTHAND NOTE.—[1] *Volney said so.*

" Marshal Ney, when on the point of marching to take the position assigned him, halted in consequence of a report that the English and Prussian armies had effected a junction in the environs of Fleurus." [1]—Page 314.

P. S. NEY'S NOTE.—[1] *Not so.* Had no command.*

" Had it not been for the delay of Marshal Ney." [1]—Page 315.

P. S. NEY'S SHORTHAND NOTE.—[1] *Delay! say (or as) the Emperor took away my reserve.*

" The loss of the French [at Ligny] was 6950[1] killed and wounded."—Page 315.

P. S. NEY'S NOTE.—[1] 16,950.

" Ney fixed his headquarters at Quatre Bras, his line being two cannon-shot distant from the enemy. He was joined by Count Erlon[1] with the corps of reserve. The loss of the English troops was estimated at 9000, that of the French at 3400." [2]—Page 316.

P. S. NEY'S SHORTHAND NOTE.—[1] *Count d'Erlon was called off (or away) by Napoleon, who crippled my movement.*
[2] *5000.*

" The third division of the second corps having suffered much at the action at Ligny, remained to watch the field of battle and take care of the wounded." [1]—Page 317.

P. S. NEY'S SHORTHAND NOTE.—[1] *This was the fatal error.†*

* Ney had just joined the army. His troops had not arrived. Napoleon alone was responsible for the delay.

† It may have been. After the battle of Ligny Girard's division numbered about three thousand men. If at Waterloo Napoleon could have sent Ney a reinforcement of three thousand men when the marshal captured La Haye Sainte, or, later, when he penetrated into the very heart of the English position, the result might have been different. Certainly Napoleon would not have suffered so serious a defeat.

"About an hour after this dispatch the Emperor received a report from Marshal Grouchy, by which it was with surprise and astonishment he learnt that instead of his being at Wavre, in close pursuit of Blücher, he was at Gembloux at five the preceding evening, and ignorant of the course Blücher had taken." ¹—Page 318.

P. S. NEY'S NOTE.—¹ *Aye.*

"Grouchy concluded he should be able to be before Wavre in season." ¹—Page 318.

P. S. NEY'S NOTE.—¹ (Shorthand.)

"A primary object of the Emperor at the commencement of operations was to attack and destroy each [army] separately.¹ . . . The three hours' delay of Grouchy prevented the Emperor from attacking the British on the afternoon of the 17th, as he intended to have done." ²—Page 319.

P. S. NEY'S NOTES.—¹ *No, no.*
² *No.*

"Six thousand men had recently landed at Ostend from America." ¹—Page 319.

P. S. NEY'S NOTE.—¹ *Bah!*

"Deeply occupied with thoughts which his situation suggested, the Emperor, at one o'clock at night, left his quarters on foot, accompanied only by his grand marshal, to see if he could discover any movements of the enemy. He went the round of the Grand Guard. . . . On approaching the woods of Chateau Hougoumont, he heard a noise as of a column in march. . . . He had determined if the English army was retreating to pursue and attack it, notwithstanding the darkness of the night. . . ." ¹—Page 319.

P. S. NEY'S SHORTHAND NOTE.—¹ *This is new to me.*

"The English were estimated at ninety thousand men;

they had lain under arms during the night, exposed to a severe rain, accompanied with thunder and lightning.[1] . . .

P. S. NEY'S NOTE.—[1] *Good.*

"The Emperor felt confident of victory. . . . 'We have,' said he, 'ninety chances in our favor, and not ten against us.' . . . 'Without doubt,' said Marshal Ney, who had just entered, 'if the Duke of Wellington were simple enough to wait for your Majesty.'[1] . . .

"The army commenced its march in eleven columns, four of which were destined for the first line, four for the second, and three for the third. The artillery marched on the flanks of the columns, and the wagons in the rear. The four columns designed for the first line arrived on the spot . . . at the same time the seven other columns were seen defiling from the heights. . . ."[2]—Page 321.

P. S. NEY'S NOTES.—[1] *By* . . . .
[2] *What stuff!*

"Soult and Ney acted as lieutenant-generals, and the Emperor himself, placed in a central and commanding position, directed every manœuvre. All the reserve were at his command, which could be ordered wherever the urgency of circumstances might require their presence."[1]—Page 323.

P. S. NEY'S NOTE.—[1] *Right.*

"The Emperor ordered Count Lobau with two divisions of ten thousand[1] men to march to support the light cavalry."—Page 325.

P. S. NEY'S NOTE.—[1] 5000.

"The victory will be more decisive, for Bülow's corps will be entirely cut up.

"It was now twelve o'clock.[1] . . .

"While this attack was going on, a large body of the enemy's cavalry, on his left, charged and repulsed a column of infantry, took two eagles and seven pieces of cannon, and advanced on to the plain."[2]—Page 326.

P. S. NEY'S NOTES.—[1] 1 P.M.   [2] *Picton.*

"The balls fell on the road before and in rear of the Belle Alliance, where the Emperor was stationed with his guards. The Prussians had advanced so near as to pour their grape on this road." [1]—Page 326.

P. S. NEY'S NOTE.—[1] *No.*

"Grouchy did not commence his march from Gembloux until ten in the morning. At half-past twelve he had advanced half-way to Wavre, when he heard the tremendous cannonade between the contending armies at Waterloo. General Excelmans . . . advised him to march toward the direction of the fire. The marshal was of the same opinion, but hesitated to disobey his orders. Count Gérard then came up and gave the same advice. The marshal was convinced. . . . At this moment he received information that his advanced cavalry had arrived at Wavre, and were engaged with the Prussians, whose forces then it was stated amounted to eighty thousand men. This determined him to continue his march for that place." [1]—Page 328.

P. S. NEY'S SHORTHAND NOTE.—[1] *Damn Grouchy.*

"It was not the defection of the marshals of the army that corrupted the soldiers and secured success to the enterprise. Even Ney, who was executed for betraying Louis, did not declare for Bonaparte until all his troops . . . manifested the most mutinous spirit, and showed that *they*[1] were determined to join his standard. It was not Ney, nor Massena, nor any of the marshals. . . ."—Page 353.

P. S. NEY'S NOTE.—[1] *They* [shorthand] *hesitated—decided long before the event.*

"Marshal Soult, Cambacérès, Savary, Fouché, Carnot, and many others were astonished at the development of public opinion." [1]—Page 353.

P. S. NEY'S NOTE.—[1] (Shorthand.)

A VOICE

FROM

ST. HELENA.

Voilà l'homme!

21st April, 1817.—NAPOLEON has been for some days in very good spirits On Saturday, the 19th, some captains of East Indiamen came to see Count and Countess Bertrand. Captains Innes, Campbell, and Ripsley, with Mr. Webb, stationed themselves at the back of the house in such a situation as to be likely to see Napoleon on his return from Bertrand's, where he had gone about

FACSIMILE OF P. S. NEY'S WRITING IN O'MEARA'S "NAPOLEON IN EXILE." VOL. II., PAGE 1.

pushed on at that time, my father-in-law would not have been against me."

Napoleon then said, that notwithstanding the occupation of Paris by the allies, he should still have succeeded had it not been for the treachery of Marmont, and have driven them out of France. His plan was arranged. He was to have entered Paris in the dead of the night. The whole of the *canaille* of the city were at the same time to attack the allies from the houses, who, fighting against troops acquainted with the localities, would have been cut to pieces, and obliged to abandon the city with immense loss. The *canaille* were all ready. (I think he also said that he would have cut off the allies from their park of artillery.) Once driven from Paris, the mass of the nation would have risen

FACSIMILE OF P. S. NEY'S NOTE IN O'MEARA'S "NAPOLEON IN EXILE." VOL. II., PAGE 100.

SPECIMENS OF POETRY

BY PETER S. NEY.*

For the *Western Carolinian*.

ON the 15th August, 1769, Napoleon Bonaparte first opened his eyes; on 6th May, 1821, he closed them forever.

"*Potentia regia defloruit,
Fama præclare viget.*"
    His regal potency is gone,
    His fame augments with clearer tone.

    Fortune may smile on others now
      As fondly as she nurtured him ;
    Through life she had his ardent vow,
      But Fortune always had her whim.

    Awhile she was a gracious dame
      And strew'd with crowns his upward path,
    Urg'd to the heights of pow'r and fame,
      Then left him with a frown of wrath.

    Forthwith from her prolific womb
      Disgrace and honor, splendor, gloom,
    Defeat, despair, hope, triumph came,
      To prop his pow'r or blast his name.

    They who had storm and battle braved
      In agonizing throes expired ;
    In frost and famine, phrenzy raved
      Of glory ! Men in death admired
    The author of their fate. *His* mind
    Had not its lust of pow'r resign'd.

* At the top of the first page of his scrap-book, from which these selections are made, P. S. Ney wrote "Original Poetry, &c." (by P. S. Ney). The scrap-book belongs to Dr. J. G. Ramsay, Cleveland, N. C. P. S. Ney's prose and poetic writings would make a large book. A few selections only are given.

He knew his intellects had rul'd
  The storms enthusiasts had rais'd ;
And though her ardor had been cool'd,
  Still Freedom on his Eagles gaz'd.

With hope and partial love, on high
  Again their fearful pinions spread ;
" Napoleon" was the battle cry,
  And myriads found a gory bed.

Dame Fortune now no longer true,
But tantaliz'd at Waterloo ;
An instant his proud standards crown'd
With vict'ry, then more darkly frown'd—
  Oh, let the fickle jade be gone !

Why be deluded day by day ?
Let Reason hold his rightful throne,
Stand at the helm, direct the way
To realms where Fortune cannot come—
To temples, which she cannot build
Above the clarichord of fame,
  Or the red glories of the field.

Terror, reverse press on his rear,
For him there's no asylum here ;
But if departed spirits can
Be charm'd by eulogy from man,
Or odium have any pow'r
To wring, beyond the mortal hour,
An age to come can hardly tell
Whether he *feel a Heav'n or Hell.*

The reverie is darkly deep—
Peace, peace be on thy final sleep !
  No more by trembling kings oppress'd ;
The euphony of Ocean's wave
  Compos'd thy mighty mind to rest,
And Nature form'd thy Island grave.

When monuments, rear'd to thy foe
  Shall feel the crumbling touch of time,
Thy undecaying tomb will show
  A grandeur similar to thine.

To the remotest date thy name
  In living characters shall pass—
In vain engrav'd is deedless fame
  On stone or perishable brass.

For the *Pee Dee Gazette.*

WATERLOO AND ITS MONUMENTS.

"How are the mighty fallen!"

Hosts burning to commence the fray,
With gleaming steel in long array,
And riders fierce and fiery steeds
Rush furiously to desperate deeds.

Tremendously the dreadful strife
Divides the slender ties of life ; .
A pang, a momentary throe—
Brief harbingers of joy or woe—
Plunge man at arms and chiefs of pride
Into the sanguinary tide
That sweeps o'er ruin's steep cascade
To realms of light or Pluto's shade.

Battalions retrograde—advance
Fresh columns close—the chargers prance—
Squadrons aloof in skirmish join,
Or flank the long, disordered line,
As when two gladiators stand
With watchful eye and ready brand,
A faltering step, averted eye,
Dooms one antagonist to die.

Wide carnage indicates the path
Where cannon issue—instant death ;
But dauntless in the fatal storm
More proudly swells each martial form ;
Vengeance and rivalry impart
A stronger pulse to every heart :
The Eagle perch'd on standard high
Seems pleased to view his foemen die ;
Unruffl'd in the van, his glance
Prolongs the energies of France !
Apt emblem of the warlike great,
The idol of a sinking state,
Whose stern commands and genius wield
The fearful movements of the field.
Britannia shakes—her visage pale
Implies her hopes of conquest fail.
Awful suspense—still valiantly
Her sons repulse each charge or die.

The Prussians on the flank appear
In masses dense, approaching near.
The imperial guards their standards wave,
Led by the "*bravest of the brave!*"
Oh, brief and brilliant was the charge!
Fresh troops the British lines enlarge!!!
The Gallic squadrons thunder on,
Exclaiming, "*Vive Napoléon.*"

Flank, front and rear, at once assailed,
To wild uproar the conflict swelled;
The blushing sun descends—the night
Augments the horrors of the fight;
Distraction and delirium high
At random strike, at random die—
The combatants, both high and low,
In mingled carnage, friend and foe.

The agonies of strife subside,
And roll in one promiscuous tide
Of fitful tumult from the field,
Where *thousands* fell, where *few* did yield.
 "*How* are the *mighty fallen!*"

And now, upon the silent plain,
 With art magnificently gay,
Huge monuments arise in vain
 To mark the struggles of the day.
In vain do sculptured tombs arise
To indicate where valor lies:
The partial epitaph may lie,
But great achievements never die.

The sage narrator, *Time*, shall tell
Who bravely fought, who nobly fell—
The motives, and the men that led
To infamy or honor's bed.
Did love of glory urge them on,
Or blind obedience to a throne?
Or did the cause of law and right
Impel them to disastrous fight?
'Tis not a finely sculptured tomb
That gives the wreath perennial bloom:
All motives base make actions mean,
Howe'er of glory mad men dream.

Thus when some mighty villains die,
Proud cenotaphs ascend on high,

Which pompous blazonries adorn
With marks of mockery and scorn.
Not so when intellectual light
To higher regions wings its flight ;
It leaves warm sympathy behind
In every great and noble mind.
Where is the chieftain of thy pride,
O Gaul ! who did thy fortunes guide ?
To him arise no work of art—
His urn is every valiant heart.

Stupendous in the Ocean's wave,
His mighty monument and grave,
An island rears her giant form—
His requiem is the thunder-storm.

These puny works must yield to Time,
But his is durable—sublime :
The *Appian Way*, renowned in song,
Was but a path for pleasure's throng.

Lo ! where the Alpine mountains rise
In snowy masses to the skies—
The broad *Simplon* on high sustain
The chariot swift or loaded wain—

Prodigious, durable, and grand—
  An epitaph that cannot lie ;
The fruitful harvest of his brand—
  The signet of his heraldry.

S———

EPITAPH.

"*Napoleon, Maximum historiæ decus.*"

UPON thy self-erected throne
Thy genius like a meteor shone ;
The world beheld thee, and admired ;
Kings trembled, flattered and retired
Before thy withering glance ; they found
Thy mental volume too profound
For common kings to scan : in fear
They placed thy mortal relics here,
Lest from the grave thy mould'ring bones
Might rise and blast their rescued thrones.

S.

For the *Western Carolinian.*

MR. EDITOR: What mind does not feel melancholy and indignant at the result of the contest for freedom in Spain? My first feelings and ideas, on hearing the sickening catastrophe, are submitted to your disposal:

> IBERIA, who can deplore
> That freedom has fled from thy shore,
> And left thee to suffer the fate
> Of thraldom, of priestcraft, of hate!
> The heroes who rose in thy cause
> For Liberty, Verity, Laws,
> In peril abandon'd by thee :
> Thou never deserv'st to be free!
> Go, bow to the tyrant who has thee betray'd ;
> Go, worship the puppet that has thee enslav'd ;
> Go, purge thy delusions by *auto da fé!*
> Iberia, thou never deserv'st to be free!
> The brave shall abhor thee, the noble shall spurn ;
> Go, bend to the priesthood who treat thee with scorn!
> Reflect on the tombs of thy heroes, and then
> Say who *are* the dastards and who *were* the men?
>   And thou, too, France!
> Beneath thy victor Eagle's eye,
> Where do thy crimson'd banners fly?

    *   *   *   *   *   *

> Fatuity and self may lead,
> Short space, astray the thoughtless head ;
> But Freedom will not wear a chain,
> Freedom cannot brook disdain,
> Though the hand that binds it round her
> Were with garlands to surround her.

    *   *   *   *   *   *

> The selfish passions may betray
>   The holy rights of man,
> But when the Mind resumes her sway
>   They grasp the sword again.
> Iberia, has the spirit fled
>   That should redeem thee now,
> And once so bright a lustre shed
>   Around thy ancient brow?

                                  O. F.

ROWAN, Dec. 18, 1823.

For the *Western Carolinian.*

TO ALL MEN IN ALL CLIMES.

ROAM over the mountain,
  Sail on the wide sea ;
Go drink at the fountain
  Of Freedom—be free !
Maintain in your manhood,
  Retain in decline,
Your birthrights as *Man* should ;
  Be never supine.

But sailing the ocean,
  Traversing the shore,
With purest devotion
  Dame Freedom adore :
Whether Moslem or Catholic,
  Gentile or Jew,
AT LIBERTY'S ALTAR
  Forever be true.

Submit to no tyrant,
  Succumb to no king ;
Put down the aspirant,
  Cut off Treason's sting ;
Repel the aggressor,
  Be true to your friend ;
Destroy the oppressor,
  The feeble defend.

Reflect on the Roman
  And masculine Greek ;
The former is no man,
  The latter is weak ;
You may be a giant—
  A giant may fall ;
If reckless, compliant,
  A dwarf might enthrall.

Be cautious in council,
  Be brave in the field ;
Give power to no numskull
  Or scoundrel to wield ;
And your days in the land
  May long be, and blest,
And Freedom will flourish
  When you sink to rest.

Republics are giants
　When govern'd aright
By rulers of energy,
　Principle, light :
Devoid of such guides,
　They are pigmies of pride,
Whom faction divides
　And monarchists deride.

All pactions are vellum,
　All Freedom uproar,
When minds intellectual
　Do *grovel*—not *soar*.
Sound culture must polish,
　Strong sympathy rule
The State that would flourish
　In Liberty's school.

　　　　　　　　　　　BRUTUS.

For the *Spectator*.

MISSOLONGHI.

" Who would be free, themselves must strike the blow."—*Byron*.

'Tis not with Homer's strength I sing,
　To tell the triumphs of the brave
Who erst did lofty Ilion bring
　To ruin and a gory grave.
Oh, sad reverse !　On Attic plains
The Greek has fall'n, the Moslem reigns.
　　＊　　＊　　＊　　＊　　＊
Missolonghi has fallen, but Greece must not fall,
Nor Moslem the Grecian again put in thrall,
While civilized man has a heart that can feel,
Or courage has vigor to brandish the steel.
　　＊　　＊　　＊　　＊　　＊
In thine own arm, O Greece ! confide ;
Strike down the ruthless homicide :
Though Missolonghi is no more,
Behold thy mountains, rocky shore,
　Each island, gulf and sea ;
Revive ! let not thy courage droop—
Action alone produces fruit ;
　Be valiant and be free.
　　＊　　＊　　＊　　＊　　＊
Thy gulf, O Salamis ! can tell
How Grecians fought, how Persians fell ;

Twelve thousand ships, destroyed in thee,
Evince the triumphs of the free.
Think on Themistocles, O Greece !
Charge home, and thou shall conquer peace !
Not *peaceful bondage !*—treat with scorn
A lot to which no *man* was born.

When thou, by factions rent apart,
   Went'st forth with Philip's conquering son,
Didst thou not show the lion heart
   That empires at Arbela won ?
Strike, modern Greece ! oh, why not be
As great, as valiant, and *more free !*

   *   *   *   *   *

Expel the tyrant from thy coast ;
   In Europe what have they to do ?
Succumb, divide, and all is lost :
   Arise, strike home, thou must subdue !
O'er Hellespontus let them fly.
Come on ! they must retreat or die.

                                                 O.

CATASTROPHE AT TERNI.*

In consternation and defeat,
Masses discomfited retreat ;
The bridge above the falls they gain ;
No exhortation could restrain
The headlong, rush-confus'd career,
By foes assaulted in the rear :
The overloaded fabric fell :
   One shriek of sorrow, mortal throe,
   An instant mark'd this scene of woe,
Amid the rapid, rolling swell
The surface of the raging flood
Exhibited no hues of blood ;
The cataract, abrupt and dense,
Held agony in brief suspense,
Plunging its victims, at a sweep,
From light and life to endless sleep.
No corse emerg'd, nor human sound
Has yet escap'd the gulf profound.

---

* " The falls of Terni are on the river Velino. Near these falls, General Pepe took his position against the Austrian army in 1821. Pepe was defeated : his disordered troops attempted to retreat over the bridge, a short distance above the falls. The bridge gave way, and several hundred men were swept over the tremendous cataract into a gulf of unknown depth by the irresistible velocity of the current. No bodies were ever found ; that gulf of *unknown depth* is their sepulchre."

Ah! had they stood in battle firm,
With dauntless front and valiant arm.
Proud victory or honor's grave
Had saved them from the ruthless wave.
Short-sighted mortals often run
Upon the fate they aim to shun.
The love of glory and a name
The head obscure, the heart inflame ;
Allure them out of reason's path,
To crime, fatuity and death.
That morning many hearts beat high,
   And boasting tongues were loud ;
Ere evening shadows veil'd the sky
   They sank without a shroud—
Not gloriously in battle strife,
Fighting for liberty and life,
   For kindred and dear native land ;
But ere the martial conflict rose
To war's last tug and desp'rate blows,
   Flying before a tyrant's band.
The hardy will mourn
   Over horrors so drear ;
The heroic will scorn
   The emotions of fear
Which urg'd them to fly
   From the face of a foe,
Whom, by stern bearing high,
   They might have laid low.

OMEGA.

For the *Pee Dee Gazette*.

"From thy own selected spot of burial, who shall dare to remove thy bones, O Washington!"

*   *   *   *   *

THOU wast no *common man!* Some few
Thy sculptur'd monument might view ;
But when old Time shall ruin bring
Over this *purposed marble thing*,
When works of art shall disappear,
Corroded by each passing year,
Posterity shall think of thee,
And hail thee champion of the free.

Should tyranny hereafter reign,
   To *splendid tombs will freedom* fly ?
On Vernon's mount she will complain,
   Where her great father FIRST *did lie*.

Then rear his mausoleum high
 Upon that site, but let no eye
 Pervade the sanctity and gloom
 Which shroud *his self-selected tomb*—
 So holy, so impressive made
 By Nature's deep, surrounding shade.

'Tis not respect which moves the throng
 To disinter his dust renown'd ;
 'Tis *pride*—'tis *vanity*—'tis wrong !
 Stir not his grave ! *'tis holy ground!*

ON READING OF THE DEATH OF SIR PHILIP SIDNEY.

WHO has not heard of Sidney's name,
 In manhood's bloom, and rich in fame ?
 On Zutphen's bloody plain he found,
 In freedom's cause, the mortal wound :
 The soldier's friend, the warrior's pride,
 At thirty-two Sir Philip died.

For the *Western Carolinian.*

" Good poetry is perfectly consistent with no high degree of precision of thought or accuracy of expression ! ! !"—*Jamieson's Rhetoric.*

DEEP-THINKING, melancholy man,
 Why for a fleeting phantom sigh !
 Thy weary vigils never can
 Unload thy heart, re-light thine eye.
 Go, mingle with the thoughtless gay,
 An antidotal charm to find
 Against the inauspicious day
 Which blasted former peace of mind.

*   *   *   *   *

Philosophy asserts in vain
 That minds of strength can triumph o'er
 The keenest intellectual pain,
 Above the freaks of fortune soar.

Fallacious!—the reverse is true :
 The mind obtuse naught can annoy.
 With anguish clearest heads review
 Their withered hopes and ruin'd joy.
 Rude imbecility will soar
 Where cultur'd energy would sink ;
 The servile bend and aid implore—
 The free are brave on ruin's brink.

Did Cato, in his dread extreme,
  Accept of Cæsar's proffered boon ?
Did Regulus become so mean
  As to avoid his certain doom ?
Corporeal ailments have their balm ;
  But what physician yet has found
An opiate the mind to calm,
  Or close an intellectual wound ?

   *   *   *   *   *

For the *Western Carolinian.*

FOURTH OF JULY, 1827.

"To be unanimous is to be great !
When right's own standard calmly is unfurl'd,
The PEOPLE are the sovereigns of the world."
—*Pilgrims of the Sun.*

THE eagle builds not in the vale,
  Nor sparrows on the mountain pine,
The linnet dares not stem the gale,
  Or mount the storm on " wing sublime ;"
So servile hearts have not the pow'r
  To grasp that magnitude of mind
Which in the dark and deathful hour
  Supports the champions of mankind.

   *   *   *   *   *

This day commemorates the DEED
  Of spirits ardent, lucid, stern,
Who freedom to this land decreed,
  And maim'd Britannia's potent arm.

   *   *   *   *   *

Then raged the conflict, hearts beat high,
  Warm kindred blood like water ran ;
" *Death! Liberty!*" the battle cry,
  Till TRIUMPH crown'd the rights of man.
Long, long that triumph shall resound,
  Its principles by age sustain'd,
Congenial sentiments be crown'd,
  Or every noble heart be drain'd.

   *   *   *   *   *

Mock not with monumental spires
  The deathless memories of men
Who toil'd through famine, flood, and fire
  For " *Freedom's guiltless Diadem ;*"

Their deeds live in the high renown
  To dauntless hearts alone assign'd ;
The warrior-wreath, the civic crown,
  Our *fathers'* temples ever bind.

Shall not their offspring worthy be
  Of such progenitors as they ?
Indomitable—lofty—free !
  Till earth and empire pass away ?
Fill high the wine-cup to the brave
  Who rear'd in blood this *Commonweal ;*
Forever like your *sires* behave !
  The EAGLE *builds not in the vale.*

O—— D.

For the *Pee Dee Gazette.*

EIGHTH JANUARY, 1815.

"*Bella, horrida bella.*"

ON tented field and forest lone
The parting beams of Phœbus shone ;
At New Orleans in luckless hour
The Briton landed with his power,
His heart elate—his ardent sigh,
His fervid pulse, his glistening eye.
Were quenched upon the gory plain
Before those beams return'd again.

Beneath the royal lion's eye]
Warr'd martial knights and barons high,
Battalions which had borne away
The palm on many a bloody day ;
Their leader tried, and culled beside
From chivalry's heroic pride.

Warm and precipitantly rash,
Upon our lines their columns dash ;
But, soon astounded, roll away
As from the rocks recoils the spray.

Collected in the dreadful strife,
As in the calmest scenes of life,
Jackson surveyed with skillful eyes
The aspect of the dread emprise ;
Sagacious, unappall'd and firm,
Prompt to repel, quick to discern,
He deem'd not that the vet'ran host
Repuls'd—conceive the battle lost.

Inur'd to war, the valiant band
Retreat apace, then bravely stand,
Promptly their broken ranks reform,
More firmly re-advance to storm,
And with Columbia's sons engage
In deadlier ire and fiercer rage.
Their leaders fall ! their boldest die !
Again they retrograde ! they fly ! ! !
In purple torrents rolled the flood
Of Mississippi with their blood.

With plumage unruffled the Eagle ascended ;
His pathway the plaudits of conquest attended !
The Lion, reluctant, retired from his slain,
Divested of laurels, and shorn of his mane.

For the *Western Carolinian*.

THE EQUINOX.

"*Insanire Juvat.*"—Hor.

The tempest raves without, and I
   Will rave in unison within ;
From constant gravity to fly
   Can be no deep or deadly sin.
Pour out the cheering wine, my boy,
We mean to pass a night of joy.

Incessant study sours the mind,
   As ceaseless sunshine taints the air ;
Nature is provident and kind—
   She only frowns to be more fair.
Then let us have a storm of mirth,
To give serene ideas birth.

Another peal, another glass.
   That flash how awful and sublime !
How fleet the coruscations pass—
   Bright emblems of the light Divine !
This nectar gleams before my sight,
A Pharos in this dreadful night.

'Tis not in levity or fear
   We treat this dread tremendous hour,
But in deep confidence and cheer,
   Submissive to the ruling power.
Let trembling guilt its head conceal—
True hearts no trepidation feel.

The storm subsides—the midnight chime
  Has struck—the ground is drenched with rain ;
"Tis time to sleep ; put by the wine,
  We'll drink when tempests rave again ;
For they must be devoid of flaws,
Who thus conform to nature's laws.
                                        O.

DUELING.

1. DUELING can derive no sanction either from laws human or divine. The laws of nature condemn it ; reason condemns it ; prudence condemns it.
2. Passions are its parents, public opinion its nurse.
3. Duellists equally detest themselves and those whose fastidious punctilios urge them to the alternative of death or disgrace.*

DURING A THUNDER-STORM ON THE NIGHT OF MAY 30, 1828.

Terrific is the stormy night ;
How grand, how brilliant is the light !
Flashing in sheets of living flame
The index to Jehovah's name.
The mightiest man is nothing now—
Awe crouches on the loftiest brow ;
From nerveless hands the sceptres fall
Which keep innumerary hosts in thrall.
The rich, the poor, the meek, the proud,
In one promiscuous group is bowed
At thy tremendous presence, Lord !
In storms alone Thou art adored.

"QUID STAT?"
                    —Horace.

To youth and health in vain we trust
To guard us from our parent dust ;
Deform'd and fair, and old and young,
Are doom'd to mingle there erelong.

Our guardian genius may defend
  From dire mishaps our brief career,
But death will level foe and friend,
  And leave the wreck of nature here.

Then, mortals, be prepar'd to go
  Where all the Godly hope to rest ;
You cannot long remain below :
  Perhaps this change is for the best.

* Probably written after the duel between Wellington and Lord Winchilsea in 1829.

FAME.

* * * * * * *

And thus heroes would perish much rather than fly,
And their greatest desire is in triumph to die.

Thus Nelson, the Briton, when navies were sinking,
Received his death-wound without sighing or shrinking ;
When the flag of his foeman was laid at his feet,
He smiled, and considered his glory complete—
His spirit enraptured to know that his name
Should blazon forever the tablet of fame.
Thus Wolfe, valiant Wolfe, the young, ardent and brave,
Would not have commuted his own gory grave
For the crown and the sceptre his monarch then swayed :
His name is eternal, his king's *has decayed.*

" *Give unto the Lord the glory due unto his name ; worship the Lord in the beauty of holiness.*"—*Ps. xxix.* 2.

When virgin voices sweetly blend
With manly tones, and both ascend
Harmonious on the dulcet air,
How soooth'd is then the listening ear !
Sweet symphonies the heart disarm
And all our sterner passions charm.

When brooding over former climes,
And perils passed in distant climes,
Defeat and glory all are gone,
Like dreams, before Louisa's* tone ;
Harsh thunders of the battle-field
To soft, melodious accents yield.

But when the holy anthem swells
That speaks where Christ in glory dwells,
When *hope* and faith united say :
" Leave worldly schemes and come this way,"
Thrones, dynasties, and martial pow'r
Appear the playthings of an hour—
Seducing, evanescent, vain,
The pompous phantoms of a worldly brain.

18 May,† 1831.

---

* Madame Ney's Christian name was Louise Aglœ. The Marshal probably called her Louise—Louisa in English. She had a remarkably sweet voice.—*Memoirs of Madame de Rémusat.*

† On the 18th day of May, 1804, Cambacérès, as President of the Senate, " proclaimed Napoleon Bonaparte Emperor of the French."

THE CABBAGE PARBOILED!!!

Best of the garden, why should we
Withhold a stanza due to thee?
Roses may entertain the eye
 And gratify the smell:
With *cabbage* and good *bacon* I
 Can hunger's tooth repel.
Pride of the kitchen, why should we
Withhold the praises due to thee?

Let emblematic flowers imply
 Emotions tongues cannot explain;
Good cabbages well cook'd defy
 Keen appetites, and life sustain.
Boast of the dinner-table, we
Award these praises due to *thee*,
We could give thee a *sweeter name*,
But still thy *virtues* are the *same*.

CABUS.

TO FALLEN AMBITION.*

Where is that lofty spirit now
 That swell'd to rule thy fellow-man—
The coronet that graced thy brow,
 When once triumphant in the *van*,
Vast armies followed thy behest,
And crowned with victory thy crest?

Gone, where all human things must go,
 Beneath *Time's rotatory* wheel!
Perhaps 'tis best that it is so,
 To give thee space thy heart to heal
Of those deep wounds Ambition made
In thy poor heart, which turn'd thy head.

REPLY—BY THE FALLEN MAN.†

Freedom, to thee I most atone,
 For quenching *once* thy innate flame;
My bosom is thy native home,
 Thy triumph is my highest fame.
Forgive me if I once did stray
Unconscious from thy splendid way.

* Dedicated (in cipher) to Napoleon Bonaparte.
† In cipher.

TO MISS J. E. T——
The Ruling Passion.

Jesting aside, my doubting heart
Endures for him the keenest smart.
Love, if thou wilt intrude upon us,
I wish thou wouldst not *Hope* take from us.
Zenobia, it is said, disdain'd
A captive to be led enchain'd
Before Aurelian's gorgeous car,
Environ'd by the pomp of war.
True—for the female heart disdains
Hymen, if he come with chains.
Tell *him*, Eros, I'll be free,
Even though he marry me.

Love I will, but not obey,
Unless he let me have my way.
He has paid on bended knee
Homage duly sworn to me !
Why then should a *subject rule* me ?
No, by Jove, he shall not fool me.
Wife or *maiden*, I must still
Be supreme and have my will.

C'EST VRAI !*

The coldest heart that ever beat
Has some emotions warm—
Some little, secret, sweet retreat.
That has a latent charm.

A cold exterior may display
To superficial eyes
A breast in which Love's vivid ray
Just enters in and dies.

Yet in that bosom's deep recess.
Volcanic flames may burn,
Which disappointed hopes repress,
And feelings fine inurn.

CUPID.

Cupid is a changeling
Requiring much art,
To keep him from mangling
The chords of the heart.

* From an album which belonged to Miss Margaret E. Graham, Salem Academy, N. C., 1845.

"A Friend" wrote in Miss Allison's album that the man whose heart music could not melt was

"the Muses' scorn—
Fit only to delve
In Mammon's dirty mine—
Sneak with a scoundrel fox,
Or grunt with glutton swine."

REPLY BY P. S. NEY.

Is there a female heart who can
Duly estimate the man—
Not by *music's* dulcet tone,
But by *moral* worth alone ?
* * * * *
Testing virtue by the *ear*
Is a standard wond'rous queer !
By that *rule*, this *Friend* of thine
Dooms to grovel with the swine
Many minds *acute* and *clear*
That can *think*, but can *not hear*.
My spirits with emotion swell
At Music's voice attemper'd well ;
Yet many men, profound, sublime,
Are strangers to the tuneful nine.
Therefore, *sweet friend*, forbear to blame
Great numbers who have soar'd to fame.
                Whom does the cap fit ?—NESCIO.

21 Jan'y, 1839.

TO MISS SARAH ——*
* * * *
THY sparkling eyes and temples fair
May feel through life some of my care,
But if I dare a prophet turn,
They ne'er with agony shall burn
Or feel that soul-consuming flame
That scorch'd me on the steeps of fame.

May, 1838.

"WESTWARD THE STAR OF EMPIRE TAKES ITS WAY."
—*Bishop Berkeley.*

WESTWARD the star of empire takes its way,
Eastward the shadows darken fast—
An infant realm is rising on the day
Far mightier than mighty past.

* From P. S. Ney's School Register.

EPITAPH ON HON. MICHAEL HOKE,* LINCOLNTON, N. C.

(*By request.*)

AMONG the manly, Hoke was foremost found,
Of mind capacious and of morals sound ;
In public spirit and in private worth,
His State ne'er gave a nobler being birth,
All mourned the exit of his early prime,
But all must yield to the decrees divine.

April, 1845.

EGOTISM—AH !†

VAST Genius laid his hand
Upon this shining page,
And here his MARK shall stand
Distinct from age to age.
Away prim manikins will pass,
But *Ney* remains an age of brass.

"GONE, WITH THEIR GLORIES GONE."‡

THOUGH I of the chosen the choicest,
To Fame gave her loftiest tone ;
Though I 'mong the brave was the bravest,
My plume and my baton are gone !

The Eagle that pointed to conquest
Was struck from his altitude high,
A prey to a vulture the foulest,
No more to revisit the sky.

One sigh to the hope that has perished,
One tear to the wreck of the past,
One look upon all I have cherished,
One lingering look—'tis the last.

And now from remembrance I banish
The glories which shone in my train ;
Oh, vanish, fond memories, vanish !
Return not to sting me again

May 26, 1835.

* A man of great ability, and of high character, the grandfather of Secretary Hoke Smith.
† From Mrs. Stircwalt's album. The last line was afterwards changed to :

"But *Ney* remains a man of brass."

‡ From Mrs. Dalton's album. See p. 156, note at bottom. P. S. Ney wrote the same piece of poetry in Miss Allison's album ; it is entitled " Farewell," and was written in March, 1838. He copies " Napoleon's Farewell," by Byron, and then writes his own Farewell.

From the *Charlotte Chronicle*.*

"The following was published forty-seven years ago in the *Charlotte Journal*, and was composed by a man who called himself Marshal Ney:"

A ROVER.

"'An me!' said Hannibal, when recalled from Italy."

An atom on the atmosphere,
Tossed here and there and everywhere ;
No female hand to press my head
Or close mine eyes when I am dead ;
No feeling friend to whisper peace
And bid my erring passions cease
Their wild uproar—no kindred—none.
An exile from my native home,
A wanderer, like Cain, am I,
And only agonize to die.
   Yes, agony must be my lot
While sensibility is mine !
   Yet shall I never be forgot,
Or silent sink to latest time.
High on the pyramid of fame,
The bravest of the brave, my name
Shall shine. Oh, sweet, consoling thought !
When I am gone I shall not be forgot.

* Date torn off ; probably published in 1890.

NAPOLEON IN EXILE;

OR,

𝕬 𝖁𝖔𝖎𝖈𝖊 𝖋𝖗𝖔𝖒 𝕾𝖙. 𝕳𝖊𝖑𝖊𝖓𝖆.

1817.—SEPTEMBER.

have of what was my opinion at that time about Wright, is faint; but as well as I can recollect, it was, that he ought to have been brought before a military commission for having landed spies and assassins, and the sentence executed within forty-eight hours. What dis-

except to him, was imperatively necessary, and indeed the chief requisite."

His excellency then told me, in order, as he said, to show the good opinion that he entertained of me, that

VOL. I. 23

SUMMARY.

THE evidence presented in the preceding pages proves conclusively, I think, that Peter S. Ney was Marshal Ney.* Of course the evidence must be considered as a whole and not in detached portions.† The physical resemblance between P. S. Ney and Marshal Ney is perfect. Marshal Ney was large, tall—a little more than five feet, eleven inches high ("*cinque pieds, cinque pouces*")—athletic, broad-shouldered, full-chested, symmetrically built. "Each attitude and motion denoted health and strength of muscle." His head was very large, partially bald, high behind, flattish on top, oval, long from front to back; hair auburn or red; complexion florid; forehead high, broad, full; eyebrows heavy, jutting, prominent ("his face," says one writer, "was slightly disfigured by his beetling brows"); eyes blue or gray, sunken, not ungentle in repose, but keen, piercing, flaming, terrible when excited; nose high, broad at the base, and slightly turned up (*retroussé*) at the end; mouth medium, straight, firm; lips compressed, the under lip a little thicker than the upper; jaws massive;

---

* See "Memoirs of Marshal Ney;" Goodrich's "History of Napoleon and his Marshals;" "Court and Camp of Bonaparte;" "The Conscript," Erckmann-Chatrian; "Memoirs of Miles Byrne, Chef de Battalion," etc.; "Reflexions sur les Notes du Moniteur et Notes Biographiques, par un Ami de la Vérité, London, 1810;" Thiers' "History of the Consulate and Empire;" Headley's "Napoleon and his Marshals;" Lever's "Tom Burke of Ours;" "Le Maréchal Ney, le Soldat," etc.; Fezensac's "Memoirs;" Maiseau's "Life of Marshal Ney;" Ségur's "Russian Campaign;" Capefigue's "Europe During the Consulate and the Empire;" Lamartine's "History of the Restoration;" Welschinger's "Le Maréchal Ney, 1815;" Sir Robert Wilson's "Secret History of the Russian Campaign of 1812;" Napier's "History of the Peninsular War;" statues and portraits of Ney; encyclopædias, etc.

† Very much of the evidence cannot be specifically alluded to in a summary like this.

chin large, round, prominent; neck large and rather short; step quick and active; face marked with small-pox; voice deep, guttural, rich, strong; expression open, stern, thoughtful, commanding. This is an accurate description of Marshal Ney. It is an accurate description of Peter S. Ney.

Again, Peter S. Ney was like Marshal Ney as to his mind, character, disposition, manners, habits, tastes, temperament, etc. Marshal Ney had a sound, strong, clear, acute, vigorous, practical mind. He was brave, bold, daring, intrepid, calm, and cool in the hour of peril or need, active, energetic, prompt, painstaking, methodical, self-denying (though heady at times), modest, kind, gentle, affectionate, tender, honest, just, generous, frank, open, blunt, rough (though not coarse*), impulsive, quick-tempered, sometimes offending his best friends by the plainness and severity of his language, yet always careful to make the amplest reparation for any wrong done when the excitement of the moment had passed away—a good, though not implacable hater, a true friend, grave, dignified (yet witty and humorous at times), plain (despising the fashions and fripperies of life), proud (though not haughty), independent, yet grateful for the smallest attention or kindness; patriotic, an ardent lover, nay, a devout worshipper of Freedom, ready to die at any moment in defence of her holy cause—a man of great personal magnetism and immense moral power, who exercised a controlling influence over almost all persons who were brought into association with him. Such was Marshal Ney. Such was Peter S. Ney.

Peter S. Ney used tobacco, and drank wine and spirits—sometimes to excess. Marshal Ney used tobacco and drank wine and spirits, though not to excess, so far as I know. His busy and eventful life left him little time or opportunity for dissipation of any kind, even if he had been so inclined. Alexander Dumas says that at the battle of Waterloo, about three o'clock P.M., Napoleon, Ney, Soult, and Jerome—Ney and Jerome covered with dust and blood—discussed a bottle of Bordeaux wine. "Napoleon, with that soft voice of his, which he knew

* I draw Byron's distinction. Byron says that Burns was *rough*, but not *coarse*.

so well how to use upon occasion, said to Ney, 'Ney, my brave Ney'—*thou*ing him for the first time since his return from Elba—'thou wilt take the twelve thousand men of Milhaud and Kellermann; thou wilt wait until my old grumblers have found thee; thou wilt give the *coup de boutoir;* and then, if Grouchy arrives, the day is ours. Go.' Ney went and gave the *coup de boutoir*, but Grouchy never came." *

At the battle of Bautzen, in May, 1813, Ney was slightly wounded in the right foot. He spent the night after the victory in a chateau near the battlefield; † and " disdaining to use a bedstead, he pulled a mattress to the floor and threw himself upon it. One of his aides-de-camp and the officer of the guard at the chateau ransacked the building in search of food, but only succeeded in finding a considerable quantity of rare old *Tokay*, which they at once *confiscated.* When the marshal awoke he was informed of the 'find,' and as the night was inclement, he, with his characteristic warm-heartedness, ordered all the guard except the pickets to take up their quarters in the chateau, as they would be more comfortable there than around their bivouac fires. He also invited all the officers in the neighborhood to come and share his hospitality. They all ' worshipped the rosy god' that night, but of course there was no dissipation. They left early the next morning, the Emperor and Marshal Ney leading the way." ‡ In his " French Revolutions," Redhead says Ney " took a copious draught of wine just before he started to the place of execution, having previously smoked a Havana cigar, as was his custom."

Peter S. Ney's surroundings were entirely different from those of Marshal Ney prior to his supposed execution in 1815. It is known that Peter S. Ney was not at all intemperate until the death of Napoleon, in 1821, when he said to Colonel

---

* " Excursions sur les Bords du Rhin," par Alexandre Dumas.

† The marshal's foot was " bound up in a napkin. He had been wounded in the battle, but said nothing about it. Doubtless he considered any wound that did not break a bone a mere nothing."—" Memoirs" of Miles Byrne.

‡ " Memoirs" of Miles Byrne, Chef de Battalion, etc.

Rogers, "With the death of Napoleon my last hope is gone." Marshal Ney worshipped Napoleon. Peter S. Ney worshipped Napoleon. Marshal Ney possessed so strong and hardy a constitution that he seemed to be able almost to defy the ordinary laws of nature. He ate sparingly of the plainest and simplest food, and required very little sleep or rest of any kind. No amount of toil, or care, or privation, or suffering, or exposure to heat or cold, or wind, or sleet, or storm could break him down. So Peter S. Ney ate sparingly of the plainest and simplest food, and slept but four or five hours out of the twenty-four. He was little affected either by heat or cold. In the coldest weather he would not sit near the fire. He was an indefatigable, proud, ambitious worker. "A soul of fire seemed to be contained in a frame of iron." Marshal Ney's filial love was very great. His mother was especially dear to him. He loved his wife with that old-fashioned, knightly devotion of which the brave alone are capable. He was tenderly attached to his children. He was a model son and husband and father. So Peter S. Ney often spoke of his mother and wife and children, and always in terms of the utmost affection and tenderness. He was true to his wife during his long residence in this country, and almost with his dying breath he said, "Oh, I can't stand it any longer. If I get well I must go back to France to see my wife and children."

Marshal Ney was a fair musician, and had some artistic talent. Lavalette says, "The marshal played tolerably well on the flute, and repeatedly played a waltz," etc. So Peter S. Ney often played on a flute and played "tolerably well." Marshal Ney had little time to cultivate his artistic talent. Peter S. Ney's drawings and paintings possessed considerable merit. Marshal Ney was noted for the ease and grace with which he rode the most vicious and fiery horses. So was Peter S. Ney. Marshal Ney was the finest fencer in Europe, with the exception, perhaps, of Marshal Murat, and he was fully equal to him. So Peter S. Ney was a perfect master of the art of fencing. He was far superior to any man, soldier or civilian, in the United States. Marshal Ney was thoroughly acquainted with everything pertaining to the art of war. So was Peter S. Ney. I do not know whether Marshal Ney had any poetic talent or not. But there is more or less poetry in every one's nature ; and a man of Ney's brains and energy was capable, especially under favorable conditions, of accomplishing almost anything. Some of the plainest, sternest, most illustrious warriors, in whom the poetic faculty is supposed not to reside, have been very fond of poetry, and capable of writing it too. Moses, David, Cæsar, Frederick the Great, Napoleon*—all courted the muse, and some of them with decided success. Many men who have won fame in some particular calling are exceedingly anxious to do that for which they are generally supposed to have little ability or no ability at all. Good, old, brusque, homely, clumsy Dr. Johnson was one day persuaded to go out rabbit-hunting. He was given a fleet, spirited charger, which the doctor was wholly unable to control. He outstripped perforce all his competitors, and was loudly and enthusiastically proclaimed the hero of the day. Dr. Johnson afterward said that he was prouder of that compliment than of any he had ever received. Wellington one day, in a thick forest, killed with his own hands, unaided, an enormous wild boar, " of which feat," says one of his friends, " he was prouder than of Waterloo." Peter S. Ney wrote poetry, and was proud of the accomplishment. He wrote some very good poetry.

Marshal Ney was wounded several times—in the foot, knee, thigh, hand, arm, chest, neck. Peter S. Ney was wounded in the foot, knee, thigh, hand, arm and chest—no one recollects that he had a wound in the neck. But one of the witnesses who was with him when he died says, " He had wounds all over him, but I cannot recollect the location and character of every wound." The sabre cut on the left side of his head, to which so many witnesses refer, cannot historically be accounted for. Marshal Ney, so far as I know, had no wound of this kind. Peter S. Ney told a few witnesses that he re-

* At St. Helena Napoleon wrote a poem suggested by the portrait of his son.

ceived the sabre wound at the battle of Waterloo. In a poem referring to the battle of Waterloo he says :

" Where broken bones and fractured skull
Had all but ruined this poor hull."

(See Mr. Ervin's testimony.) Mr. W. M. Reinhardt says : " Mr. Ney told me one day, while I was cutting his hair, how he received the sabre wound. He said that during the battle of Waterloo he happened to come in contact with an English officer named Ponsonby—I think he said General Ponsonby—and that in the *mêlée* Ponsonby gave him this wound, but that he cut Ponsonby down, and broke his sword in doing so. This is my recollection of the matter, and I do not see how I can be mistaken." Now, General William Ponsonby was killed in a cavalry charge at Waterloo, and Colonel Frederick Ponsonby was badly wounded. He was disabled in both arms by sabre blows, and fell from his horse apparently dead. He lay upon the ground unconscious for several hours. Marshal Ney in all probability encountered, face to face, in actual personal combat, one of these men or both. According to Dumas, Ney was " covered with dust and *blood.*" Victor Hugo says, " Ney, one of his epaulettes half cut through by the sabre cut of a horse guard, and his decoration of the great eagle dinted by a bullet—*bleeding*, muddy, magnificent, and holding a *broken sword* in his hand, shouted, ' Come and see how a marshal of France dies on the battlefield. . . . Oh, is there nothing for *me !*' "* Ney himself says, " Constantly in the rear guard, which I followed on foot, having all my horses killed, worn out with fatigue, covered with contusions, and having no longer strength to march, I owe my life to a corporal who supported me on the road, and did not abandon me during the retreat." †

Of course there was no official record of wounds received even by the higher officers, as Napoleon and his empire were completely overthrown. Peter S. Ney understood the English language, and spoke it well, with very little foreign accent.

* " Les Misérables." † Letter to Fouché, June 26th, 1815.

Marshal Ney understood the English language, and spoke it easily and fluently. When Marshal Grouchy was in this country in 1819 he was asked this question : " Could Marshal Ney speak the English language ?" " Certainly he could," replied Grouchy. And he mentioned that on one occasion, in the early years of the French Revolution, when he and Ney served together in the same army, some English prisoners were taken, and that Ney talked with them in their own language. General Lallemand, of the French army, also said that Ney understood the English language. Mr. William Leigh (naval officer), of Martinsburg, W. Va., in a letter written in 1887, says : " The Hon. Thomas Spalding, of Georgia, was in Washington, D. C., shortly after Napoleon's downfall. There were in the city at that time two French general officers on whom Mr. Spalding called, with the intention of making some inquiries about Marshal Ney. These officers did not like Marshal Ney. One of them used some expressions about Ney which induced Mr. Spalding to say, ' But Ney could not speak a word of English.' ' Not speak English ! ' the other replied, ' why, he spoke it like a native.' These facts were related to me several years ago by Mr. Spalding himself. Mr. Spalding also called my attention to the peculiar bearing of Count Ney, who had not long before made a visit of some duration to this country." * Peter S. Ney was a highly educated man. He was a superior mathematician, a fine classical scholar, well informed on all subjects of general interest, and thoroughly acquainted with the French, German, and perhaps other languages. Peter S. Ney said that when he came to the United States he had a good though not a classical education ; that, during his first three years and a half stay in this country, while he remained in seclusion, he prepared himself for teaching by studying the classics and the higher mathematics. In that length of time a man of Ney's parts could have completed the usual college course. And he was at all times a diligent student. The idea generally obtains, even among educated people, that Marshal Ney was an

* *Vide Southern Literary Messenger*, 1847 ; *Southern Quarterly Review*, 1853 ; " History of Cecil County, Md.," by George Johnston, LL.D.

ignorant man who could scarcely read or write his name. But nothing could be farther from the truth. He was much better educated than most of Napoleon's marshals. He wrote a book on the Art of War, which is universally acknowledged to be a work of transcendent merit. In 1802 Napoleon appointed Ney Minister Plenipotentiary to the republic of Switzerland. Of course he would not have appointed an illiterate man to so important and responsible a position as that. And, as shown elsewhere (see biography), Ney proved himself to be as great a diplomatist as he was a warrior. I have several letters and reports of Marshal Ney written entirely by himself, and I do not hesitate to say that as to correctness, force, and even elegance of composition, they will compare favorably with similar papers written by Wellington or Napoleon. Indeed, Ney's style is much less stilted and poetical than that of Napoleon. It is conspicuously clear, concise, and forcible, especially when he wrote upon military subjects. So was Peter S. Ney's style.

But, it is asked, if Peter S. Ney were Marshal Ney, why did he adopt the name of Peter Stuart Ney ? The French soldiers called Marshal Ney "Peter the Red." It was their pet name for him. "Courage, the Red Lion is coming ; all will soon be right, for Peter the Red is coming" ("Memoirs"). This name, therefore, must have had for Ney the most delightful, the most tender, even the most sacred associations. As to his middle name, P. S. Ney said (according to some witnesses) that the maiden name of his mother was Stuart, and that he chose Stuart on that account. According to other witnesses he chose this name because his mother was related to or in some way closely connected with a family of Stuarts. But *Ney*—why did he adopt that name—a name of worldwide fame, and therefore almost certain to create suspicion and to lead to discovery—a name which no one would expect him to take ? He took it in all probability simply because it was famous throughout the world ; because no human being would expect him to take it. It was his greatest protection, his best foil against suspicion or recognition. It was in keeping with Ney's bold, daring, shrewd, practical character. Besides, there was magic in the name. NEY! It awoke a thousand precious, hallowed memories. It thrilled one through and through like an electric shock. It was the synonym of bravery, and heroism, and immortality. Ney could not give up that name. It was his life, his glory, his all.

It is claimed by some persons that if P. S. Ney were the marshal he could have returned to France when a general amnesty was granted by the Bourbon government. It is true that most of the exiled officers—Grouchy, Lallemand, Vandamme, Kellermann, etc.—returned to France when this general amnesty was granted; but if Marshal Ney were alive the amnesty could not possibly apply to him, because Marshal Ney, legally and formally, was a dead man—not an exiled officer—and therefore no amnesty was intended to apply to him. Indeed, the amnesty was granted simply because Marshal Ney was, in the eye of the law, a dead man. He was the one victim that had to be offered to appease the Bourbon wrath and hate. If he had returned at any time prior to 1848 he would have been given over to public vengeance, and every Frenchman who aided in his escape would have been shot or hanged. Besides, P. S. Ney said that he could not return to France unless Wellington gave him permission to do so. Certainly he was most anxious to go back to his home and country. The evidence undoubtedly proves this. For some years after the Revolution of 1830, Dupin, of counsel for Ney, General Excelmans, Armand Carrel, Odilon Barrot, and others labored most faithfully to procure from the Chamber of Peers a reversal of the sentence of death against Marshal Ney, but they were unsuccessful. The Peers were frightened and refused to reverse the sentence. They were afraid of another revolution. Had the sentence been reversed P. S. Ney of course could have returned to France. Marshal Ney's presence in France at any time after 1831 would in all probability have been the signal for an uprising of the people against the government of Louis Philippe. In May, 1835, soon after Dupin and his friends appeared to have lost all hope of obtaining a reversal of the sentence against Ney, Peter S. Ney wrote in Mrs. Dalton's album that remarkable poem entitled,

"Gone, with their glories, gone!" a poem which, as I shall show, alone proves that Peter S. Ney was Marshal Ney.

I have found but one serious difficulty in the entire investigation. History states that the Christian name of Marshal Ney's mother was Marguerite or Margaretha. P. S. Ney said the Christian name of his mother was Catharine Isabella (see testimony of Mrs. Hughes, General Hill, Mrs. Hill, Mrs. Irwin). In 1891 I visited Saar-Louis, Lorraine, the historic birthplace of Marshal Ney. I examined the official "Register of Marriages, Births, and Deaths." I quote from it as follows :

"Michel Ney, son of Peter Ney and Margaretha Gräffin, was born at Saar-Louis on the 10th day of January, 1769. The parents were married on the 13th day of January, 1767 ; the same are registered in the marriage contract as Peter Neu, twenty-nine years of age, son of Matthias Neu and Margaretha Becker, of Ensdorf District, Saar-Louis, and Margaretha Groewelinger, twenty-eight years of age, daughter of Valentin Groewelinger and Margaretha Denis, of Bidingen, diocese of Trier."

In the marriage contract Ney's mother signed her name *Margaretha Greblinger.* On Bier Street stands a small, plain house, in which, it is said, Marshal Ney was born. Over the front door is a small marble or slate panel with this inscription : "Here was born Marshal Ney." In this village I found two distinct families of the name of Ney, but in no way related to each other. Each family, however, claimed to belong to that from which Marshal Ney descended. Mrs. Schafer, wife of Professor Schafer, of Saar-Louis, belongs to what I may call the unhistoric family. She said she was related to Marshal Ney, and that the name of his father was not Peter, but Nicholas, and the name of his grandfather was Anton, and not Matthias. I then asked her what was the Christian name of Marshal Ney's mother. She answered without a moment's hesitation, "*Catharine.*" Her family, she said, originally came from Wachendorf, Würtemberg. I went to Wachendorf. I there made the acquaintance of the Baron and Baroness of Ow. They received me with charming courtesy, and gave me some valuable information respecting the unhistoric Ney family. The baron said that his father, Baron John Charles, had fully investigated the claims of the two families, and was thoroughly convinced that Marshal Ney was descended from the Wachendorf—Anton Ney—family. The opinion of Baron John Charles is entitled to great weight, for I learned from high authority that he was a man of excellent judgment and a most careful, painstaking, and conscientious investigator. Above the front door of the old house in which Anton Ney lived is a tablet with this inscription: "Original Mansion of Marshal Ney's Family" (or "Ancestors").

Mrs. Elizabeth Schliter, of Wachendorf (née Ney), belongs to the Anton Ney family. She said: "Our family is very old. My ancestors settled here many years ago, though several of them have since emigrated to other places in Europe. The family name has always been spelled *Nëy*—with the two dots above it. There are several families of the name of Neu, both in Germany and France, but this name is entirely different from that of Ney. I have often heard my father speak of Marshal Ney as one of his relatives. Marshal Ney's father was named Nicholas, and he emigrated to France about the year 1760."

Pastor Knittel, of Wachendorf, says: "It has always been believed here that Marshal Ney's family originally lived in Wachendorf; that his grandfather was named Anton and his father Nicholas."

In the "Official Paper for Würtemberg," published at Stuttgart, bearing date of April 1st, 1866, I find the following: "It is an undoubted fact that the famous French Marshal Ney, the 'bravest of the brave,' descends from Swabia, and that his family continues to live at Wachendorf, where it was settled some centuries since. The grandfather of the marshal was Anton Ney, and he reared a large family of children at Wachendorf. His son Nicholas emigrated to France and settled in Saar-Louis,* where he followed the calling of a

* There was a Saar-Louis in Alsace.

cooper. He married a French girl, and from that marriage sprang Marshal Michael Ney."

The following extract is taken from the "Official Paper of Ravensburg for 1825," to wit: "The grandfather of Marshal Ney is Anton Ney, born May 24th, 1699, who married, at first, Anna Faiss, November 25th, 1725. There were five sons. The first, John, born October 2d, 1728, removed to Alsace. The second, Joseph, took possession of the household and paid to each brother forty florins. The third, Fidelis, removed to Hungary. The fourth, named Nicholas, removed to Alsace. Nicholas was born October 27th, 1738, and is recognized all over this country as the father of the French Marshal Ney."

A genealogical table of the Ney (Wachendorf) family was prepared by Pastor Bok. The facts were chiefly taken from the official records of the town of Wachendorf. From this table (kindly furnished me by the Roman Catholic priest of Wachendorf) I extract the genealogical record of the Ney family found on the following page.

Let us go back to the *historic* Matthias Ney family. In the "Official Register of Marriages, Births, and Deaths" at Saar-Louis we find that Marshal Ney's father was Peter *Neu*, not Ney; that his grandfather was Matthias *Neu*,* not Ney; and that his mother had three different names. Now, here is a regular *olla podrida*: Michel Ney, Peter Neu, Peter Ney, Matthias Neu, Margaretha Gräffin, Margaretha Groewelinger, Margaretha Greblinger! I asked the polite registrar to explain the matter. He shook his head. "It's very strange," said he, "but I can't explain it." †

I had written thus far when I received the following letter from the Mayor of Friedrichshafen, Würtemberg:

FRIEDRICHSHAFEN, WÜRTEMBERG, February 19, 1895.

WORTHY SIR: The official records here show that Nicholas Ney married Catharine Rossman, of Buchhorn. The grand-

---

* Neu and Ney, it must be remembered, are entirely different names. When was Neu converted into Ney, and for what reason?

† In writing the biography of Ney I simply followed the accepted historical accounts as to his birth, parentage, etc.

GENEALOGY OF THE NEY FAMILY,
WACHENDORF, WÜRTEMBERG.

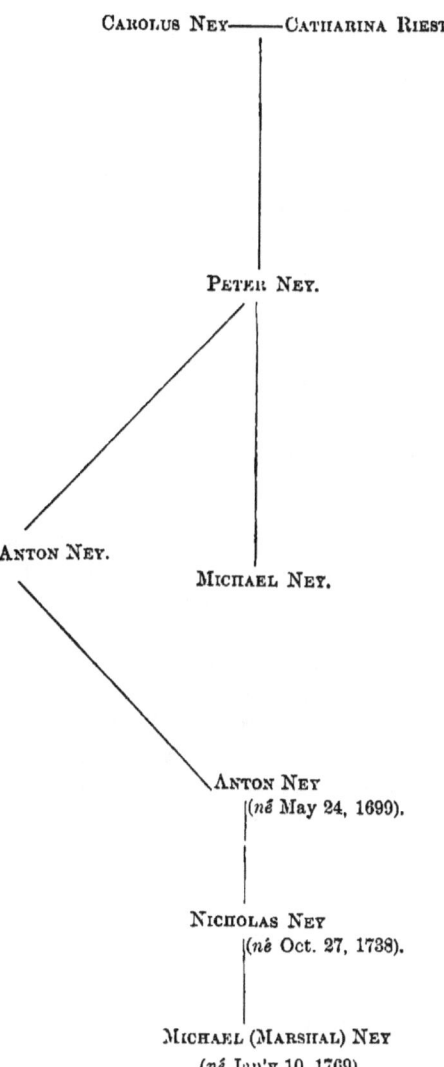

father of Catharine Rossman was Michael Rothmund. His daughter, Anna Maria Rothmund, married a Rossman in France. From that marriage sprang Catharine Rossman. Catharine Rossman married Nicholas Ney, a cooper at Saar-Louis. They had two children :
1. Michael, Field Marshal of France, Duke of Elchingen, Prince of the Moskowa.
2. Margaretha, who married Claude Monnier.

Francisca Rothmund died at Markdorf in 1798, and left a legacy of two hundred florins to her niece, Catharine Ney, *née* Rossman, mother of the French Marshal Ney. The legacy remained unpaid for many years, and was finally paid to two poor relatives of Catharine Ney, *née* Rossman, who were then living at Friedrichshafen. I enclose copies of two official documents which may be of service to you :

Transcript.

" I, the undersigned, Aglae Louise Auguié, widow of Monsieur Michel Ney, Prince de la Moskowa, Duke of Elchingen, declare by these presents, in the name of my sons, Napoleon Joseph Ney, Prince de la Moskowa ; Louis Felix Ney, Duke of Elchingen ; Eugene Michel Ney, and Napoleon Henri Edgar Ney, that I renounce in favor of the natural heirs of Madame Francisca Rothmund, deceased in 1798, at Markdorf, grand baillage de Tettnang, Royaume de Würtemberg, that part which comes to my sons of a sum of two hundred florins bequeathed by the Dame Francisca Rothmund to her niece, Madame Catharine Ney, *née* Rossman, mother of the late Monsieur le Maréchal, Prince de la Moskowa, Duc d'Elchingen. Done at the Chateau of Coudreaux, near Chateaudun, Department of Eure and Loire, the 15th day of June, 1823.

" (Signed.)   A. L. Auguié,
                     " *Princess de la Moskowa.*
" Attest : Léan Foucault, *Maire.*"

Transcript.

" I, the undersigned, Marguerite Ney, widow of Monsieur

Claude Monnier, declare by these presents that I renounce in favor of the natural heirs of Madame Francisca Rothmund, deceased in 1798, at Markdorf, grand baillage de Tettnang, Royaume de Würtemberg, that part which falls to my share of a sum of two hundred (200) florins, bequeathed by said Dame Francisca Rothmund to her niece, Madame Catharine Ney, *née* Rossman, my mother.

"Done at Malgrange, near Nancy, the 29th day of June, 1824.

"(Signed.)   VEUVE MONNIER.
"Attest : JEAN JOSEPH ABRY, *Maire.*"
I have the honor to be, etc.,
             SCHMIDT, *Mayor of Friedrichshafen.*

According to the statements of the *historic* Matthias Ney family, Margaret Ney was the sister of Marshal Ney, and married Monsieur Claude Monnier.

These documents then prove, beyond the shadow of a doubt, that Marshal Ney's mother was *Catharine* Rossman, not Margaretha Gräffin, or Margaretha Groewelinger, or Margaretha Greblinger.

The documentary evidence is very strong—I may say conclusive. It cannot be overthrown. It greatly strengthens the testimony of the witnesses. Indeed, it makes it substantially unassailable from any standpoint whatever. The handwriting of P. S. Ney is remarkably like that of Marshal Ney, yet altogether unlike it in the sense of servile imitation. I care little for expert opinion as to the value of comparative handwritings. The authorship of the Junian letters, says a high authority, has been "attributed by professional experts to thirty-seven persons.'' * There is an expression, an individuality, a life about handwriting that cannot be explained or de-

* I have not the slightest doubt that Burke was Junius. Sir Philip Francis could not have written the Junian letters. Macaulay's argument is as weak as water. Contemporary opinion ascribed the authorship to Burke, and "contemporary opinion," says Burke's biographer, "as formed from a variety of minor circumstances, which do not come within the knowledge of future inquirers, is perhaps on such occasions the truest." Contemporary opinion pointed strongly to P. S. Ney as Marshal Ney.

scribed. The handwriting of every man or woman is of necessity informed or saturated with the writer's own personality, and cannot be recognized by strokes, turns, curves, angles, flourishes, etc. In all such matters every one must judge for one's self. Professional opinion is not seldom of far less value than non-professional. The skull and chin of P. S. Ney, so far as I am able to judge by the illustrations, were precisely like those of Marshal Ney. The statement of Colonel Melody as a *Mason* is very significant. It is sufficient to say that its importance cannot be overestimated. The testimony of Mr. R. A. Henderson is of the highest value. Of no less importance is the fact, attested by several witnesses, that P. S. Ney was recognized as Marshal Ney by persons of reputable character who had known him or seen him in France or other portions of Europe. The most valuable witness is Peter S. Ney himself. By all the rules of evidence his statements, oral and written, are entitled to the highest credibility. The testimony of the witnesses without exception (to say nothing of the circumstantial evidence) is that P. S. Ney's mind was sound, clear, and strong, and that his character was pure, honest, and upright. There could be no more capable, competent, truthful witness. Peter S. Ney, when perfectly sober, said to a few confidential bosom friends that he was Marshal Ney. When in wine—intoxicated or *entre deux vins* —he often publicly declared he was Marshal Ney. Such declarations must have much weight with thinking people. Men under the influence of intoxicants have no delusions. They are imprudent and indiscreet, but they tell the truth. One's real character comes out when one is intoxicated or partially intoxicated. "In wine is truth." This old saying comes down to us strengthened and fortified by the universal observation and experience of mankind. The poem which P. S. Ney wrote in Mrs. Dalton's album, and afterward in Miss Allison's album, alone proves (as I have stated) that he was Marshal Ney. Take the first stanza:

> "Though I of the chosen the choicest,
> To fame gave her loftiest tone,
> Though I 'mong the brave was the bravest,
> My plume and my baton are gone."

Marshal Ney was called the bravest of the brave—a name given him by Napoleon himself, and by which he was universally known. A marshal only was entitled to the baton. The last two lines prove conclusively that P. S. Ney was Marshal Ney. Again, in his poem entitled "A Rover," we find evidence of the same character :

> " High on the pyramid of fame,
> The bravest of the brave, my name
> Shall shine . . . . ."

But the strongest evidence (with the single exception, perhaps, of P. S. Ney's dying declaration) is to be found in the " Memoirs of Napoleon" referred to in the documentary evidence. On page 315 the author says, " Had it not been for the delay of Marshal Ney he might have secured this position," etc. P. S. Ney replies : " Delay ! *Say the emperor took away my reserve !*" The italicized words are written in shorthand. On page 316 we read in the text : " He [Ney] was joined by Count d'Erlon with the corps of reserve." P. S. Ney says, " Count d'Erlon * *was called away* (or off) *by Napoleon, who crippled my movement.*" The italicized words are written in shorthand. P. S. Ney's dying declara-

---

* It is well known that Ney's reserve of twenty thousand men, commanded by Count D'Erlon, was called off by Napoleon. If Ney had had D'Erlon's troops at Quatre Bras he would have defeated Wellington. Napoleon gained a barren victory at Ligny. The Prussians fought well, and if they had been commanded by a first-class general Napoleon would have been defeated. Even Blücher would have been victorious if Bülow had been present, as he ought to have been, and would have been but for an inexcusable and criminal blunder. Napoleon owed most of his great victories to the fact that the opposing armies were commanded by third-rate generals. Suppose a man like Wellington had been in command of the enemy's forces at Arcola, at Marengo, at Ulm, at Jena, at Eylau, at Essling, at Borodino, at Dresden, at Ligny ; every fair-minded man must admit that Napoleon would have been badly whipped. It is high time to assign Napoleon his proper place in military history. Napoleon himself acknowledged that Wellington was a better general than he was. To General Bertrand he said, " The Duke of Wellington, in the management of an army, is fully equal to myself, with the advantage of possessing more prudence." To Captain Paget, of the English army, Napoleon said, " I have no hesitation in saying that Wellington is a better general than myself."

tion is confessedly of the highest possible value. In the presence of death, with an unclouded mind, with a full sense of the responsibility which he assumed, he solemnly declared to his attending physician and others that he was Marshal Ney of France.

To me the fame of Marshal Ney is very dear—it is sacred. If Peter S. Ney had lived a bad, a dishonorable life in this country I would not have touched the investigation. I would have left the "bravest of the brave" "alone in his glory." But if P. S. Ney was Marshal Ney, as I firmly believe he was, then his career in the United States reflects as much credit upon him as his management of the rear guard in the Russian retreat. The great soldier wished to redeem his life, and he did redeem it gloriously. If possible, he was greater in peace than he was in war.

A few minutes before his death P. S. Ney became delirious. In this condition he died. Mr. O. G. Foard says that his last words, spoken in delirium, were these : "Bessières is dead and the Old Guard is defeated ; now let me die." * Marshal Ney had often led the Old Guard to victory, and they had gone down with him on the battle-field of Waterloo. Marshal Bessières, the loved and honored commander of the Old Guard, was killed at the defile of Rippach in 1813, the day before the battle of Lutzen. Napoleon and Ney, who was much attached to Bessières, for they were very much alike in character, were riding by the side of the marshal at the time of his death. A white cloth was instantly thrown over his body to conceal the knowledge of his death from the army, and from the Old Guard in particular. The death of Bessières made a deep, a profound impression upon Napoleon, Ney, and the entire army. The Old Guard loved Bessières with the tenderest, the most devoted affection. It was natural that Ney, in his last moments, should link them together— Bessières and the Old Guard. Like Stonewall Jackson,† de-

* Correspondent of the New York *Herald*, Turnersburg, N. C., 1879.

† Wellington, Ney, Stonewall Jackson—soldiers like these can conquer the world.

lirious and dying : " A. P. Hill [his right arm], prepare for action." " Bessières is dead, and the Old Guard is defeated ; now let me die." With these words upon his lips the war-worn soldier passed over the river.

Peace.

Rest.

APPENDIX A.

(See P. S. Ney's note, page 229.)

ALL this is doubtless true. Napoleon himself, according to Emerson, was a "boundless liar," and little confidence is to be placed in his statements about the matter. Besides, as P. S. Ney intimates, Napoleon had special reasons for telling these falsehoods—reasons which if not good *in foro conscientiæ*, might be considered as valid or venial by the world at large. That there was a conspiracy or plot to bring Napoleon back to France is now admitted by all candid historians. Indeed, I think it was never seriously doubted at any time. Napoleon at Elba was in constant communication with France. His old soldiers were sent from Elba to France to corrupt the army, and to prepare the way for his coming. These were his vanguard. Signs and watchwords had been agreed upon between him and his friends in France—"signs," says Lamartine, "which he alone could read, and of which the emissaries who brought them, under various pretexts, did not themselves know the importance or signification." Three persons especially had promised Napoleon at Fontainebleau to "inform him of what was going on in France, and to give the signal for his return." These were Maret, Duke of Bassano, Savary, and Lavalette. In the following fall and winter the friends of Napoleon became very bold and confident, and seemed almost openly to defy the government itself. Full details of the conspiracy were communicated to the French Government, but it took no notice of them. Bonaparte cared nothing for his abdication. He told General Kohler and others that he would revoke it in a moment if he thought he could succeed in regaining his throne. This was some days after the abdication had been formally and authoritatively made and ratified. He said his abdication was *forced*; that he was overwhelmed by foreign mercenaries and traitors; that as it was extorted from him by force and treason, it was not binding, and he had a right to revoke it or annul it at any time for the good of France. The safety and welfare of the State was the supreme law. Of course arguments of this kind might easily be made to apply to Ney and the other officers who took the oath of allegiance to Louis XVIII. There can be no doubt that there was a perfect understanding between Bonaparte, Ney, and others that Bonaparte was in due time to return from Elba as the Emperor of France, whose reign had been interrupted, but not overthrown and destroyed. There can be no doubt, as P. S. Ney says, that "the scheme of the plot was formed," that the " return was preconcerted before Napoleon quitted Fontainebleau for Elba." Marshal Ney on his trial said he knew nothing of Bonaparte's return until several days after his disembarkation at Cannes ; that there was no plot, no conspiracy to bring him back from Elba ; that he (Ney) was entirely loyal to Louis XVIII. until March 14th, when he saw that the king's cause was hopeless, and that he then went over to Napoleon to prevent the breaking out of a civil war. But these statements which Ney made on his trial (to save his life) are at variance with those which he made before his trial. Baron Capelle said that Marshal Ney told him that the return of Bonaparte was contrived by him (Marshal Ney), other marshals, the Minister of War (Soult), and Madame Hortense. Generals Bourmont and Lacourbe said Ney told them that everything had been arranged for three months for Bonaparte's return, and that if they had been in Paris they would have known it. The Count de la Genetière said that after Ney had read the proclamation, he said to the persons around him, " The return of Napoleon has been arranged for three months."

Count de Faverney said that Marshal Ney informed him that measures had been taken beforehand to render the defection of the troops inevitable.

Captain Casse, of the Forty-second Regiment, stated that Ney said to him, " I had no idea of fighting for the king. Had he given me twenty times the value of the Tuileries, I would not have served him. I bore the emperor in my heart." Other witnesses stated that the marshal said Bonaparte's return had been concerted a long time ; that he had been in correspondence with the isle of Elba, and knew of Napoleon's intended departure, etc.

Now it is impossible to doubt the truth of these statements, considering the character of the persons who made them, and considering all the circumstances of the case. Marshal Ney, on his trial, solemnly declared they were false in order to save his life. That is the simple truth of the matter. But it may be said that I am dragging down my hero, that I make his treason greater than it was before. So be it. Let us have the truth. Ney's character is so solid, so grand that it will bear a great many flaws. After all, the flaws may not be so great as they appear to be. Marshal Ney was the truest of patriots. He loved his country with a devotion which has never been surpassed, perhaps never equalled. His whole life was bound up in his country's welfare. Even amid the horrors of the Russian retreat he thought only of the honor and glory of France. His love of France dominated every other feeling, and seemed to elevate his character above human environments, to make him indeed almost more than man. " Everything for France." That was Ney's motto, Ney's creed, Ney's religion. He could say, as no other man perhaps could say,

"I know my country, for her soul is mine."

So when Napoleon abdicated at Fontainebleau, Ney very readily entered into his plans. He felt that the Bourbon rule would be utterly ruinous to his country, that Napoleon was the rightful ruler of France, that the people had solemnly repudiated the Bourbons and had chosen Napoleon as their lawful sovereign, and that the " voice of the people was the voice of God."

Napoleon, though in chains, was still the Emperor of France, and Ney believed it was his highest duty to aid in restoring him to that throne to which the people had elevated him, and from which he had been treasonably and unlawfully expelled. He would take the oath of allegiance to the Bourbon Government because the good of his country for the time being seemed to demand it. He would be loyal to the king so long only as the king was loyal to France. Fidelity to France was the only fidelity he acknowledged. Such was Ney's position. Patriotism was, as I have said, his master passion; it swallowed up every other feeling, every other thought. Ney was a child of the Revolution, impulsive, trained in camps, little accustomed to reason on abstract principles of right and wrong; and, above all, he was under the influence of Napoleon, his master, almost his god, who had taught him that any crime, however great, is justifiable in the interest of the State, for the good of one's people and country. I cannot say Ney was right. I believe he was wrong; but no one can question the purity and sincerity of his motives. He was honest; there was no treason in his heart. We can but admire and commend his conscientious devotion to duty as he understood it. He erred, like Wellington, but it was an error of the head, and not of the heart. He was not so bad as the great Duke of Marlborough, who, while professing unlimited loyalty to his sovereign, corresponded regularly with the Pretender, and acted grossly a double part. In war and in times of high political excitement many persons of good reputation will commit gross offences against morality and honor for the "good of their country," which they would not think of committing as private individuals. Even the Duke of Wellington half-way justifies Talleyrand's treachery at the Congress at Erfurt, when, as Napoleon's confidential adviser and minister, he went secretly every evening to the house of the Emperor Alexander, and gave him a full and detailed account of everything that Napoleon had said to him (Talleyrand) during the day. It was the grossest kind of treason, without any mitigating circumstances whatever, and yet Wellington calls it a sort of treachery, as not exactly justifiable, but somewhat *excusable* under the circumstances. Wellington also said that many men, and RESPECTABLE ones, in employment under Napoleon had been in constant communication with the Duke of Orleans. (See "Greville Memoirs.")

Sir Walter Scott states that if the Pretender had succeeded in his designs on England, many Englishmen of character and influence would have taken the oath of allegiance to him with the deliberate intention ultimately to dethrone and destroy him. Judge Gaston, of North Carolina, in 1832 argued himself into the belief (honestly, I doubt not) that he had a perfect right to do that which the Constitution of North Carolina expressly forbade him to do. I once mentioned this subject to Judge Ruffin the younger, the ablest lawyer, in my opinion, the State has ever produced—not even excepting Chief Justice Pearson. I said to Judge Ruffin, "Judge Gaston's argument seems to me to be unworthy of so great a man. It is the veriest hair-splitting. How could Judge Gaston say that he believed all that Protestants believe, when the very life blood of Protestantism is its opposition to very much of Roman Catholic faith and Roman Catholic teaching ? That is an essential part of the *truth* of the Protestant religion. Roman Catholics deny that Protestants teach the truth. How, then, could Judge Gaston, as a Roman Catholic, say that he believed all that Protestants believe ?" Judge Ruffin's face was a study. He straightened himself up and looked off in the distance for a few moments. Then he turned to me and said, with an emphasis which no one could mistake, "Well, he said it anyhow."

Some of the greatest reformers in this country—men occupying the highest positions in Church and State—openly countenance the most flagrant violations both of the laws of God and man because of the probable good that may result from such immoralities and crimes. I cannot excuse Ney, but I have put him in very respectable company. After all, it is the *only* dark spot in his whole career. What a grand testimony to the greatness of the man! We cannot excuse him, but we love him and we honor him.

APPENDIX B.

P. S. NEY'S SHORTHAND ALPHABET.

Letter	Symbol	Words
a, e		an, any, one.
b		be, by, because.
d		do, due, done.
f, v		if, off, of, often.
g, j		go, gone, joy, again.
h		he, have, high.
i		I, eye, idea.
k, c hard		can, know, known.
l		all, the whole.
m		me, my, may.
n		in, on, no.
o, u		O! owe, owing.
p		People, persons.
qu		question, quality.
r		are, or, our, ear, air.
s, z, c soft		say, see, as, so, us, use.
t		it, at, to, too.
w		we, with, way.
x		example, except.
y		ye, you, your, yea.
ch		such, each.
sh		she, shall, show.
th		the, thee, they.
wh		who, which.

The world   O̱

And   U

Mute letters and medial vowels omitted.

A dot (•) over any character means em, im, in, etc.   Thus: ė̸   emperor

Ċ   impose

etc.

Many characters are omitted.

APPENDIX C.

Mrs. MARY C. DALTON, in her testimony (see page 154), says: "One day, about dark, a stranger rode up to our gate and asked father if he could stop with him that night. We had a good deal of company at the time, and every room was occupied. My father told him that he was sorry he could not accommodate him; but the young man insisted, and said he was willing to sleep on the floor, and that his horse being tired and completely worn out, he could go no farther. My father then told him that if he could suit himself to circumstances he would be glad to have him remain. The stranger, a fine-looking man, thanked him and went in. When he was conducted in to supper he took a seat at the table opposite Mr. Ney, who was occupying his usual seat on the left hand of my father. They glanced at each other, and though not a word was spoken it was evident to all present that it was a glance of recognition. My mother said a sign passed between them. Immediately after tea Mr. Ney and the stranger, taking their hats, left the house together, and were not seen by the family any more that night. An old negro man (Frederick) reported that he saw them near midnight sitting behind a straw stack in the field in close conversation, and, although unobserved by them, could hear them distinctly, but could not understand a word they said. The stranger ordered his horse very early the next morning and left. He gave no information about himself except in a general way. After the man had gone Mr. Ney went to his room and remained in it all that day, reading and writing. He never made any allusion to the matter, and we had too much respect for him to question him about it. The stranger had black hair, black eyes, and a dark complexion. This incident happened, I think, in 1834 or 1835."

Since this book went to press the author has received a letter from a foreign gentleman of high character and position, in which he says: " I am acquainted with the history of Peter S. Ney prior to his escape to the United States of America. Many years ago, when I was a young man, I visited your country for the express purpose of communicating with him. I found him in Rowan County, North Carolina, teaching school. He was boarding with a planter. After supper we retired to a straw stack, where we spent the night in talking over past matters. I never saw him afterward. The identity of Peter S. Ney has been a profound secret. He was a fugitive from justice, and many persons in France were accessory to his escape. If Peter S. Ney had revealed his identity in America his friends in France who aided in his escape would have suffered death. Even now, perhaps, his identity cannot fully be made known. . . . He was born January 10th, 1769."

The name of this writer cannot be given. It is known only to my publisher, Mr. Thomas Whittaker, and myself.

INDEX.

A.

Adams, Dr. J. R. B., Testimony of, 165.
Allison, Dr. J. A., Testimony of, 181.
Almeida captured, 43.
Alphabet, Shorthand, of P. S. Ney, 303, 304.
Andrews, James, Testimony of, 186.
Arunca River, English driven to, 45.
Angulé, Mlle., Ney married to, 21.
Aurillac, Ney arrested near, 91.
Austin, Mrs. E. D., Testimony of, 221.
Auxerre, Meeting of Ney and Napoleon at, 82,83

B.

Bancroft, George, Letter from, 175.
Barber, Joseph, Testimony of, 186.
Barber, Rev. R. W., Testimony of, 215.
Barringer, Hon. V. C., Testimony of, 180.
Bautzen, Battle of, 74.
Beale, Mrs. G. N., Testimony of, 199.
Beresina, Passage of the, 70.
Bernadotte, Army of Observation of, 11.
    routs Marshal Oudinot, 76.
Bertrand serves under Ney, 77.
Bingham, Dr., Testimony of, 201.
Borodino, Battle of, 54-57.
Boulogne, Marshal Soult at, 28.
Bournonville's letter to Minister of War, 9.
Brevard, Alexander F., Testimony of, 200.
Briqueville, Ney rescues, 64.
Bunn, Hon. H. G., Testimony of, 164.
Busaco, Masséna repulsed at, 43-45.
Butler, John A., Testimony of, 195.

C.

Cain, P. H., Testimony of, 180.
Cambronne's surrender, 99.
Campbell, Mrs. S. A., Testimony of, 172.
Cauchy informs Ney of his sentence, 93, 94.
Celorico, Masséna and Ney quarrel at, 49-51.
Chamber of Peers, Trial of Ney by, 92, 93.
Charles, Archduke, defeated, 18.
Ciudad Rodrigo captured, 43.
Claveau, Statement of, 120.
Clement, Mrs., Testimony of, 139.
Coa, Battle of, 43.
Cole, General, at Redinha, 46.
Conciergerie, Ney imprisoned in the 91.
Condeixa, Ney blamed for burning, 48.
Corunna, Ney stations himself at, 43.
Crawfurd, General, defeated by Ney, 43.

D.

Dalton, Mrs. M. C., Testimony of, 153.
Dalton, Dr. Robert H., Testimony of, 170.
Danikowa, Ney's stratagem at, 63.
"Danville Times," Testimony of Editor of, 169.
Davout, General, at Borodino, 55.
Dennewitz, Ney defeated at, 75.

Deppen, Retreat from, 38.
D'Hénin, General, at the Dnieper, 65, 66.
Dierdorf, Action near, 10.
Dnieper, Ney crosses on ice, 63, 64.
Documentary evidence as to P. S. Ney's identity, 227-256.
Dresden, Napoleon surprised at, 75.
Duke of Elchingen (see " Ney"), 34.
Dupin's effort to save Ney, 92.

E.

Elchingen, Ney's brilliant victory at, 32, 33.
Ems, Ney's stratagem at, 20.
England, Plans for invading, 25, 26, 28-30.
Ennis, J. H., Testimony of, 181.
Ervin, Witherspoon, Testimony of, 162.
Evidence, Documentary, as to P. S. Ney's
    identity, 227-256.
    summary of, 279-297.
Eylau, Battle of, 38.

F.

Fezensac's march to the Dnieper, 65-67.
Fleurus, Battle of, 5.
Foard, Archie, Testimony of, 223.
Foard, Mrs. O. G., Testimony of, 224.
Folk, Colonel G. N., Testimony of, 200.
Foote, Major J. H., Testimony of, 193.
Forchheim, Surrender of, 7.
Fraser's, Sir William, account of Ney's execution, 118.
    doubts of Ney's death, 120.
Friedland, Ney at the battle of, 39.
Friedrichshafen, Mayor of, Letter from, 290, 292, 293.

G.

Gaither, Burgess, Testimony of, 139.
Gaither, David, Testimony of, 192.
Galicia occupied by Ney, 42, 43.
Gamot, Madame, visits Ney in prison, 94.
Gay, Rev. J. L., Testimony of, 177.
Genealogy of Ney family, 288-293, (table) 291.
Giessen, Defeat at, 10.
Gillot's, General, letter to Ney, 17.
Girard, General, defeated at Leibnitz, 76.
Graham, A. H., Testimony of, 205.
Graham, Colonel C. C., Testimony of, 180.
Graham, Thomas D., Testimony of, 222.
Gross-Beeren, Battle at, 76.
Guarda Mountain, Repulse at, 51, 52.
Guntzburg, Battle at, 31.

H.

Hall, Hon. J. G., Testimony of, 170.
Hall, Mrs., Testimony of, 184.
Hall, N. F., Testimony of, 208.
Harlee, General W. W., Testimony of, 169.

Haslach, Battle of, 31.
Haye Sainte, La, Capture of, 88.
Haynes, William M., Testimony of, 183.
Heidelberg, Victory of Ney at, 18.
Heilbronn, Engagement at, 15.
Helper, H. H., Testimony of, 200.
Henderson, R. A., Testimony of, 220.
Hill, General D. H., Testimony of, 208.
Hill, Mrs. D. H., Testimony of, 209.
History, Notable errors in, 98-103.
Hoche, Ney's letter to, and reply, 9-11.
Hohenlinden, Battle of, 20.
Hohenlohe, Prince, defeated by Ney, 18, 19.
Houston, Colonel Thos. F., Testimony of, 147.
Hughes, Mrs. S. N., Testimony of, 210.
Hutchinson's, Madame, efforts to save Ney, 111, 112.

I.

Ingolstadt, Victory of Ney at, 19, 20.
Ireland's, W. H., account, 121.
Irwin, H. M., Testimony of, 209.

J.

Jena, Battle of, 34, 35.
Jetton, John L., Testimony of, 198.
John, Archduke, retreats to Vienna, 34.
John Charles', Baron, opinion concerning Ney's ancestry, 289.
Jones, M.D., Rev. Basil G., Testimony of, 201.
Jourdan and Kléber, Quarrel of, 6.
  writes to Ney, 8, 9.
Junot, General, at Valoutina, 54.
Jurney, Dr. P. C., Testimony of, 196.

K.

Katzbach, Macdonald defeated at the, 76.
Kaya, Attack at, 74.
Kléber and Jourdan, Quarrel of, 6.
  praises Ney, 8.
Klix, Victory at, 74.
Knittel's, Pastor, testimony concerning Ney's ancestry, 289.
Königsberg, Ney's foraging near, 37.
Koutousoff, General, demands Ney's surrender, 60.
Kowns, Defence of, 71-73.
Krasnoi, Battle of, 60, 61.

L.

Lamarche, General Ney under, 5.
Landamman's, The, letter to Ney, 23, 24.
Lavalette, General, Escape of, 134.
Lecourbe, General, assumes command, 18.
Lefol, Adjutant-General, at Manheim, 16.
Legrand's, General, letter to Ney, 18.
Leibnitz, Defeat at, 76.
Leinster, Frederick, Testimony of, 185.
Leipsic, Ney's energy at, 78, 79.
Lestocq, General, at Soldau, 36.
  at Eylau, 38.
Leval's, General, letter to Ney, 17.
Lichtenstein, Prince, defeated by Ney, 18.
Lille, Ney sent by Napoleon to, 83.
Lingle, Moses, Testimony of, 208.
Loison, General, Ney's command given to, 49.
Louis XVIII. insults Wellington, 112, 113.
Lugo, Ney ordered to fortify, 43.
Luneville, Treaty of peace at, 20.
Lutzen, Battle of, 73, 74.
Luxembourg, Ney's execution near the, 116.

M.

Macdonald, Marshal, defeated, 76.
Mack surrenders to Ney at Ulm, 33, 34.

Maestricht, Ney at the siege of, 6.
Magdeburg, Surrender of, 36.
Manheim, Capture of, 11-13.
  Evacuation of, 16.
Masséna, Marshal, Ney compared with, 1.
  writes to Ney, 15.
  quarrels with Ney, 49, 51,
  moral weakness of, 49.
Maternité, Hospital of the, Ney's body taken to, 121.
Mayence, Ney at the siege of, 6.
McBee, Vardry A., Testimony of, 165.
McCulloh, James, Testimony of, 174.
McKnight, Joseph, Testimony of, 186.
Merlin's Letter to Ney, 7.
Miles, Pliny, takes P. S. Ney's papers, 148, 159, 173, 176, 195, 225.
Miller, George A., Testimony of, 204.
Montbrun, General, at Coa, 43.
Montreuil, Ney appointed commander-in-chief of, 25.
Moreau, Ney serves under, 19.
  killed at Dresden, 75.
Morrison, D.D., Rev. R. H., Testimony of, 179.
Moscow, Retreat from, 57.
Moskva, Battle of the, 54-57.
Müller, General, recalled, 16.
Mumford, Giles B., Testimony of, 173.
Murat, Prince, Ney's quarrel with, 31-33.
  at Borodino, 55.
Murcelha, Ponte de, Ney abandons, 48.

N.

Napier, Major, Ney's kindness to, 41.
Napoleon Bonaparte, Emperor of France, 28.
  Ney's letter from, 21.
  at Madrid, 39, 40.
  at Borodino, 55, 56.
  esteem for Ney, 68, 69.
  surprised at Lutzen, 74.
  abdication of, 79, 80.
  last campaign of, 83.
  untruthfulness of, 290.
Neu, General, at Ingolstadt, 19.
Ney, Madame (see also "Auguié").
  character, 80, 81.
  last visit to Marshal Ney, 94.
  death of, 130.
Ney, Marshal, Duke of Elchingen, 34.
  Prince de la Moskowa, 54, 55.
  birthplace, 3.
  early training, 3.
  leaves home, 4.
  arrival at Metz, 4.
  duel with a fencing-master, 4.
  aide-de-camp to General Lamarche, 5.
  wounded at Mayence, 6.
  brigadier-general, 8.
  prisoner at Giessen, 10.
  horsemanship, 11.
  at Manheim, 12.
  general of division, 13, 14.
  letter to war minister, 13.
  war minister's letter to, 14.
  transferred to Army of Switzerland, 14.
  wounded at Winterthur, 14, 15.
  ordered to Army of Rhine, 15.
  wounded at Manheim, 16.
  commander-in-chief, 16.
  circular upon assuming command, 16, 17.
  marriage to Mlle. Auguié, 21.
  minister-plenipotentiary, 22.
  writes his "Military Studies," 27.
  marshal, 28.
  campaign in the Tyrol, 34.
  bold incursions of, 37.

INDEX.

Ney, Quarrel with Masséna, 49-51.
  at battle of Borodino, 54-55.
  bravery at the Borysthenes, 57, 58.
  bravery at Kowno, 73.
  saves Marshal St. Cyr, 75.
  letters to Napoleon after Dennewitz, 78.
  dislike for society, 80, 81.
  rejoins Napoleon, 81.
  flight after Waterloo, 90.
  Turkish sabre of, 90, 91.
  arrest at Bessonis, 91.
  imprisonment of, 91.
  letter to Wellington, 108.
  trial of, 91-93, 300.
  conviction of, 93.
  last hours of, 93-95.
  execution of, 95-115.
  official report of execution, 118.
  death of, 97.
  burial of, in Père la Chaise, 122, 123.
  grave of, 130.
  statue of, 130.
  genealogy of, 288-293.
  patriotism of, 301.
Ney, Peter, 3.
Ney, Peter Stuart, 97.
  account of himself, 133.
  age of, 141, 205.
  appearance (personal), 135, 136, 138, 139, 140, 147, 149, 165, 166, 171, 172, 181, 184, 191, 193, 202, 279.
  battle of Bautzen, after, 281.
  burial-place of, 166.
  burns his papers, 136, 138, 145, 148, 182.
  character of, 146, 153, 280.
  choice of name, 286, 287.
  death of, 108, 222, 223.
  drinking habit of, 139, 146, 149, 155, 161, 169, 280.
  execution described by him, 144, 150, 183, 188, 219.
  fencing skill, 137, 143, 151, 182, 194, 196, 208.
  foreigners recognize him, 136, 151, 159, 211, 213.
  handwriting of, 293, 294.
  horsemanship, 136, 161, 169, 181, 182, 206, 207, 208.
  languages, knowledge of, 140, 141, 201, 202.
  Louis XVIII., his contempt for, 142.
  mathematics, knowledge of, 140, 192.
  military knowledge, 137, 193, 217.
  stranger, visit of a, to him, 154, 182.
  Napoleon, his opinion of, 141, 153, 171.
  sorrow on the death of, 145, 148, 173, 174, 189, 202.
  Ney, Marshal, his claim to be, 133, 144, 149, 155, 224, 225.
  orator, as an, 138.
  Russian expedition, his account of, 141, 150, 187.
  scars, 137, 147, 208, 222.
  scholarship of, 140, 149, 285, 286.
  seclusion, desire for, 147, 194.
  shorthand alphabet, 303, 304.
  shorthand notes, 295.
  stenography, knowledge of, 148, 193, 195.
  suicide, attempt at, 136, 138, 162.
  teacher, sternness as a, 146, 160, 167, 168, 180.
  visit of stranger to, 305, 306.
  Waterloo, his description of, 142, 188, 190, 200, 284.
  Wellington, references to, 142, 190.
  words, last, 296.
  wounds, 137, 143, 161, 168, 188, 283.
Niemen, Crossing of the, 72.
Nuremberg, Ney's capture of, 8.

O.

Oporto, Soult's defeat at, 2.
Oudinot, Marshal, routed, 76.
  serves under Ney, 77.

P.

Pack, General, at Redinha, 46.
Paris, Surrender of, 79.
  Capitulation of, 90.
Partisans, The, 5
Peers condemn Ney, 103.
Père la Chaise Cemetery, Ney buried in, 181, 121, 122.
Philipsburg paroled, 13.
Picton, General, at Redinha, 46.
Platoff's, General, attacks on Teolino, 67.
Plotho's account of retreat from Deppen, 38.
Poclinitz, Charles A., Testimony of, 138.
Poetry and prose by P. S. Ney, 257-277.
Pombal, Combat at, 45.
Portugal, Invasion of, 43.
Prince de la Moskowa (see "Ney"), 54, 55.

Q.

Quatre Bras, Engagement at, 85-87.

R.

Ramsay, Dr. J. G., Testimony of, 217.
Redinha, Battle of, 46, 48.
Regnier, General, Conduct of, 48.
  disobedience of Ney's orders, 77.
Reinhardt, Wallace M., Testimony of, 160.
Rhine, Ney ordered to Army of the, 15.
Richelieu, Duke de, pleads for Ney, 104, 105.
Rockwell, D.D., Rev. E. F., Testimony of, 174
Rogers, Captain F. M., Testimony of, 158.
Rogers, Colonel John A., Testimony of, 135.
Rohan, Prince of, 34.
Russia, Expedition to, 53.
  Retreat from, 57.
Russian treachery, 60.

S.

Sanders, J. W., Testimony of, 211.
Schliter's. Mrs. Elizabeth, testimony concerning Ney's ancestry, 289.
Schwartzenburg, General, Ney's stratagem with, 20.
  advances upon Dresden, 75.
Shepherd, Mrs. George F., Testimony of, 223.
Sloan, Elizabeth P., Testimony of, 208.
Smolensko, Council at, 54.
  Triple danger near, 58.
Smorgoni, Napoleon returns to Paris from, 71.
Snyder, Daniel, Testimony of, 212.
Soldau, Capture of the village of, 36.
Soria, Napoleon blames Ney at, 40.
Soult, Marshal, compared with Ney, 1.
  jealous of Ney, 42.
Spain, Ney ordered to, 39.
Spainhour, Dr. James M., Testimony of, 218.
Spencer, General, at Redinha, 46.
St. Cyr, Marshal, at Dresden, 75.
St. Louis "Republic," Testimony of, 221.
Steele, John M., Testimony of, 224.
Stettin, Ney defeats Austrians at, 19.
Stevenson, William S., Testimony of, 213.
Stirewalt, Valentine, Testimony of, 219.
Swain, Hon. David L., Testimony of, 173.
Sweden, Crown Prince of, defeats Ney, 75.
Switzerland, Army of, Ney transferred to, 14.

T.

Teolino, Defence of, 67, 68.
Testimony concerning Peter S. Ney, 135-225.
Thorn, Capture of, 36.
Trott, W. H., Testimony of, 184.
Turkish sabre, Ney's, 90, 91.
Turner, Wilfred, Testimony of, 185.
Tyrol, Ney's campaign in the, 34.

U.

Ulm, Surrender of Mack at, 33, 34.
United States, Ney in the, 132.

V.

Valoutina, Conflict at, 54.
Vandamme's loss near Kulm, 76.
Vandermassen, General, at Manheim, 16.
Viazma and Smolensko, Fighting between, 57.

Vienna, Retreat of Austrians to, 34.
Vistula, Passage of the, 36.

W.

Wachendorf, Ney family in, 289, 290.
Waterloo, Battle of, 87-90.
Wellington, Duke of, at Redinha, 47.
   attacked at Quatre Bras, 87.
   at Waterloo, 87.
   insulted by Louis XVIII., 113.
   Ney's letter to, 108.
   power of, 114.
Wheeler, Colonel J. B., Testimony of, 158.
Winterthur, Ney wounded at, 14, 15.
Wislok, Ney's victory at, 19.
Wood, Dr. Daniel B., Testimony of, 217.
Wood, Thomas S., Testimony of, 167.
Wood, D.D., Rev. William A., Testimony 196.
Worth, Mrs. B. G., Testimony of, 172.
Wurtzburg and Forchheim, Ney at, 7.

www.ingramcontent.com/pod-product-compliance
Lightning Source LLC
Chambersburg PA
CBHW020306240426

43673CB00039B/721